COERCIVE GEOGRAPHIES

Studies in Critical Social Sciences Book Series

Haymarket Books is proud to be working with Brill Academic Publishers (www.brill.nl) to republish the *Studies in Critical Social Sciences* book series in paperback editions. This peer-reviewed book series offers insights into our current reality by exploring the content and consequences of power relationships under capitalism, and by considering the spaces of opposition and resistance to these changes that have been defining our new age. Our full catalog of *SCSS* volumes can be viewed at https://www.haymarketbooks .org/series_collections/4-studies-in-critical-social-sciences.

Coercive Geographies

Historicizing Mobility, Labor and Confinement

Edited by

Johan Heinsen, Martin Bak Jørgensen
and Martin Ottovay Jørgensen

Haymarket Books
Chicago, IL

First published in 2020 by Brill Academic Publishers, The Netherlands
© 2020 Koninklijke Brill NV, Leiden, The Netherlands

Published in paperback in 2021 by
Haymarket Books
P.O. Box 180165
Chicago, IL 60618
773-583-7884
www.haymarketbooks.org

ISBN: 978-1-64259-620-5

Distributed to the trade in the US through Consortium Book Sales and
Distribution (www.cbsd.com) and internationally through Ingram Publisher
Services International (www.ingramcontent.com).

This book was published with the generous support of Lannan Foundation and
Wallace Action Fund.

Special discounts are available for bulk purchases by organizations and
institutions. Please call 773-583-7884 or email info@haymarketbooks.org for more
information.

Cover design by Jamie Kerry and Ragina Johnson.

Printed in the United States.

10 9 8 7 6 5 4 3 2 1

Library of Congress Cataloging-in-Publication data is available.

Contents

Preface and Acknowledgements

The humble origins of this volume date back to a few informal lunch and afternoon chats in our departmental lunchroom. A subsequent interdisciplinary workshop eventually yielded the volume you are now reading. Hopefully, you will gain as much from engaging with it as we did when bringing it together.

Despite working in different fields as well as on different topics and time periods, we all followed the (often joint) intensification and militarisation of borders and migration monitoring and control in Europe, the Middle East and the US. Against this backdrop, our informal discussions on mobility, labor and coercion across time and space soon led us to the realisation of a need for a formal interdisciplinary workshop centred around the notion of 'coercive geographies' to link these issues together past and present.

The workshop (Coercive Geographies: Historicising Mobility, Labour and Confinement) was held in Aalborg, Denmark, in October 2018. Above all, the presentations and discussions at the workshop confirmed, to us at least, both the importance of the overall issue and the relevance, flexibility and strength of the notion 'coercive geographies. Accordingly, we pursued this volume with most of the workshop attendees and a few additional contributors. In doing so, we have faced the usual challenges of trying to practise interdisciplinarity, navigate chapter logistics and deadlines and, not least, securing a balance between the volume's overall cohesion and the directions of the individual chapters. However, the timeliness of putting together an interdisciplinary volume became clearer and clearer along the way. On the one hand, the plethora of diverse but interconnected neoliberal coercive geographies—from Northern Africa and Southern Europe and the Middle East to South East Asia and Central America—mutated, connecting and bringing to light the deeper histories of the modern state, capitalism and imperialism. On the other, people's unyielding and resourceful ways of resisting these spatial assemblages of confinement and immobility also highlighted not only their incredible tenacity and immense will, but also the importance for all of us of refusing to accept these coercive geographies as fair, normal or acceptable.

We are grateful for the support of David Fasenfest for the opportunity to publish this book in Brill Series *Studies in Critical Social Science* and for his encouragement during the process. We also thank the contributing authors in this book for their effort and contribution to enrich the perspectives on the issue at stake.

Putting the last pieces of the volume together from the comfort of our homes during the COVID-19 lockdown has only added, we think, to the need to practise global solidarity and engage with the global dynamics and histories of immobility, confinement and coercion going forward. Hopefully, the global pandemic will make us rethink what is important and the type of world we want to create. We therefore wish to dedicate this volume to people on the move, everywhere.

Illustrations

Figures

Table

Notes on Contributors

Irina Aguiari
is a Ph.D. candidate at the Faculty of Political and Social Sciences at the Scuola Normale Superiore based in Florence, and member of COSMOS – Centre of Social Movement Studies. She holds an MA in International Migrations and Ethnic Relations and Global Gender Studies at Aalborg University. She is currently working on peasant protests, action and contentious repertoires in Southern Italy.

Abdulkadir Osman Farah
is a lecturer at Aalborg University where he teaches Migration, Development, Transnational Encounters and Connections, Transnational NGOs, New-regionalism and Transnational State Formation. Dr. Farah is a founder of the Analysis Centre for Transnational Encounters and Connections (AC4TEC) in Denmark and North Eastern African-Nordic Network (NEANOR). He serves as an associate editor of Somali Studies Journal as well as the editorial review boards of a number of journals focusing on political development and political sociology. His latest books include: *Somalis: Transnational Communities and the Transformation of Nation and State* (Adonis & Abbey Publishers Ltd, 2016); *Transnational NGOs: Creative Connections of Development and Global Governance* (Aalborg University Press, 2014) and *China-Africa Relations in an Era of Great Transformations* (Ashgate Publishing, 2013).

Leandros Fischer
studied Social Anthropology at the University of Cologne and holds a Ph.D. in Political Science from the Philipps University of Marburg. In recent years, he has conducted research on migrants and refugees from the Middle East to Cyprus for the project 'Cyprus as a Place of Exile and Asylum in the Middle East'. He is currently a postdoctoral fellow in Aalborg for the DIGINAUTS project, focusing on migrants' digital practices vis-à-vis the European border regime. He has taught at the universities of Marburg, Nicosia (University of Cyprus), and Aalborg. His research interests include migration, citizenship studies, social movements and political parties of the contemporary European Left.

Konstantinos Floros
is a Ph.D. candidate at the IT University of Copenhagen. He holds a B.Sc./MA Degree in Political Science and Public Administration from the National and Kapodistrian University of Athens. He is currently investigating Danish digital

labor platforms and the intertwining of digital platform work with the digitalized welfare state and the Danish industrial relations system. In the past he has conducted research on digital citizenship and public sector digitalization in the Greater Copenhagen and Skåne Region. He has recently collaborated with Associate Professor Martin Bak Jørgensen of Aalborg University on a research project about the institutionalization of migrant precarity in the Danish and the Greek context and co-authored 'Tracing the future of migrants' labor relations. Experiences of institutionalised migrant precarity in Denmark and Greece.' published in *Political Geography*.

Johan Heinsen

is Associate Professor at the Conflict, Coercion and Authority in History (CCA) research group at the Department of Politics and Society, Aalborg University. He works on the history of labor coercion and punishment across the early modern world. He has written extensively on the history of Danish colonialism as well as on the history of convict labor in Denmark. He is the author of the books *Mutiny in the Danish Atlantic World* (Bloomsbury, 2017) and *Det første fængsel* (Aarhus Universitetsforlag, 2018). He is currently vice-chair of the COST-action Worlds of Related Coercions in Work (www.worck.eu).

Martin Bak Jørgensen

is Associate Professor at the Research group on Democracy, Migration and Society (DEMOS) at the Department for Culture and Learning, Aalborg University, Denmark. He works within the fields of sociology, political sociology and political science. He has published the following books *Politics of Dissent* (Peter Lang, 2015; co-authored with Óscar García Agustín), and *Solidarity Without Borders: Gramscian perspectives on migration and civil society alliances* (Pluto Press, 2016) and *Solidarity and the 'Refugee Crisis' in Europe* (Palgrave, 2019) both co-authored with Óscar García Agustín. He has published articles in journals like *Internal Migration Review, Critical Sociology, Journal of International Migration and Integration* and *British Journal of International Politics*.

Martin Ottovay Jørgensen

Ph.D. in International History, has previously been an Assistant Professor in International History at the Conflict, Coercion and Authority in History research group at at the Department of Politics and Society, Aalborg University and a visiting research fellow at the Department of Politics and International Relations at Goldsmiths, University of London. He is currently a voluntary postdoctoral researcher with the Department of History, Ghent University, making ends meet teaching international politics and global history at various educational institutions in London. His research explores how international peacekeeping within the context of an international system significantly influenced by multiple imperial regimes is linked to inequality and insecurity.

Apostolos Kapsalis

is a lawyer and labor relations researcher at the Labor Institute of the General Confederation of Greek Workers. In 2015 he served as Executive Secretary of the Greek Labor Inspectorate Body. His articles and studies have been published in journals and collective volumes on labor law, industrial relations, migration policy, labor market discrimination and trade union movement. In 2018 he published the book *Migrant Workers in Greece: industrial relations and migration policy in time of Memoranda* (in Greek, Papazisis). He holds a Masters Degree (DEA) in Labor Law from the University of Strasbourg and a Ph.D. from the Department of Social Policy of the Panteion University. Currently, he has been awarded a state scholarship to conduct post-doctoral research on Labor Relations of Agricultural Workers at Panteion University and is an Adjunct Lecturer of Migration Policy at the Department of Social and Educational Policy of the University of Peloponnese.

Karin Krifors

Ph.D. in Ethnicity and Migration, works at the Institute for Research on Migration, Ethnicity and Society (REMESO) at Linköping University, Sweden. Her research concerns migration systems, labor, moral economy, anti-/racism, intersectionality and social exclusion. In her post-doc project, Krifors studies social movements in small Swedish communities that work with migrant inclusion. She analyses how activists aim to create alternative communities and how forms of anti-racist and convivial practices negotiate an notion of national belonging and local identities. In a project launched in 2020 Krifors will investigate how biometric data is used in migration systems and stored across EU information technology systems.

Sven Van Melkebeke

Ph.D. in History, is affiliated to Ghent University where he works as a postdoctoral researcher on a voluntary basis. His research focusses on the development of commodity frontiers (coffee, rubber, cotton), especially in Africa; labor; rural; and environmental history. In 2019, he published 'Divergence in rural development: the curious case of coffee production in the Lake Kivu region (first half twentieth century)' in *African Economic History*. He is currently preparing his first monograph *Dissimilar Coffee Frontiers: Mobilizing Labor and*

Land in the Lake Kivu Region, Congo and Rwanda (*1918–1960/62*) which will appear in 2020.

Susi Meret
is an Associate Professor at the Department of Politics and Society, Aalborg University, Denmark. Her main interest is within populist radical right parties in Europe, populism, political violence and extremism and civil society reactions hereto. Among her latest publications: 'The Politics and Act of Solidarity: The Case of Trampoline House in Copenhagen' (with B. Siim; in Baban, F and Rykiel, K. (eds.), *Fostering Pluralism through Solidarity Activism in Europe: Everyday Encounters with Newcomer*, Palgrave, forthcoming); '"What Can We Learn from Gramsci Today?" Migrant Subalternity and the Refugee Movements: Perspectives from the Lampedusa in Hamburg' (in Antonini, F., Bernstein, A., Fusaro, L. and Jackson, R. (eds.), *Revisiting Gramsci's Notebooks*, Brill, 2020).

Vasileios Spyridon Vlassis
is currently a Research Assistant in the IT University of Copenhagen. He holds a Bachelors Degree in Mathematics from the University of Crete, a Masters in Philosophy and History of Science and Technology from the National and Kapodistrian University of Athens, and recently received his Ph.D. from the Business IT department of the IT University of Copenhagen. His thesis, titled 'Registration of irregularized migrants in the EU in times of "crisis"' focuses on practices of border guards and their use of technologies in the identification and registration process, as it occurred in the border between Greece and Turkey. The thesis is placed in the intersection between Science and Technology Studies (STS), Surveillance Studies and Critical Border Studies.

CHAPTER 1

Coercive Geographies: Historicizing Mobility, Labor and Confinement

An Introduction

Johan Heinsen, Martin Bak Jørgensen and Martin Ottovay Jørgensen

1 Introduction

In late November 2018, the Danish nationalist Party (Danish People's Party) eagerly presented a political agreement with the ruling liberal-conservative coalition government to the press. The Party had secured the deal in return for support of the government's annual budget. Concretely, the agreement would confine two groups of people on the small and remote island of Lindholm: migrants who had been convicted, had served their sentences and were to be deported but were not yet able to leave; and Danish citizens convicted of fighting with Islamic militant organisations (Nielsen, Jenvall, and Ingvorsen 2018). On the one hand, the agreement reflected the Party's overall strategy of gaining parliamentary influence by regulating the mobility and increasing the insecurity of migrants and refugees: people, the Party, racialices as fundamentally different from Danish people, as taking hard-working Danish peoples' jobs, as preying on Danish welfare services and as criminal by nature. On the other, the agreement also placed legislative emphasis on a particular small group of people who the Party expected to find few, if any, allies in public debate and parliamentary politics. To stress these peoples' unwantedness, the island, journalists reported, had predominantly been used for research on infectious diseases on animals, which were cremated on the island once deemed no longer useful. Moreover, the only means of access to both the island and the envisioned facility was by ferry (Ritzau 2018a). With no ambiguity, the agreement and what it entailed was thus to engender a strong sense that those to be placed there were undesirable both among those voting for them to be there and among the people to be confined themselves. Keen to be seen as acting within international law and not doing the nationalists' bidding, however, the liberal-conservative government made sure to explain that the island was not actually a prison and that the people to be placed there would only have a duty to report daily and stay on the island overnight (Nielsen, Jenvall, and Ingvorsen 2018). Yet, the government and the nationalist parties clearly went as far as they could before being in breach of international human rights law. Tellingly, both the Danish Institute of Human Rights and the United Nations Commissioner of Human Rights voiced their concerns with regard to the envisioned regime's breach of human rights (Abend 2019; Ritzau 2018b).

For various reasons, the Danish government and nationalist parties not only failed to translate their political agreement into policy, but also lost both their political majority in parliament and governmental power. To the government that succeeded it, the expense in the excess of one billion Euros was too much to stomach. Nevertheless, the initial agreement between the liberals and the nationalists is exemplary of how 'undesired' people across every region in the world are not only increasingly constrained, confined or detained on a mass-scale at this moment, but also kept in conditions that frequently test international human rights conventions and laws. At the same time, the agreement also connects to the centuries-long racialized, classed and gendered global history of states, empires, colonial states, paramilitary organisations, companies, international organisations, criminal organisations and others monitoring, constraining, coercing or deporting, for example, itinerant laborers, refugees, homeless people, vagrants, migrants and other people in vulnerable positions and in different ways at odds with, or contesting, the political and economic order of the day.

In some ways, Lindholm emerged almost out of nowhere. On the surface, the xenophobic biopolitics it was projected to enact appeared at odds with Scandinavia's welfare states and the core tenets of social democracy and liberalism on which they were built. While, political nationalism has been on the rise for decades, Lindholm seemed extreme, and the complicity of a large political spectrum unsettling. It felt as if history was twitching erratically. Yet, at the same time, Lindholm's appearance can be read in a different way. Perhaps it did not represent a sudden discontinuity, but rather the opposite: the realisation of deep historical linkages. In such a perspective, this was not the emergence of something new, but rather the repetition of something old. History seemed to reverberate in that idea of the island and the logics of displacement and confinement that it made possible.

For at least five centuries, European states have turned islands into prisons for disposable populations (Anderson 2018). Such islands were intrinsically linked to the emergence of prisons as such, but also to the history of forced labor camps (Gibson and Poerio 2018). The totalitarian (and disconcertingly, non-totalitarian) states that in the twentieth century saw the institutionalisation of states of exception in camps had experimented for ages with the techniques they put to new work. Those experiments expressed themselves in myriad ways. Thus, to the liberal insistence that Lindholm was not a prison, historians might have retorted that punitive confinement has had many forms, and that Lindholm in fact did look just the part.

Many of the theatres in which contemporary struggles of migration and confinement are playing out, are steeped in historical significance on these subjects too. The history of the Mediterranean offers perhaps the most striking parallels to our present. Throughout recorded history this ocean has been defined by migrations and, for almost as long, conflicts about mobility. In the Middle Ages a ransom economy developed which saw camps of enslaved people confined as a result of endemic warfare and piracy on both sides of an ocean that was already then divided by cultural and religious differences. Some of these sites later turned into sites for convicts and other marginals, displaced across oceans. Such was the case of Spain's possessions in Northern Africa – Melilla, Oran and Ceuta among others which in the early modern period became sites for displacement and labor coercion tied to disciplinary and penal systems (Pike 1983). In that way, the development of the prison itself was intrinsically tied to this coercive geography. Another facet in that story was the prevalence of galleys. All Mediterranean powers manned the benches of their vessels with forced oarsmen and very often combined different groups. Thus, enslavement and sentencing were two different ways to the same chains. By the mid-eighteenth century, the galleys mutated and most of the forced rowers were instead interred in labor camps on the shores of the ocean. Those camps formed early experiments in mass incarceration and were formative for how states would marry displacement and confinement. The labor performed in the Gulags carried the name 'Katorga', derived from the Greek word for galley, because its initial emergence was this geography (Gentes 2008).

Scandinavian states also experimented with these forms. Galley servitude never became widespread – mostly because galleys were less common in Northern waters – but islands were key to the formation of their imaginaries of confinement. Denmark – until 1814 tied to Norway through the absolutist King – experimented in a range of settings. St. Thomas in the Caribbean was initially settled with a mix of convicts and indentured migrants. A similar, but ultimately failed, experiment unfolded in Greenland in the late 1720s. Closer to home, military outposts Christiansø in the Baltic was used as a prison in the same period. So were several Norwegian island fortresses. The Swedes used the island of Marstrand near Gothenburg to the same purpose. Even today, Norway maintains a minimum-security prison on the island of Bastøy. Meanwhile, Denmark no longer have island prisons, but the twentieth century saw islands in The Great Belt (Sprogø) and The Limfjord (Livø) were used to inter mentally disabled people judged to be dangerous to the population. Thus, when Danish nationalist and liberal politicians conjured Lindholm, they at the same time evoked a deep history of coercive displacement putting the spatial to work for the state.

2   Contemporaneity and History

Responding to the deteriorating situation of migrants today and the complex assemblages of the geographies they navigate, this anthology examines historical and contemporary forms of coercion and constraint exercised by a wide range of actors in diverse settings. It links the question of spatial confines to that of labor. This fraught nexus of mobility and work seems self-evidently relevant to explore. At this moment in time, it takes an active choice to ignore the frenzy of images and testimonies about coercion appearing at alarming rates from the multifarious worlds of migrant laborers. Whether the images that fill our heads are those of oxygen deprivation in a shipping container, drowning just out of sight of a Mediterranean beach resort or the nauseating realities that enable the overabundance of cheap produce available in grocery stores, the illusion of global capitalism's benign modernity is impossible to maintain.

Yet, said urgency also threatens the interpretation of this nexus. The feeling that these are issues so important that we cannot stop in our tracks to reflect on their deep lineages needs to be fought. Contemporary scholars interrogating coercion risks reading the quickly evolving systems of control, surveillance and exploitation as phenomena whose current states of rapid necropolitical twitching dislodge them from history. However, the speed with which an object moves does not mean that it does not come from somewhere. Instead, said speed might sometimes be better understood if we ask what put said object unto its current trajectory.

This means to engage critically with myriad histories that unfold what has become our contemporary moment – to produce genealogies in all their varied meanings. One path in this endeavour is currently being laid out by what has become known as 'global labor history.' This might seem surprising. With its focus on organized (often male, almost exclusively white) workers and their politics, labor history seems eminently unhelpful as a tool with which to interrogate the present. However, while that branch of historical writing stagnated in the 80s and 90s then withered in the 00s, new approaches grew in its wake. At the core of this turn were responses to the simple fact that historians began interrogating their own biases, coming to the unsettling conclusion that what they had envisioned as giving a voice to those fighting to create decent conditions in labor markets, had only succeeded in a very small part of the world. As history in general gained a global perspective in the last decades of the twentieth century, labor history suddenly appeared Eurocentric by design. At the same time, feminist scholars tore the male-centric gaze on the past of labor historians to pieces. It was time to start over.

That new beginning did not have the firm footing in Marxism that traditional labor history had enjoyed. Historical materialism had dictated that capitalism was to be understood as a system of exploitation in which the worker had been kicked off his land and now had nothing but his labor to sell. He was the protagonist of history. Ironically, traditional Marxism shared its automated identification of capitalism with free labor with classical economics. As social historians started to consider seriously the issue of work outside of Western labor markets, it became clear to them that their math was flawed. Traditional labor historians assumed that global heterogeneity could be explained teleologically by simple arguing that economies outside of the west had not yet fully reached modernity, but eventually would. Global labor history was born from the premise that maybe capitalism did not always equal a free, but proletarianized workforce with the potential to unsettle the political (were it simply to realise its strength).

What followed was a radical diversification of the study of work across history. Where traditional labor history had a clearly defined actor and a timeframe defined by that actor (modern history), the emerging histories of work have expanded the list of subjects and obliterated any temporal preferences. Even ten years ago, it would have been hard to find a medievalist or even early modernist that would argue that they were pursuing 'labor history', but now studies framed as labor history are regularly emerging on subjects such as enslavement, serfdom, servitude or penal labor before any sort of industrial revolution (De Vito and Lichtenstein 2015; Donoghue and Jennings 2016). And the days in which only organized labor was of interest seem a distant past in light of the plethora of historical works dealing with as diverse subjects as sex work, care work or military labor (García et al. 2017; Hoerder et al. 2015; Zürcher 2014).

Jürgen Kocka recently suggested that "it is not yet clear what the leading questions and viewpoints structuring the history of work as a general field might be" (quoted in Eckert 2016: 7). However, some common themes are clearly emerging. These themes are rooted in contemporary issues, but also appear directed at the shortcomings of other disciplines (economics especially) to understand their histories.

3　　Conceptualizing History of Work

One such theme – if we can call it that – is *space*. As global labor history emerged in light of many of the same critiques of eurocentrism that gave rise to the broader tradition of global history, this is not surprising. Global history has principally conceptualized space in two ways. One was a totalizing perspective that took the entirety of the globe as its starting point. This has produced rich histories on specific topics viewed through a lens seeking to show how the global scale of whatever topic is being studied. Synthesizing vast amounts of previous scholarship but viewing such scholarship in a new light can produce radical new insights, as seen for instance in a recent volume by Sven Beckert who reads the emergence of global capitalism in light of the long and globe-spanning history of cotton production. Thus, as the nominally free laborers whom traditional Marxism favoured entered the textile factories so emblematic of industrialization, they worked materials that had traversed the globe and, in the process, helped created a wide range of very different labor relations (Beckert 2014). Increasingly, it is becoming unacceptable to write histories of western labor without reflecting on such multiplicities. Meanwhile, however, other global historians have envisioned the global not as 'globe-spanning' but as connected. Traditional labor history was often methodologically nationalist, writing the history of the *English* working class or *German* unions. However, the worlds of work were defined by mobility – of objects, capital and people, as well as technologies of production and control. While the global labor histories that aim to tell a story spanning the globe have appeal in their encompassing scope, it is perhaps the histories that start from the premise of interconnectedness that have produced the richest histories. It is also the mode most interesting in light of this volume as it interrogates the mobility (or lack thereof) of workers. In a recent volume, Christian G. De Vito and Anne Gerritsen argued convincingly for the need for historians to be "aware of the role of spatial dimensions in the construction of history, the ways in which multiple connections among places and temporalities construct spatiality, and the need for methodologies that overcome the local/global divide" (De Vito and Gerritsen 2018: 4). What they envisioned as micro-spatial history can take a number of forms but begins from the premise that we should begin by historicizing the evolving practices that created spaces. Doing so means to start with empirical studies of circulations, networks and mobilities working from the specific towards an understanding of what space has meant or continues to mean in a given locality. It is our contention – as we hope this volume demonstrates – that this conceptualisation of histories of labor is compatible with and might gain further momentum from engaging productively with the work of ethnographers, anthropologists and mobility scholarship working on the present.

The new spatialities of labor history work to consider different, entangled spaces *within* a given setting as well. Thus, the inquiries of labor historians are no longer restrained to the work done at something we can define as work, but also at activities that take place in other spheres. Thus, much scholarship on labor no longer takes the labor market as its natural arena but encompass a host of interconnected spaces. The household is one such unit. The barracks or camps might be another. That focus has come as a logical extension of the impetus to study labor beyond wage labor (van der Linden 2008). In general, it can be observed that historians no longer understand the worker in light of one single relationship to an employer, but rather as an individual engaged in a host of different productive practices and relations. This has gone hand in hand with a focus on previously neglected topics such as care work, housework or child labor. It has also led historians to engage with concepts such as 'informal work' and, more recently *precarity*. As precarity became a publicly debated concept it was loaded with an unfortunate chronological idea that the precariat was a fundamentally new phenomenon whose labor relations stood in contrast to workers of the past who enjoyed much more stable working lives (cf. Standing). Historians have argued strongly against this historical myopia. In a compelling study, Italian historian Eloisa Betti has argued that "women, as well as migrants, experienced a significant level of precariousness even in the so-called golden age of the twentieth century" (Betti 2016: 64). Thus, the kinds of struggles and insecurities denoted by the term, have long histories as soon as we take a moment to gaze away from the breadwinning, white, male proletarian of the twentieth-century West. As put emphatically by one of the field's founding members, Marcel van der Linden, "standard employment under capitalist conditions is an historical anomaly" (van der Linden 2014: 20). This has led some to suggest a new conceptualisation of precariousness that point to the need to study the experiences of precariousness as understood by workers themselves. For instance, a recent article argues to define the concept as "the workers' own perception of their lack of control over their labor power in relation to other workers, the labor market, and the social reproduction of the workforce" (Schiel, De Vito and van Rossum 2020: 10).

A similarly contested concept is that of 'modern slavery.' While this concept has served to mobilize political awareness to questions of labor coercion, global labor historians have been critical of the way it structures our conceptualisation of such questions. Not only is slavery a particular (Western) concept with its own deeply problematic legacy, it also tends to dichotomize our understanding of working relations. Thus, the concept lends itself to an often analytically unfruitful divide between free and unfree labor. Simply put, the concept leads to the unfortunately lazy thought that a person is either a 'slave' or a free person. However, the experienced realities of labor coercion remain much more complicated. These shortcomings have resulted in attempts at re-conceptualisation such as the attempt to talk broadly of 'slaveries', or 'practices of slaving' thus building a concept that reminds us that unfreedom has taken many forms other than what was found in eighteenth and nineteenth-century Atlantic world (Miller 2012). Others have abandoned 'slavery' as an analytical concept altogether, favouring concepts such as bondage and *labor coercion*. (Stanziani 2014; Schiel, De Vito and van Rossum 2020). The latter trend has been defined by a push to historicize coercion by studying its historical or con-temporary specificity. This has expressed itself in several ways. One is a push to study the linguistic figurations of coercion (sometimes labelled as 'grammars of dependency'). This approach studies concrete linguistic practices – what were the words used – nouns but also verbs – in specific contexts about pro-cesses of coercion and how were they productive of specific social relations. This perspective "helps to understand the grammatical structure of a specific modality of domination and dependence in a particular social formation (...) and enables us to abstract from concrete situations of word usage in a way that may bring about a new analytical language" (Schiel, De Vito and van Rossum 2020: 8–9).[1]

A similarly situated approach seeks to study what Marcel van der Linden dubbed "moments" of coercion in the life of a labor relation (van der Linden 2016). This approach studies the specific modalities of coercion at entry into a labor relation, during the extraction of labor and at exit. The analytical reward comes in studying how specific form of entry, extraction and exit link together in a given historical setting, presenting a way to conceptualize how coercion shaped the lives of workers in a diachronic way. Thus, a migrant worker might enter voluntarily into a working relation but accrue so much debt during the extraction process that exit becomes impossible by legal means – violation of which might then lead to new forms of coercion at a later point. In this way, we can – at one and the same time – blur the analytical lines between different types of labor and understand their historical specificity. The diachronic per-spective on the lives of workers it opens up also allow us to sense how coercion and agency can be understood relationally. It is no coincidence, that some of the richest studies of labor coercion in the field of global labor history are in

---

1   This approach is heavily inspired by Ågren 2017 (for more see www.worck.eu/organisation/wg1).

fact studies of runaways (van Rossum and Kamp 2016; Rediker, Chakraborty and van Rossum 2019).

What is shared by these attempts to develop new analytical frameworks with which to think through the deep histories of labor coercion is an insistence not to begin from a priori concepts (such as the laden concept of Slavery) and instead historicize labor coercion. However, as hinted above this also means to study the lives of those who experienced moments of coercion diachronically. In regards to the subjects in this study – as with many subjects both today and throughout history – that means to study coercion in light of mobility. Thus, the second major source of inspiration behind this volume is current trends in conceptualizing *mobility* and examining the intersections with precarity.

4   Conceptualizing Mobility

The scientific study on migration can be dated back at least to Ernst Georg Ravenstein's studies in the 1880s (Greenwood and Hunt 2003). From these early steps, the understanding of migration was somewhat linear. Basically, it was assumed that people moved from one place to another. End of story. Over the decades, different explanatory models were developed showing how economic structures were decisive for people's decisions to move. First through quite simplistic push-pull models, later through household economics and choices. Despite the change of analytical unit, the understanding of migration as such remained the same. The last decades have given us more nuanced or sophisticated perspectives, such as attempts to understand the transnational dimensions of migration (compared to understanding international migration solely as the movement from one nation-state to another) (e.g. Faist 2012). The transnational perspective calls for a new perspective on migration and settlement, which argues that the traditional approaches social scientists use to understand individuals who move and settle abroad no longer are suitable for understanding moving populations in an increasingly complex world (Fink 2011). Vic Satzewich argues that "concepts like immigrant no longer suffice because they imply a permanence to migration that no longer exists" and furthermore calls for "a labor history that pays attention to both the local and the transnational can temper claims about the unprecedented nature of contemporary transnationalism, particularly as it relates to the understanding of immigrant lives" (2011: 39). The transitional turn implies that sociocultural groups no longer can be seen as territorially defined but rather are defined through migrations. At the same time, it opens up for a new global ethnography. Thomas Faist makes a bridge between globalisation studies and migration studied when he develops the notion of transnational social spaces (1998). This notion is helpful for understanding how coercion is spatialized, which is one of the analytical foci in this volume. Faist argues that transnational social spaces consist of:

> Combinations of social and symbolic ties, positions in networks and organizations and networks of organizations that can be found in at least two geographically and internationally distinct places [...]. Transnational social spaces are constituted by the various forms of resources or capital of spatially mobile and immobile persons, on the one hand, and the regulations imposed by nation-states and various other opportunities and constraints, on the other [...].
>
> FAIST 1998: 216–217

If the transnational turn of migration studies is one important development within – or even correction to – migration studies, the other conceptual development comes with the mobility turn. The mobility turn highlights various forms of spatial mobility.

The mobility turn emphasizes the historic and contemporary importance of movement on individuals and society. This paradigm incorporates new ways of theorizing about how mobilities lie "at the center of constellations of power, the creation of identities and the microgeographies of everyday life" (Cresswell 2011: 551). The mobility paradigm is pivotal for conceptualizing the dynamics of precarity among migrants but also contains its own pitfalls. We should be aware to critically reflect underlying political assumptions about the nexus between spatial and social mobility (Faist 2013). Likewise, should this paradigmatic turn be used to examine the mechanisms underlying the production of social inequalities.

Inequalities between and within countries play a significant in shaping migration dynamics and patterns (Vickers et al. 2019). This has less to do with the incentives presented to the individual than with the structural inequalities. Alice Bloch and Sonia McKay rightly argue that "uneven opportunities to migrate, with border controls aimed at excluding some groups while the global elite can move freely; the growth of forced migration as a consequence of North/south relations and the need for of capitalism for low-paid and often precarious workers" (2016: 5). Along the same lines, Harald Bauder notes that, the political economy of neoliberal globalisation creates a condition where the excluded are unsafe and vulnerable, but not superfluous – they are indeed valuable due to their vulnerable position and thus particularly exploitable (Bauder 2006). The key interest of this volume is how to understand intersections between mobility, precarity, coercion and constraint. Geographical mobility has been in focus in studies examining immigrant precarity, which often identify international migrants as precarious workers (e.g. Casas-Cortés 2014; Floros and Jørgensen 2020; Vickers et al. 2019). The reason for this is, as Marcel Paret and Shannon Gleeson argue, that migrant experiences due to being marked by various forms of exclusion, "provide a crucial window into the origins and institutionalization of precarity" (2016: 277). Access to mobility is not a given. On the contrary, migration and mobility regimes set up differential access to mobility depending on a person's legal status. Mobility is necessary coupled with immobility and mobilities and immobilities are embedded within and constrained by asymmetrical power relations (Wyss 2019). Recent studies have shown how migrants become stuck in mobility (Floros and Jørgensen 2020; Marcu 2019; Wyss 2019). Despite the positive connotations often associated with mobility (as in the rhetoric of the European Union) mobility obviously has its downsides. Structural barriers push migrants with precarious legal statuses into mobility and deny them stability (Wyss 2019). In this context immigration controls function both as "a tap regulating the flow of labour" and as "a mould shaping certain forms of labour" (Anderson 2010: 301). There is an interplay of entrant categories, employment relations and construction of institutionalized uncertainty steered by immigration controls to form particular types of labors and relations to the employers and labor market (Floros and Jørgensen 2020). This understanding also problematizes rigid binaries, such as 'free vs. forced' (migrant) labor and opens up for examining how (legal) immigrant categories structure mobility and immobility (Vickers et al. 2019). The contributions in this volume are interested in the political economies and geographies constraining mobility and institutionalizing precarity both historically and contemporary.

Struggles over mobility and struggles against labor exploitation are connected, as is the question of agency in these struggles. In Multitude, Michael Hardt and Antoni Negri argue that: [...] most migrations are driven by the need to escape conditions of violence, starvation, or depravation, but together with that negative condition there is also the positive desire for wealth, peace, and freedom. This combined act of refusal and expression of desire is enormously powerful (2004: 131). Multitude is for Hardt and Negri the lived experiences and alternative to this characterized by an embedded urge for resistance against exploitation and repression and the struggle for a democratic society. Can we recognize this when examining the intersections and relations between migration, mobility, precarity and coercion? Hardt and Negri, like scholars as Sandro Mezzadra, regard the migrant as the emblematic figure in precarity struggles. Mezzadra has argued that migrant struggles prefigure the struggles of the precariat (2007). The migrant in this type of studies becomes a central figure in both the understanding of precarity and processes of preca-risation and in the strategies and struggles developing from this condition (Jørgensen 2016). Collective campaigns like 'A Day Without Immigrants' in 2006 organized by Latino immigrants in the United States and the *24h sans nous* in France in 2010 where migrants stopped working and stopped consum-ing to show what life would be like without immigrants, or other self-organized manifestations of collective protests demonstrate the emergence of new po-litical subjectivities – and how agency is captured (Jørgensen 2016). Mobility can be analysed in this perspective as well. In regard to refugees and irregular migrants, Nick Gill and colleagues argue that "in contrast to the volitional mo-bility of the nomad, mobility is the last-ditch attempt to exercise agency" (Gill et al. 2011: 303). There is huge difference between the expat and the irregular migrant worker – mobility for the latter becomes a drive for circumventing the regime of immobilization framework constituted by the labor and migra-tion regimes (Wyss 2019).

5   Coercive Geographies

It is with a leg in each of these traditions and approaches that this volume studies what we conceptualize as *coercive geographies*. Coercive geographies is our attempt to bring together space, precarity, labor coercion and mobility in an analytical lens. We define coercive geographies as *spatialities that work to create moments of coercion through practices that limit or otherwise define the mobility of a subject*. Precarity emerges in particular geographical and histori-cal contexts, which are decisive for how it is shaped. Hence, coercive geogra-phies can be analysed as localized and spatialized intersections between labor regulations and migration policies, which become detrimental to existing mo-bility frameworks.

Perhaps we can best illustrate how we understand a coercive geography through an example. In 2004, a tragic incident happened in the UK, known as the Morecambe Bay cockling disaster. The disaster left at least 24 Chinese workers dead after the incoming tide after picking cockles at the Lancashire coast (Cohen 2004). A local father-son business had unlawfully hired a group of Chinese workers to pick cockles. The Chinese migrants had entered the UK without papers. They were given payment far below the standard and exposed to very low living conditions. They were smuggled into Liverpool hiding in con-tainers in a run organized by the Chinese triads here adding human trafficking to their business roster. The workers were underpaid and exploited by the local business. The pickers had no experience or training in picking cockles, could not swim, did not wear any lifesaving equipment and had no local knowledge of the geography, when the tide arrived or how fast, they did not know English and thus could not understanding the warning British cockle pickers tried to give them. David Anthony Eden, Sr., and his son David Anthony Eden were cleared of helping the Chinese workers breaching the immigration law. The Chinese gang master who had brought the workers to the UK and further onwards to Lancashire was convicted to prison sentence. "Sometimes, the [global] chain leads to satisfaction all round — cheap labor in Britain, remittance money to build new houses back in China.... Sometimes it ends in tragedy, as on the sands of Morecambe Bay..." journalist Richard Spencer afterwards wrote in The Daily Telegraph (here quoted from Song 2004: 137). As noted by Miri Song

> [T]he global chain cannot be characterized as 'satisfaction all round' if migrant workers, who are working inhuman hours, and living in poor conditions (reportedly 40 people to a house), are suffering and paying the cost of what is effectively indentured labor.
>
> SONG 2004: 137

What were the Chinese cockle pickers? Victims of human smuggling tricked to organized gangs seeking to exploit them? Or were they clients of people smugglers paying their way out of poverty in the Fuijan Province, ready to endure hardship to make a better life? (Olsen 2008). We do not know if their mobility was voluntary of forced. Neither can their work be seen as completely free or unfree. Rather is characterized by a spatialized coercion shaped by the particular conditions of the local possibilities, the mobility trajectories and the immigration regime. Morecambe Bay in that way becomes an example of a coercive geography.

6   Structure of the Book

Putting the concept coercive geographies to use in different ways, this volume explores the production of and resistance to precarity and coercive geographies. While one part of the chapters in the volume examines the spatial constrains of labor and mobility, another part examines resistance towards and against labor, migration, mobility and penal regimes. The four chapters in the first part examine how different legal, political, economic and administrative frameworks in various coercive geographies across Europe and the Middle East institutionalize and preserve precarious work and life conditions for people fleeing interventions, war, climate change and collapsing societies.

Zooming in, Konstantinos Floros, Apostolos Kapsalis and Martin Bak Jørgensen explore the workings of a particular agricultural coercive geography on the Greek mainland in their chapter *Migrants' Entrapment in a 'State of Expectancy': Patterns of Im/mobility for Agricultural Workers in Manolada, Greece.* Combining interviews with, amongst others, Bangladeshi strawberry pickers and readings of recent controversial legislation, they explore the workings of Greek labor and migration legislation in the coercive geography of the strawberry village of Manolada. Through their analysis, Floros, Kapsalis and Jørgensen demonstrate how the highly regulated access to the labor market and deportation postponement both enable and institutionalize dependencies and particular forms of exploitation of both legally and 'irregularly' residing migrants in Manolada.

In his chapter, *Constructing Immobility: Border Work and Coercion at the Hotspots of the Aegean,* Vasileios Spyridon Vlassis shifts the focus to the Greek islands of Lesvos and Chios as part of the EU's external border and its 'Hotspots' approach. Using data from non-participant observation and interviews with staff of NGOs, the Greek police, Frontex and the EU 'Hotspots.' Vlassis explores the EU bordering practices in the 'frontline member state.' In this analysis, the 'Hotspots' not only create temporal spaces of exception for irregularized migrants caught in immobility. The 'Hotspots' also intensify EU migration surveillance in that they discipline Greece's bordering practices on the one hand and represent an enhanced surveillance of migrant bodies to be 'datafied' and enrolled in the EU database assemblage on the other.

Turning to Cyprus, Leandros Fischer examines the assemblages of power that not only confine people fleeing wars and persecution in the Middle East but also render them an exploitable workforce in various coercive geographies across Cyprus in his chapter, *"Cyprus Is a Big Prison": Reflections on Mobility and Racialization in a Border Society.* Linking the EU external border regime, the Schengen-area (in which Cyprus is not partaking) and Cypriote labor regulation, Fischer classifies Cyprus as a geopolitical borderland between Europe and the Middle East in which asylum seekers who are unable to gain refugee status in Cyprus have been, and are, both entrapped and exploited to the extent they have been a noteworthy part of securing Cyprus' recovery after the 2013 financial collapse.

Turning to Scandinavia in the last chapter of the first part, Karin Krifors offers an analysis of the precarity of seasonal Thai workers navigate when picking wild forest berries in Sweden in her chapter *'When the Snow Falls, They Have All Left': Infrastructures of Seasonal Labor in Migration Corridors.* Centring

gender and race, Krifors' ethnographic study links global labor migration circuits and the personal aspirations of the Thai migrant workers to historical
examples of other groups of berry pickers in Sweden such as unemployed
Swedish women in the early 20th century, Polish seasonal workers in the 1980s
and contemporary Roma berry pickers. Emphasizing transnational complexity, Krifors argues that the forms of coercion experienced by migrant laborers
within the logistics of the supply chains might at the same time enable them
to engage in different forms of emancipatory projects.

As in the first part, the chapters in the second part of the book apply the lens
of coercive geographies in different ways. Here, however, emphasis is placed
on investigating how individuals, families, groups of people and communities
in different ways navigate and challenge the different legal, political, economic, administrative and military assemblages of coercion they face in various
geographies across Europe, the Middle East and Africa.

Focusing on migrant workers in Italy, Susi Meret and Irina Aguiari connect
past and present forms of the forced labor in their chapter, *Turning Migrants
into Slaves: Labor Exploitation and* Caporalato *Practices in the Italian Agricultural Sector*. Tracing the history of the 'caporalato' system, Meret and Aguiari
argue that the current coercive labor involving migrants is not only an adaptive
form of the 'caporalato' previously involving Italian poor from the South but
also that it is enabled by the legislative marginalisation and criminalisation of
as well as the physical segregation of poor migrants. Using interviews, however,
Meret and Aguiari also show how migrant agricultural workers find ways to
resist and build opportunities within these coercive geographies through, for
example, cooperative practices of farming and distribution.

In his chapter, *Strategies of Overcoming Precarity: The Case of Somali Transnational Community Ties, Spaces and Links in the United Arab Emirates*, Abdulkadir Osman Farah explores how Somali migrants work to overcome precarity in the United Arab Emirates by engaging in the building of transnational
community-generated platforms and networks. Using both individual and
group interviews with Somalis and extended (insider) participant observation
in the UAE, Abdulkadir Osman Farah examines how the Somali communities
in UAE turn to the transnational formation of diversified and multi-facetted
community ties, economic spaces and links to overcome precarity. In doing so,
he shows how these strategies not only help the migrants in UAE overcome
precarity through socio-economic 'bridgeheads' but also offer important humanitarian and development support to communities and relatives in Somalia
as well as Somali youth seeking education beyond both Somalia and UAE.

Martin Ottovay Jørgensen remains focused on the Middle East in his chapter, *Negotiating Displacement, Precarity and Militarized Confinement in the*

Middle East before Neoliberalism: The Gaza Strip, 1957–1967. Using records from the United Nations, Ottovay Jørgensen explores how the Israeli, Egyptian and UN regimes of military surveillance and confinement turned the Gaza Strip into a highly militarized coercive geography defined by displacement and precarity and how Palestinians and Bedouin negotiated this multilateral assemblage in everyday life from 1957 to 1967. In doing so, he demonstrates the deep but overlooked linkage between the emergent regimes of migrant confinement and expulsion in the Middle East, southern Europe and south-eastern Europe to the Ottoman and British imperial regimes of militarized migration regulation, surveillance and policing in the same regions as well as the resistance to both.

In his chapter, *Science as the Handmaiden of Coerced Labor: The Implementation of Cotton Cultivation Schemes in the Eastern Congo Uele Region, 1920–1960,* Sven Van Melkebeke examines the role of science in the forced labor regime of the cotton industry in the former Belgian colony of Congo. Van Melkebeke brings together the notion of coercive geographies within a commodity frontier framework and records from the African Archives of the Federal Public Service Foreign Affairs, Foreign Trade and Development Cooperation. He demonstrates how the overlapping Belgian colonial agricultural production systems (ab)used agronomy to coerce people to cultivate a cash crop according to imposed regulation and how people responded to these coercions, thereby also highlighting the deeper lineages of current agricultural systems' exploitative practices.

(Re)turning to Scandinavia in his chapter, *Life on the Run: Coercive Geographies in Denmark–Norway, 1600–1850,* Johan Heinsen examines how convict workers on the run from the coercive geographies of the Denmark–Norway's state penal labor institutions' confinement, labor control and exploitative practices faced border patrols, passport controls and other newly installed measures. Using records from the Danish penal system, Heinsen not only demonstrates that prison breaking was from a marginal phenomenon as thousands of convicts most of whom were from the lowest rungs of society managed to escape their confines and retain their autonomy. He also highlights how modern democracies' efforts at controlling mobility, policing crime and disciplining labor often share deep ties to the prison factories and other types of punitive labor institutions from their former absolutist lives.

In summary, this book is an attempt to link scholars from a broad range of disciplines to bring together space, precarity, labor coercion and mobility in the concept of coercive geographies against the backdrop of an increasingly volatile global regime of migration surveillance, confinement and exploitation. As we hope to have shown, the concept can be employed to explore historical cases, examine lineages of current practices and, not least, challenge current and emergent systems around the world.

References

Abend, L. (2019). "An Island for 'Unwanted' Migrants Is Denmark's Latest Aggressive Anti-Immigrant Policy," *Time*, 16 January 2019. https://time.com/5504331/denmark-migrants-lindholm-island/.

Anderson, B. (2010). "Migration, immigration controls and the fashioning of precarious workers," *Work, Employment and Society* 24(2): 300–317.

Anderson, C. (ed.) (2018). *A Global History of Convicts and Penal Colonies*. London: Bloomsbury.

Bauder, H. (2006). *Labor Movement: How Migration Regulates Labor Markets*. Oxford: Oxford University Press.

Beckert, Sven (2014). *Empire of Cotton: A Global History*. New York: Knopf.

Betti, E. (2016). "Gender and Precarious Labor in a Historical Perspective: Italian Women and Precarious Work between Fordism and Post-Fordism," *International Labor and Working-Class History* 89: 64–83.

Bloch, A., and McKay, S. (2016). *Living on the Margins: Undocumented Migrants in a Global City*. London: Policy Press.

Casas-Cortés, M. (2014). "A genealogy of precarity: A toolbox for rearticulating fragmented social realities in and out of the workplace," *Rethinking Marxism* 26(2): 206–226.

Cohen, R. (2004). "Chinese cockle-pickers, The transnational turn and everyday cosmopolitanism: Reflections on the new global migrants," *Labour, Capital and Society/ Travail, capital et société*: 130–149.

Cresswell, T. (2011). "Mobilities I: catching up," *Progress in Human Geography* 35(4): 550–558.

De Vito, C. and Gerritsen A. (2018). "Micro-Spatial Histories of Labour: Towards a New Global History," in De Vito, C. and Gerritsen, A (eds.). *Micro-Spatial Histories of Global Labour*. Cham: Springer: 1–28.

De Vito, C. and Lichtenstein, A. (eds.) (2015). *Global Convict Labour*. Leiden: Brill.

De Vito, C., Schiel, J. and van Rossum, M. (2020), "From Bondage to Precariousness? New Perspectives on Labor and Social History," *Journal of Social History*: 1–19.

Donoghue, J. and Jennings, E. (2016). *Building the Atlantic Empires: Unfree Labor and Imperial States in the Political Economy of Capitalism, ca. 1500–1914*. Leiden: Brill.

Eckert, A. (2016). "Why all the fuss about Global Labour History," in Eckert, A (ed.). *Global Histories of Work*. Berlin: De Gruyter: 3–22.

Faist, T. (2013). "The mobility turn: a new paradigm for the social sciences?," *Ethnic and Racial Studies* 36(11): 1637–1646.

Faist, T. (2012). "Toward a transnational methodology: methods to address methodological nationalism, essentialism, and positionality," *Revue européenne des migrations internationales* 28(1): 51–70.

Faist, T. (1998). "Transnational social spaces out of international migration," *Archives Européennes de Sociologie* 39(2): 213–247.

Fink, L. (ed.) (2011). *Workers across the Americas: The Transnational Turn in Labor History*. Oxford: Oxford University Press.

Floros, K., and Jørgensen, M.B. (2020). "Tracing the future of migrants' labour relations. Experiences of institutionalized migrant precarity in Denmark and Greece," *Political Geography Journal*. Pre-print. https://doi.org/10.1016/j.polgeo.2019.102120.

García, M.G., van Voss, L.H. and Meerkerk, E. (eds.) (2017). *Selling Sex in the City: A Global History of Prostitution, 1600s–2000s*. Leiden: Brill.

Gentes, A. (2008). *Exile to Siberia, 1590–1822*. New York: Palgrave.

Gibson, M. and Poerio, I. (2018). "Modern Europe, 1750–1950," in Anderson, J. (ed.). *A Global History of Convicts and Penal Colonies*. London: Bloomsbury: 271–306.

Gill, N., Caletrío, J., and Mason, V. (2011). "Introduction: Mobilities and forced migration," *Mobilities* 6(3): 301–316.

Greenwood, M.J., and Hunt, G.L. (2003). "The early history of migration research," *International Regional Science Review* 26(1): 3–37.

Hardt, M. and Negri, A. (2004). *Multitude: War and Democracy in the Age of Empire*. London: Penguin Books.

Hoerder, D., Meerkerk, E., and Neunsinger, S. (eds.) (2015). *Towards a Global History of Domestic and Caregiving Workers*. Leiden: Brill.

Jørgensen, M.B. (2016). "Precariat–what it is and isn't–towards an understanding of what it does," *Critical Sociology* 42(7–8): 959–974.

Marcu, S. (2019). "The limits to mobility: Precarious work experiences among young Eastern Europeans in Spain," *Environment and Planning A: Economy and Space* 51(4): 913–930.

Mezzadra, S. (2007). "Living in Transition: Toward a Heterolingual Theory of the Multitude," http://eipcp.net/transversal/1107/mezzadra/en.

Miller, J.C. (2012). *The Problem of Slavery as History: A Global Approach*. New Haven: Yale University Press.

Nielsen, S., Jenvall, N.L., and Ingvorsen, E. (2018). "Udvist, kriminelle udlændinge sendes til øde ø i Stege bugt," Public news broadcaster. *DR*. 30 November 2018. https://www.dr.dk/nyheder/politik/udviste-kriminelle-udlaendinge-sendes-til-oede-oe-i-stege-bugt.

Olsen, H.H. (2008). "The snake from Fujian Province to Morecambe Bay: an analysis of the problem of human trafficking in sweated labour," *Eur. J. Crime Crim. L. & Crim. Just.* 16(1): 1–37.

Paret, M., and Gleeson, S. (2016). "Precarity and agency through a migration lens," *Citizenship Studies* 20(3–4): 277–294.

Pike, R. (1983). *Penal Servitude in Early Modern Spain*. Madison: The University of Wisconsin Press.

Rediker, M., Chakraborty, T. and van Rossum, M. (eds.) (2019). *A Global History of Runaways: Workers, Mobility, and Capitalism, 1600–1850*. Oakland: University of California Press.

Ritzau (2018a). "De udvistes ø er først virusfri om to år," *Berlingske*, 6 December 2018. https://www.berlingske.dk/danmark/de-udvistes-oe-er-foerst-virusfri-om-to-aar.

Ritzau (2018b). "FN-chef er seriøst bekymret over regeringens Lindholm-center," *Jyllands-Posten*, 6 December 2018. https://jyllands-posten.dk/politik/ECE11053529/fnchef-er-serioest-bekymret-over-regeringens-lindholmcenter/.

Satzewich, V. (2011). "Transnational Migration: A New Historical Phenomenon?," in Fink, L. (ed.). *Workers Across the Americas: The Transnational Turn in Labor History*. Oxford: Oxford University Press: 39–48.

Song, M. (2004). "When the 'global chain' does not lead to satisfaction all round: A comment on the Morecambe Bay tragedy," *Feminist review* 77(1): 137–140.

Stanziani, A. (2014). *Bondage: Labor and Rights in Eurasia from the Sixteenth to the Early Twentieth Centuries*. New York: Berghahn.

van der Linden, M. (2008). *Workers of the World: Essays toward a Global Labour History*. Leiden: Brill.

van der Linden, M. (2014). "San Precario: A New Inspiration for Labor Historians," *Labor Studies in Working-Class History of the Americas*: 9–21.

van der Linden, M. (2016). "Dissecting Coerced Labor," in van der Linden, M. and Garcìa, M.G. (eds.). *On Coerced Labor: Work and Compulsion after Chattel Slavery*. Leiden: Brill: 293–322.

van Rossum, M. and Kamp, J. (eds.) (2016). *Desertion in the Early Modern World: A Comparative History*. London: Bloomsbury.

Vickers, T., Clayton, J., Davison, H., Hudson, L., A Cañadas, M., Biddle, P., and Lilley, S. (2019). "Dynamics of precarity among 'new migrants': exploring the worker–capital relation through mobilities and mobility power," *Mobilities*: 1–19. https://doi.org/10.1080/17450101.2019.1611028.

Wyss, A. (2019). "Stuck in Mobility? Interrupted Journeys of Migrants With Precarious Legal Status in Europe," *Journal of Immigrant & Refugee Studies* 17(1): 77–93.

Zürcher, E. (ed.) (2014). *Fighting for a Living: A Comparative Study of Military Labour 1500–2000*. Amsterdam: Amsterdam University Press.

Ågren, M. (ed.) (2016). *Making a Living, Making a Difference*. Oxford: Oxford University Press.

CHAPTER 2

Migrants' Entrapment in a 'State of Expectancy': Patterns of Im/mobility for Agricultural Workers in Manolada, Greece

Apostolos Kapsalis, Konstantinos Floros and Martin Bak Jørgensen

1 Introduction

The strawberry producing village of Nea Manolada, whose name has become a synonym for undeclared migrant labor coupled with violence and compulsion on behalf of the employers' side, is the popular archetype of a coercive geography in the Greek context. Institutionalized precarity, as we meet here, is situated and shaped by particular political geographies which constitute different coercive geographies producing confined, restricted spaces which create unfreedom, stuckness and immobility (cf. introduction this volume). An outcome of enduring migration/labor policies on the national level combined with social and labor market particularities on the local level, Manolada constitutes a divisive and exclusionary geography, which facilitates the emergence of severe forms of labor exploitation of both legally and "irregularly" residing migrants. In the past 25–30 years, migrants have been living there in slum settlements working under harsh and unhealthy conditions. They have been shot at while asking for their salaries in 2013, workers have been severely injured or died in accidents during their transportation to the fields and they have witnessed the conflagration of three of their settlements and the subsequent burning of large amounts of money, personal belongings and administrative paperwork. Still, as many as seven hundred Bangladeshi migrants stay there permanently throughout the year and up to nine thousand migrants (mainly of Bangladeshi origin) provide their labor during the peak of the harvesting season, which lasts from January to June.

This chapter investigates the causes which enable a steady supply of migrant labor in Manolada and outlines migrants' im/mobility (cf. Bélanger and Silvey 2019) patterns within the Greek territory. Our research is based on twenty-nine qualitative interviews with Bangladeshi migrants, through which we delve deeper into their aspirations and self-perception of their situation and agency. In order to analyse how such a geography has been stabilized for more than a decade we apply the aspiration-capability framework (Schewel 2019) into our empirical case. Moreover, we observe how legal frameworks create barriers to migrants regarding their integration in the labor market and impede their mobility. We especially focus on attempts to occupationally and geographically immobilize migrants within the Greek agricultural sector and institutionalize their precarious condition through recent policymaking (Floros and Jørgensen 2020), which introduced the concept of 'para-legality' (Kapsalis 2018a) as a new category in stratified labor and residency statuses. Our aim is to justify the terming of Manolada as a coercive geography by providing a nuanced report on a) migrants' labor and housing conditions, b) the role of restrictive migration/labor frameworks and c) migrants' personal accounts about their situation and im/mobility.

In the Greek political discourse Manolada figures as the par excellence example of a coercive geographical space, mainly because of migrant protest against the exploitative conditions and the violent incidents of 2013 (Papadopoulos et al. 2018). Nevertheless, through our research we became aware of several other coercive geographies within the Greek agricultural sector, as the same Bangladeshi migrants relocate by hundreds and by seasons across the country to work and lodge, in circular patterns more or less similar to each other and in equally degrading conditions. Their consecutive back and forth in the same exploitative routes coupled with their current or original aspirations to reach some other European country, lead us to term this pattern as 'mobility in immobility', as an ongoing mobility in the frame of an institutionalized immobility both in the country and in their occupational activity.

We conclude that Bangladeshi migrants working in the Greek agricultural sector are entrapped in a constant 'state of expectancy' created by restrictive – yet under special circumstances promising – residence permit policies, which standardize their exploitation within diverse agricultural settings in Greece. This comes as no surprise. The restructuring of European agricultural production has been premised on maintaining "vulnerable legal status and social condition(s) of migrants" (Corrado et al. 2016: 4) and Greece does not pose as an exception in this regional map of coercive geographies.

In our chapter we begin by briefly outlining the legal framework that shapes the agricultural labor market for migrants in Greece. We then introduce the concepts that constitute our theoretical framework and the methodological approach to our research. In the next part we present and analyse our empirical findings, arguing on the existence of a 'state of expectancy' and a 'mobility in immobility' pattern, before concluding by explaining the reasons for the perpetuation of Manolada's coercive geography.

2   Greece's Restrictive Legal Framework and the Introduction of
       'Para-legality'

In Greece, socio-legal constraints are the outcome of a thirty-year long restrictive immigration regime, which curbed the acquisition of citizenship and at
the same time tied residence permits and their renewal to a certain 'amount' of
declared work performed by migrants (Gemi 2013; Triandafyllidou et al. 2013).
It is not our intention here to provide a nuanced map of migration policymaking in Greece, but we need to stress out a series of policy provisions which have
shaped the agricultural labor market for migrants. Greece has forged a frag-
mentary and preventive migration policy in the past 30 years, dealing with migration in "purely instrumental terms" (Triandafyllidou 2014: 122). Migrants
cover 95 per cent of the need for waged labor in the agricultural sector (Kasimis et al. 2015), yet undeclared labor is widespread. The only legal pathway for
a migrant to enter the Greek labor market has been the invitation procedure
(in Greek metaklisi) and the seasonal work scheme, which both applied almost exclusively to agricultural labor. Nowadays, these schemes tend to be replaced almost entirely by work-permits corresponding to article 13a. According
to unpublished data obtained by the Ministry of Labor and Social Affairs, the
number of permits issued through 13a has risen from 1,100 for the period 2015–
2016 to 9,500 for 2017–2018. Permits issued for metaklisi or seasonal work for
agriculture were only 5,400 in 2017–2018.

    In 2016, an amendment (13a) to the Immigration Code provided the grant-
ing of six-month-long work permits to irregularly residing migrants, almost
exclusively for the agricultural sector. These work permits can be renewed but
are not coupled by residence permits. This new socio-legal status for migrants
has been termed 'para-legality' by Kapsalis, since 13a "constitutes a parallel
state of tolerance (of labor) into illegality (of residence) [...] as it appears that
the residence status remains irregular throughout the duration of the work
permit" (Kapsalis 2018a: 78). Migrants, who once possessed a residence permit
or whose deportation has been suspended due to humanitarian or technical
reasons, need a certificate of employment and a deportation postponement by
the police authorities. If completely undocumented, migrants first sign a deportation confirmation, followed by a 6-month postponement. The permit has
occupational and geographical limitations, since a migrant can only work in
the prefecture which issued the permit, thus entrapping possibility of legal
work in designated areas.

    Agricultural labor is almost exclusively declared through the ergosimo (Wil-
liams et al. 2016; Kapsalis 2018b), a payment voucher introduced in 2010 allowing employers to "contract" migrant workers mainly in the agricultural and

domestic care sectors. Labor according to 13a provisions is mandatorily paid through ergosimo. Nevertheless, this employment relation is not declared in the official digital registry for dependent employment (ERGANI). It only appears in social security registries, when – and if – the voucher is redeemed by the migrant. The ergosimo minimizes social security costs and facilitates employers' arbitrary behavior, given the fact that it is a means of labor payment essentially – and typically – detached from the obligation to declare real working hours, employment location, job specification or any other data on the employment relation. Flexibility and contingency are intrinsic to this voucher, since this kind of employment relation is almost uncontrollable from labor inspections. Conclusively, 13a reinforces hyper-flexibility and augments migrants' dependency on the employers, rendering migrants susceptible to exploitative labor conditions, while at the same time temporally entrapping them geographically and occupationally.

3   On Im/mobility, Unfree Labor and Precarity

The concept of globalisation as well as its contestations produced extensive theoretical debates around the turn of the millennium. Bred in this context of constant flux of people, products, ideas and information, one of the most influential contributions within social sciences was the 'mobility turn', which called for mobility to be placed at the epicenter of theory and research (Urry 2000; Cresswell 2006; Sheller and Urry 2006). Although this theoretical paradigm emphasized the existence of constraints in mobility – and especially when referring to the issue of migration – very soon scholars pointed out the need to use immobility as a theoretical lens, in order to "challenge the grand narrative of hypermobility, flux, and fluidity associated with modernity" (Schewel 2019: 5). Jørgen Carling theorized on immobility through his research in Cape Verde (Carling 2002), concluding that our times should be outlined as an age of 'involuntary immobility', an approach that contradicted the popular concept of the 'age of migration' introduced by Castles and Miller (1993).

Indeed, mobility and immobility coexist in empirical cases of migration and sometimes even share common causes, thus raising the need for reflective and nuanced approaches regarding their conceptual use. Spatial and temporal factors are key to conceptualizing accounts of immobility. A migrant may travel thousands of kilometers only to be confined in a detention camp or s/he can be stuck for a long period of time in a certain place (of origin, transit or destination) but still aspire to move. Aspirations are crucial when investigating migration. In our research we use the aspiration-capability framework (Schewel

2019), so as to investigate patterns of mobility and immobility for Bangladeshi migrants working in Manolada's strawberry-producing agricultural sector. Firstly introduced as aspiration-ability model by Carling (2002) and further elaborated by de Haas (2014), who replaced 'ability' with the more dynamic term 'capability' and Schewel (2015) who added the 'acquiescent immobility' category to it, this framework is characterized by a methodological two-step approach, which first evaluates migration as a potential action and then observes categories of mobility or immobility in a given spatio-temporal context (Carling and Schewel 2018).

Spatial dimensions of immobility have been investigated in recent literature from various different angles (e.g. Tazzioli 2018; Suter 2013; Mata-Codesal 2018). 'Im/mobility' – as an ambiguous term – has been used widely in order "to underscore the mutually constitutive relationship between particular forms of movement and the regulations and disciplinary pressures that delimit that movement" (Bélanger and Silvey 2019: 2). The same scholars engage with the term 'immobility in mobility' (ibid.) so as to highlight im/mobility patterns for migrant care workers all over the globe and describe situations of confinement or restriction of movement in employers' homes. In our case we detect a reverse condition. Bangladeshi migrants are circularly mobile within specific different coercive geographies of rural Greece, yet immobilized to a great extent inside the country's borders and moreover socially and occupationally immobilized in the aforementioned geographies. It is what we coin as 'mobility in immobility.'

Another crucial feature of migrant im/mobility is waiting (Conlon 2011). Waiting is very often imposed on migrants who 'get stuck' for indefinite periods of time in countries they originally considered as transit points, blurring distinctions between transit and final destination (Collyer et al. 2012; Suter 2013). It has also been widely enforced to asylum seekers, refugees and migrants in a number of contexts (Mountz 2011), creating what Mezzadra and Neilson (2012) have coined as 'waiting zones', namely "holding zones and funnels" which facilitate the regulation of the "timing and tempo" of migrants' differential inclusion (ibid.: 68–69). Such analysis complements Mountz's, who speaks of "fixation of mobile people in limbo through exclusionary processes" (2011: 383). Waiting, though, sometimes comes as a deliberate strategy by migrants who voluntarily enter exploitative labor conditions in order to achieve benefits regarding their socio-legal status (Axelsson et al. 2017). Through combining these two points of view, one should always consider the exclusionary processes at play, which facilitate differential inclusion of migrants in the countries of the global North. The institutionalisation of migrants' precarity is achieved through a series of constraints, fracturing of citizenship and stratification of statuses and permits (Floros and Jørgensen 2020).

In line with this literature and the theoretical approaches that take into account migrant agency in its multifarious expressions, we consider that the majority of Bangladeshis working in Manolada live and work in what we term as a 'state of expectancy.' They are not in a 'waiting zone' since they are already included in the labor market, nor do they wait for a concrete outcome, but rather share a general expectancy for the improvement of their socio-legal status. They lag in a nexus between involuntary and acquiescent immobility – or more precisely 'mobility in immobility' – with the constant hope of navigating through a tunnel of demeaning and exploitative labor conditions, appalling housing conditions and hyper-precarity. At the end of the tunnel there is a flickering light, since a few migrants finally achieve the "residency permit for exceptional reasons," nevertheless, this permit which requires seven years of consecutive and well-documented presence in Greece is not awarded to everyone and is also at stake through the change of policies or governments. This uncertainty and the behaviors that derive from it is what we term 'state of expectancy'.

Our chapter also draws on the concepts of 'unfree labor' and the 'hyper-precarity trap' (Lewis et al. 2015a) to "show how neoliberal labour markets and highly restrictive immigration regimes intersect to produce multidimensional insecurities that underpin the demand and supply of forced labour subjects" (Lewis et al. 2015b: 144). Unfree labor has been conceptualized by the ILO (ILO 2018) and various Marxist theorists (e.g. Brass 2011) in dichotomizing ways. In our analysis we follow the theoretical angle of critical unfree labor studies (McGrath 2016), which eschews strict binaries of freedom/unfreedom in order to delve deeper into the variety of unfreedoms that characterize labor relations within coercive geographies. Therefore we prefer to emphasize the multidimensional particularities of coercive labor relations by projecting our findings on continuums; what Lerche (2011) has termed the 'continuum of unfreedom' or Skrivankova (2010) 'continuum of exploitation'.

The creation and preservation of certain enclaves is frequently encountered within intensive agricultural production systems in Europe, where low-wage labor is performed by migrants, living and working in hyper-precarious conditions. The 'hyper-precarity trap' is formed at the intersection of socio-legal constraints imposed by restrictive immigration regimes within neoliberal economies and the imperative need of migrants to encounter any available employment so as to subsist on it, but also to settle their debts or cater for families back home. Their adverse incorporation (Philips 2013) in the labor market coupled by their exclusion from welfare provisions marks their 'hyper-precarious' status (Lewis et al. 2015a). Nevertheless, by highlighting this 'hyper-precarious' status we do not mean to portray migrants as mere victims of the labor market. We agree that "migration policy and research that privileges the analysis of migrants primarily as jobseekers and refugees fails to adequately represent the subjective diversity of migrant mobilities, the dynamic power of migrants themselves, and the analytical value of taking mobility seriously as a starting point for understanding border policies" (Casas Cortes et al. 2015: 896). A growing body of scholars has taken up this 'Autonomy of Migration' (AoM) approach, recognizing migrants' agency as constitutive of border, migration and labor policies (ibid. 2015; De Genova 2017). By employing AoM as an analytical tool we wish to avoid the objectification of migrants and their im/mobility.

4   Methodology

Our chapter is based on 29 semi-structured on-site interviews with Bangladeshi migrants working in the strawberry-producing area of Manolada in Greece, as well as extensive desk-based research on Greek legal texts, parliamentary debate, policy papers and existing literature on the case of Manolada. We also conducted an interview with the mayor of Andravida-Kyllini (which is the administrative municipality of the greater strawberry-production area) as well as several informal interviews with lawyers and NGO members providing legal assistance to migrants in the area. Our research benefits from insight we have already gained by investigating the enactment of recent legislation through expert interviews with officials of Greek ministries regarding 13a (Floros and Jørgensen 2020) and extensive desk-based research on labor legislation regarding migrants in the Greek agricultural sector (Kapsalis 2018a).

We decided to take a two-step approach according to the aspiration-capability model (Carling and Schewel 2018; Schewel 2019). First we evaluated potential aspirations and plans of Bangladeshi migrants regarding their mobility within and beyond Greek borders. For the second step, which requires observation of categories of mobility or immobility in a given spatio-temporal context, we did not only use qualitative data from the interviews but we also interpreted it in combination with socio-legal constraints on mobility deriving from Greek legislation. The two ways of conceptualizing migration capability are "as potential or revealed" (Carling and Schewel 2018: 955). Quantitative data on irregularly residing Bangladeshis' migration patterns are not accessible, since a lot of migrants' trajectories within and through Greece remain undocumented, so 'revealed' capability was out of this research's reach. There-fore we focused on 'potential' capability, also reflecting on the fact that all in-terviewees were obviously unable or unwilling – up to date – to migrate out of Greece.

The first three interviews with Bangladeshi migrants date back to June 2018. Another eleven were conducted in October 2018 and the last fifteen in May 2019. Our first interviews where with contacts facilitated through trade unions and antiracist organisations and where carried out in Greek. We immediately realized that our interlocutors where hierarchically above – if not exploiting – their compatriots. As we later found out, their seniority of presence in the vil-lage and their ability to communicate in Greek allowed them to hold a mastura position. *Masturas* are intermediaries between migrants and local bosses, who profit from supplying labor positions, accommodation and mediation to the rest of the labor force. In order to encounter less biased informants, we at-tempted to establish new connections at the local café, where Bangladeshis hang out. Through these connections we arranged the second on-site visit, this time with a translator. We carried out eleven interviews, three of them with *masturas*, one of which was our new liaison. In order to recruit informants avoiding gatekeepers (Sixsmith et al. 2003), we visited again Manolada in May 2019, at the peak of the harvesting season, together with a Bangladeshi NGO translator that had already worked in the field and helped us evade *masturas*. So as to circumvent the gatekeepers we went straight to the slum settlements and took a site-based approach to recruit informants. The last fifteen inter-views were divided in two groups. In order to recruit participants that would ensure a diversity in our sample (Eide and Allen 2005) we conducted eight in-terviews with migrants employed in Manolada for more than five seasons and seven with newly-arrived migrants; five of which had only been in Greece for a few months.

All participants were Bangladeshi males between the age of 24 and 50. The oldest was one of the first Bangladeshis to arrive in the village, whereas the youngest had entered Greece less than a month ago. Our questionnaire was divided in four sub-categories, namely personal information, socio-legal sta-tus, labor conditions and housing conditions. Three of the questions followed the aspiration-capability framework typology, so as to detect and evaluate a) "aspiration, desire or preference to migrate," b) "conditional willingness to migrate" and c) "likelihood of migration" (Carling and Schewel 2018: 948). We preferred semi-structured interviews to surveys, in order to ensure that partici-pants would fully engage with delicate and ambiguous concepts. Several open-ended questions were formulated in such a way so as to ensure that mi-grants could provide answers in their own terms (Qu and Dumay 2011), within a cross-cultural setting of communication. We considered vital for our research to pursue a deeper understanding of the subjective diversity of Bangladeshi agricultural workers, in line with our use of AoM as an analytical tool. Against a victimizing approach on migration, we strived to discern migrants' self-perception of concepts such as coercion, entrapment, unfreedom and agency and to gain insight in the ways they navigate, resist or succumb to the restrictive immigration regime enforced by the Greek state within Europe's neoliberal framework.

Before each interview we clearly stated the fact that we are researchers and that our only contribution through this research is the dissemination of knowledge regarding the demeaning and exploitative working and housing conditions that they experience. In conducting our research we engaged with sensitive data of people who are predominantly in a precarious socio-legal situation. We respected the anonymity of our informants and abstained from enclosing any information that could reveal their identity or in any way prove harmful to them. We wish to thank all of our informants, but especially the ones in our last visit, for welcoming us into their tents during their resting time and offering us food and tea.

5   Living and Working in the Strawberry-Producing Zone

Nea Manolada is a village in the Peloponnese with less than two thousand inhabitants. It is located in a small plain which is intensively cultivated to produce 90 per cent of Greece's strawberries (Manoladawatch 2019). The harvesting season begins in January and ends in June. During its peak more than six thousand migrants – predominantly Bangladeshi, but also Pakistani, Afghans and some of Balkan origin – live in the village and work in the surrounding fields and around three thousand more reside in nearby villages such as Lappa and Psari, also seasonally harvesting strawberries. When the season comes to an end, only seven hundred migrants remain in Manolada.

Bangladeshi workers are hardly ever accommodated in houses in the village; locals are unwilling to rent their property to groups of single men and prefer hosting migrant families from the Balkans. The Bangladeshis set up slum camps in the fields at the edge of the village, built with iron arches, reed, greenhouse PVC plastic and carton boxes. The capacity of each tent is a matter of size, cost and availability and it ranges from four to twenty people. The larger camps can host up to 700 workers during high season, without toilets, with only a non-drinkable water supply for cleaning and showering purposes. Due to the constant use of the water supply, stagnant cesspools are formed next to the settlements. Chickens and goats bought for feeding purposes also live inside and around the camps.

The interior of the tents is humid and cold in the winter, but as temperature rises in the springtime living conditions become more unbearable, especially during the daytime. Indoor temperature is ten to fifteen degrees Celsius higher during the day, flies and mosquitos are ever-present and everyday cooking in the improvised gas kitchenettes of the tents' antechambers further worsens the situation. Workers sleep on rugs or blankets on the floor, next to each other. Their belongings are stored in bags hanging from the ceiling and a big part of the free space in the tent is occupied by six-packs of plastic bottles of drinkable water.

These tents do not come for free. Each worker pays a monthly rent to the compatriot who set up the tent. A part of this money is paid to the landlord of the field. Prices in 2019 ranged from 10 to 25 euro per capita per month.

> I built the tent on my own, but do not ask for money from my fellow countrymen. I am not a scum to live on commissions. The four of us live here and pay altogether 35 euro/month to the field-owner. I am not like the *masturas* that live off other workers' sweat.
>
> WORKER B 2019

A mastura is a migrant intermediary. Also referred to as group-commanders, the *masturas* (a word deriving from the greek word mastoras, which translates into skilled craftsman) are the backbone of the migrant labor market in Manolada. They are usually veteran workers who live in Manolada throughout the year and have basic conversational skills in Greek. A mastura sets up his own group of workers, negotiates jobs with bosses by guaranteeing availability of workers and is responsible for payments and handling of claims. A mastura hardly ever performs manual labor, he is a foreman usually yelling and swearing at the workers to achieve better productivity. Bangladeshi workers pay 100 euro per season to a mastura, in order to secure an employment spot for the season. A mastura also makes money through arranging deals with field-owners for settlements, as well as from building up tents or securing declared labor for migrants striving to achieve or maintain residency permits:

> I renewed my permit last year by giving the mastura 150 euros to convince the boss to declare me. [...] Money does not guarantee you a paper. Only good relations with the mastura does.
>
> WORKER C 2019

> Nowadays bosses pay on time. It is common practice though that the last
> salary of the season gets paid the next season. So it goes, every year. The
> mastura says that this is the boss' doings. It is a common pattern this way of
> paying, so as to ensure that workers will come back the next season as well.
>
> WORKER D 2019

Wages are fixed at 24euro/day for a seven-hour shift. Overtime is hardly ever
paid for (2–3 euros per hour when it is rarely the case) and payments are performed by the mastura and usually delayed. Working conditions are harsh and
exhausting. Most of the migrants complain about back pains, respiratory problems and skin irritations. Gloves and masks are never provided, not even during the spraying of pesticides in greenhouses. Migrant protests are scarce nowadays. Claims are made to the mastura, a worker never gets to demand or
negotiate anything with the boss. Complaints and demands usually lead to a
week-long deprivation of employment:

> Whenever I protest about something... anything... the mastura cuts off
> eight to nine days of work.
>
> WORKER O 2019

> Once I asked for a mask and gloves and the mastura told me I should call
> my family back home and ask them for money to buy some gloves.
>
> WORKER M 2019

Lately, there has been an effort – with the help of an NGO – to build a trade
union of Bangladeshis working in the area. Almost all workers were aware of
this effort and said they would like to contribute and speak up against their
problems. Only two stated that they are not interested, because they said that
the *masturas* will take over the association and control it.

Except for interviewed *masturas*, who claimed that relations among Greeks
and migrants are perfect, the rest of the workers said that there is no kind of
relationship between them and the Greeks; they hardly ever speak to each
other. Everybody agreed that the police never performs paper controls inside
the village and they feel totally protected and safe within the broader
strawberry-producing area:

> The police only comes when labour inspections take place, because they
> have to. The police is being paid by the bosses. Chief K...'s daughter runs
> a farm with 700 workers.
>
> WORKER C 2019

When defining labor as unfree or terming a geography as coercive it is important to substantiate such allegations. In our case, apart from interviewees' personal narratives and judgements on unfreedom and coercion, there also exist judicial decisions on the issue. The unfreedom that characterizes migrants' labor relations in Manolada can no longer be questioned, since such forms of forced labor are defined with clarity in the decision of the European Court of Human Rights (2017) on the case of Chowdury vs Greece, which referred to the 2013 incidents. Moreover, in June 2019, a decision of the Greek Supreme Court on the same incidents, annulled the initial acquittal of the employers of the shot Bangladeshis by the local court, on the grounds of human trafficking for labor exploitation according to Greek penal legislation. Summarizing the literature regarding these court decisions, employers apparently take advantage of the vulnerability of migrants in order to exploit them. The cause of this vulnerability is migrants' irregular socio-legal status and harsh living conditions (Asta 2018; Stoyanova 2018).

Recently, 355 workers who lived in the camp which burnt down in 2018 were awarded residence permits on 'humanitarian grounds'. According to the District Attorney they worked in the strawberry-fields under "particularly abusive terms." This development was based on Greek legislation (4052/2012) which transposed into national law the European Directive 2009/52, providing for minimum standards on sanctions and measures against employers of illegally staying third-country nationals. Nevertheless, for thousands of their fellow workers, who did not lose their tents and papers in the fire, the prospect of a residence permit remains a very difficult task.

6   State of Expectancy

Do something, write something! We need legal papers and different housing conditions. Our situation here is unbearable.
>   WORKER R 2018

The desire of the majority of migrants to acquire residence permits is obvious from the fact that the ones residing for years in Greece either once had a valid permit which expired or have already filed applications to obtain 'residence permits for exceptional reasons'. Eight out of twenty-nine Bangladeshis interviewed were rejected asylum seekers. Many others wanted to file an asylum application in the past, but were told by swindlers that they needed to pay a lot of money for the application, so they never did. Even those who have never even applied for a residence permit, aspire to acquire one through a law where an application is possible once you can prove through documents that you have resided in Greece for seven consequent years.

As stated above, this 'residence permit for exceptional reasons' requires proof of strong ties with Greece and seven years of consecutive and well-documented presence in the country, but is not awarded to every applicant. All traces of existence in public documents are of extreme importance to them and especially the ones related to social security issues.

A migrant can invoke a large range of public documents such as asylum applications or even personalised monthly transportation tickets in order to file his/her application, but documents which certificate strong ties to Greece are among others Greek tax number acquisition documents, social security stamps, health cards and deportation papers, as well as redeemed ergosimo vouchers. Ergosimo vouchers are very popular as proof of administrative existence. Migrants who possess a tax registration number but have no valid residence permit can be paid with ergosimo. In any case – except for domestic labor which is almost exclusively feminized – the only possibility for irregularly residing migrant males to obtain administrative traces of existence is in the agricultural sector, where payment through ergosimo is mandatory.

Almost all Bangladeshis were aware of the existence of 13a, yet very few had realized that when applying for 13a one also signs his/her deportation postponement. The majority of them had asked their mastura or boss for a 13a spot but were denied one:

> I asked my boss in Lappa for a 13a spot. He said no. I came to Manolada to find one but I can't. I want a 13a permit so that one day maybe I will be able to acquire a proper permit.
> WORKER X 2018

> Yes, I want a 13a spot, but have no steady employer. They told me that bosses ask for 200 euros in order to file the application.
> WORKER Y 2018

Most of the migrants interviewed – except for *masturas* and the majority of the newly-arrived – said that 13a spots are awarded to people who pay for them (150–200 euros) and are selected by the mastura. Due to this fact, 13a is losing its popularity as a pathway to legalisation. Seven of the interviewees said they prefer to wait until they can document a seven-year presence so as to apply for a 'residence permit for exceptional reasons'. The possibility of acquiring such a permit dictates patterns of behavior for a lot of the Bangladeshi workers. Seeing this as their only hope of achieving a legal status that will enable them to live and work wherever they want without the threat of imprisonment or deportation, they agree on their exploitation from *masturas* and bosses in return for proof of legal existence (and waged labor off course), definitely in Manolada and also in other coercive geographies:

> Last year I was working in the Mesolonghi area (Western Greece) with some friends. The boss withheld 5000 euros from our payment. We went to the police but they told us we can't do anything, we are illegal.
>
> WORKER D 2019

This resembles the tactics of Chinese chefs in Sweden (Axelsson et al. 2017) who endure years of exploitation as part of a tactic to acquire a permanent residence permit. The difference in our case is that there is no legal certainty of a permanent residence, since small details can lead to a rejection of the application and also a change in policy can prove disastrous to seven-year planning. A conviction for some minor offence can also lead to a rejection. Nevertheless, hundreds of 'residence permits for humanitarian reasons' have been awarded to the victims of the 2013 shootings and the 2018 camp conflagration, while at the same time there are numerous Bangladeshis who already achieved 'residence permits for exceptional reasons' by documenting 'strong ties to Greece' through their presence in Manolada's labor market. According to data from the Ministry for Migration Policy, in June 2019, male migrants throughout Greece possessed 900 valid "residence permits for humanitarian reasons" (one third of which belonged to the burnt camp victims) and 13,900 for "exceptional reasons" (many of them awarded – and hundreds still pending – to male Bangladeshi agricultural workers).

Uncertainty coupled with hope shape a 'state of expectancy', which usually dictates Bangladeshi migrants' choices. One of these choices is their constant move in search of employment and administrative traces, what we term 'mobility in immobility'. Manolada is a stable point of reference in these trajectories.

7 Mobility in Immobility

An official at the Greek Ministry for Migration Policy stated in 2018 that: "If the state would properly legalize the status of these Bangladeshi workers (in

Manolada), then they would all leave to Athens in the next day, to look for a more decent job" (Floros and Jørgensen 2020).

Sixteen out of twenty-nine interviewed migrants agreed on that. They said that if they had a residency permit, they would look for a job in Athens. Five did not answer definitely and eight said that they would stay put. Four out of these eight were *masturas* who live in Manolada throughout the year. The other four justified their decision on the feeling of security and community that Manolada provides. However, Manolada is not the only agricultural labor market that provides a safe haven from police controls. Several interviewees pointed out that there are also no controls in destinations like Arta (orange production), Lakopetra (peppers), Sofades (peppers) and Thiva (beans).

> I've been in Greece for 8 months and have no papers. Most of the time I work in Manolada. I only saw police once, in Kalamata where I was picking olives. They saw I was from Bangladesh and they let me walk.
>
> WORKER J 2019

All workers are aware that in most destinations they will not face police controls, but they are very afraid of the in between journeys. When the season comes to an end, only very few labor opportunities are available in Manolada. The vast majority of Bangladeshi migrants know that they have to take the risk of a possible detention en route towards one of many destinations except for the ones already mentioned. Karditsa, Molaoi, Sparta, Monemvasia, Kalamata and Halkida are also places that attract a large number of Bangladeshis. In some of the aforementioned areas as many as three thousand Bangladeshis live and work in situations fairly similar to Manolada.

> Last year I worked at Lakopetra harvesting peppers. Early in the season it was 1 euro/crate, later on 0,5 euro/crate. The *masturas* there owe me 800 euros from last year. In Thiva the *masturas* are also very bad, actually wherever I work there exist *masturas*.
>
> WORKER C 2019

> I pay 100 euros to *masturas* in Manolada to secure a labor spot. In Arta the price is negotiable. If you cry a little, they usually cut off their commission.
>
> WORKER N 2019

A common finding in all interviews is that each Bangladeshi worker leaving Manolada tends to follow his/her[1] own route within the Greek territory and many times returns to the same employer, due to networking with certain *masturas* or to personal acquaintance with small-scale producers. In few cases labor conditions are better, but the majority of workers seems entrapped in a vicious circle of coercion: Withheld wages, *masturas*, poor housing conditions, lack of police controls, employers who do not respect labor laws. Nevertheless, Bangladeshi migrants traverse these geographies and almost every year end up in Manolada. We refer to this situation as 'mobility in immobility.'

> From January to May there are very few labor positions for Bangladeshis allover Greece. Maybe a few in Amaliada. This is the only available mass labor market.
>
> WORKER O 2019

> I am not feeling well here. I have psychological problems. I only work here because I am afraid. I have no papers and the police does not bother me. Otherwise I wouldn't stay here a day longer. Also in Sofades, from July to October, I have no fear of police controls. Only the journey is a problem.
>
> WORKER E 2019

Bangladeshi migrants are socially immobilized. For a certain part of the year they are also geographically immobilized within Manolada's labor system. The ones signing up for 13a schemes are also institutionally immobilized, both occupationaly and geographically. Hence, their mobility between Greece's agricultural coercive geographies is within a spectrum of multifarious immobility.

Almost half of the people interviewed aspired to reach another European country. Out of the ones that wish to stay in Greece, only eight would prefer to continue working in Manolada. In spite of such aspirations to exclude Manolada from their mobility patterns, all migrants were interviewed on-site. Having the aspiration but not the capability to migrate (outside Greece, or at least to an urban center like Athens), most of these migrants should be placed in the category of 'involuntary immobility' (Schewel 2019). Others, mainly *masturas*

---

1 Only one female Bangladeshi presence – and for only one season – has been recorded in the past 10 years in Manolada. She was the wife of a worker and did not work in the fields (worker P 2018).

with residency permits, have the capability but no intention of migrating; they belong to the 'voluntary immobility' categorisation. Interestingly enough, there are also several irregularly residing migrants who have no capability to migrate, yet expressed no aspiration to leave Manolada. These people, pertaining to the category of 'acquiescent immobility' justify their choice with a cynical acceptance of their status. They are either afraid of further trouble with police authorities and prefer the safety of the strawberry zone or have built bonds with Manolada's social environment and have developed a "place-attachment" (Lewicka 2011).

> I have lived here for nine years. I love the earth and the fields. I want to stay.
>
> WORKER O 2019

> I have stayed five consecutive years in Manolada and wish to stay. In Athens it is more difficult, you face problems with fascists and the police. Here, nobody bothers you.
>
> WORKER AB 2018

There is no better way to sum up the empirical part of our research than in the words of worker L. He is forty-nine years old and recently left his country for the first time. He lived in Silet province, a place deeply affected by climate changes, as he stated. L reached Greece six months ago, leaving his family and four children behind. He aspired to reach some central European country, but has been stuck in Manolada for the last six months.

> I had never imagined that I would have to live this way. I always thought of Europe as a completely different place. I want to reach France or Spain.
>   Q: What if nothing changes and you find yourself stuck in Greece for the next ten years in the same situation. Will you work here?
>   Well, yes. I have no choice. I must keep sending money back home and I still owe the money for my trip to Greece.
>
> WORKER L 2019

8   Conclusion

The labor market of Manolada bears some stable characteristics. It offers a lot of job opportunities every year within a fixed period and employers prefer hiring male Bangladeshi migrants (Floros and Jørgensen 2020). Wages are better than the ones offered in many other jobs or places, yet payments are erratic and subject to commissions withheld by *masturas*. Working and living conditions are unacceptable. These characteristics coupled with the aforementioned Greece's recent migration policies create a 'state of expectancy' for migrants. In Manolada's case this situation goes beyond the individual state and for many migrants transforms into a collective socio-spatial locus of expectancy. The entrapment of thousands of Bangladeshi agricultural workers in this exploitative geography is primarily based on these 'fetters of expectation' for a long-lasting and uncertain regularisation procedure. For the time-being, this procedure is fruitful for some of them, but for the majority it will prove to be vain hope.

Thus, Manolada – a 'de facto Special Economic Zone' (Kerasiotis 2019) – is socio-legally transformed into a geographical zone of entrapment and immobility, where migrants' capabilities (and aspirations) for further mobility remain in limbo. However, during the year, this geography expands to more agricultural spaces, where mass temporary relocation takes place. All these enclaves of seasonal work add up to create a wider interconnected geography of coercion and immobility coupled with hope. This forms a continuum of im/mobility, where migrants are mobile within short-term relocations to predefined spaces of administrative and policing tolerance, yet socially, occupationally and spatially immobilized in Greece's agricultural settings.

Conclusively, more than other factors presented and accounted for in this chapter, we argue that migrants' hope/expectancy and its reinforcement/perpetuation from state and employers through doses of moderate optimism (13a, exceptional or humanitarian residence permits) is the main reason for this constant supply of labor force, despite hyper-exploitative working conditions and inhuman housing conditions. Nea Manolada is the epicenter of a coercive geography with multiple temporary relocation inscriptions, which benefits from the existence of a strong pole of attraction: the expectancy of acquiring a residence permit, which could be used as a passport to new pathways of aspired mobility towards new geographical spaces and occupational sectors.

Of course, the state and the employers do not have the least interest in the further mobility of Bangladeshi migrants. Their main concern is the development and sustainment of the successful strawberry sector, which goes hand in hand with ensuring the continuation of labor supply in the area. It remains to be seen if this will be achieved through imposing further obstacles to the – already difficult – acquirement of special residence permits or if this phenomenon will perpetuate through the continuous arrival of new migrants from the large pool of labor force flowing in from the same country of origin.

While we were writing our final draft on the conclusions for this chapter, there was a change in office after the Greek elections. One of the first moves of the new conservative cabinet was to dismantle the Ministry of Migration and demote it to an agency under the control of the Ministry of Citizen Protection. At the same time, acquisition of tax numbers for irregularly residing migrants became inaccessible due to new legislation. Greece's migration policymaking seems to become even more restrictive and preventive. The effects that this changes in policy might have underline the fragility of migrants' 'state of expectancy' and presage further obstacles to their mobility.

References

Asta, G. (2018). "The Chowdury Case before the European Court of Human Rights: A Shy Landmark Judgment on Forced Labour and Human Trafficking," *Studi sull' integrazione europea* XIII: 195–212.

Axelsson, L., B. Malmberg, and Q. Zhang (2017). "On waiting, work-time and imagined futures: Theorising temporal precariousness among Chinese chefs in Sweden's restaurant industry," *Geoforum* 78: 169–178.

Bélanger, D., and R. Silvey (2019). "An Im/mobility turn: power geometries of care and migration," *Journal of Ethnic and Migration Studies*: 1–18. https://doi.org/10.1080/1369183X.2019.1592396.

Brass, T. (2011). *Labour regime change in the twenty-first century: unfreedom, capitalism and primitive accumulation.* Leiden: Brill.

Carling, J. (2002). "Migration in the age of involuntary immobility: theoretical reflections and Cape Verdean experiences," *Journal of ethnic and migration studies* 28(1): 5–42.

Carling, J., and K. Schewel (2018). "Revisiting aspiration and ability in international migration," *Journal of Ethnic and Migration Studies* 44(6): 945–963.

Casas-Cortes, M., S. Cobarrubias, and J. Pickles (2015). "Riding routes and itinerant borders: Autonomy of migration and border externalization," *Antipode* 47(4): 894–914.

Castles, S., and M.J. Miller (1993). *The age of migration: international population movements in the modern world.* London: Palgrave Macmillan.

Collyer, M., F. Düvell, and H. De Haas (2012). "Critical approaches to transit migration," *Population, Space and Place* 18(4): 407–414.

Conlon, D. (2011). "Waiting: Feminist perspectives on the spacings/timings of migrant (im) mobility," *Gender, Place & Culture* 18(3): 353–360.

Corrado, A., C. de Castro, and D. Perrotta (eds.) (2016). *Migration and Agriculture: Mobility and change in the Mediterranean area.* Oxford: Routledge.

Cresswell, T. (2006). *On the move: Mobility in the modern western world*. Abingdon-on-Thames: Taylor & Francis.

De Genova, N. (ed.) (2017). *The borders of "Europe": autonomy of migration, tactics of bordering*. Durham, NC: Duke University Press.

De Haas, H. (2014). "Migration theory: Quo vadis?," *Working Paper, International Migration Institute, University of Oxford*. https://www.migrationinstitute.org/publications/wp-100-14.

Eide, P., and C.B. Allen (2005). "Recruiting transcultural qualitative research participants: A conceptual model," *International Journal of Qualitative Methods* 4(2): 44–56.

European Court of Human Rights (2017). "Migrants who were subjected to forced labour and human trafficking did not receive effective protection from the Greek State," Retrieved July 28, 2019. http://hudoc.echr.coe.int/eng-press?i=003-5671464-7189869.

Floros, K., and M.B. Jørgensen (2020). "Tracing the future of migrants' labour relations. Experiences of institutionalized migrant precarity in Denmark and Greece," *Political Geography* 77, 102120.

Gemi, E. (2013). *Albanian irregular migration to Greece: new typology of crisis*. ELIAMEP.

ILO (2018). "Measurement of forced labour," 20th International Conference of Labour Statisticians Geneva, 10–19 October 2018. Retrieved July 28, 2019. https://www.ilo.org/wcmsp5/groups/public/---dgreports/---stat/documents/meetingdocument/wcms_636050.pdf.

Kapsalis, A. (2018a). "The development of Greek migration policy and the invention of "para-legality" in labour relations of immigrants," *Κοινωνική Πολιτική* 9: 67–87.

Kapsalis, A. (2018b). "Review of the 'ergosimo' service voucher system in Greece." Ministry of Labour, Social Security and Social Solidarity. Not yet published online.

Kasimis, C., A.G. Papadopoulos, and S. Zografakis. (2015). "The precarious status of migrant labour in Greece: Evidence from rural areas," in della Porta, D., Silvasti, T., Hänninen, S., Siisiäinen, M. (eds.). *The New Social Division*. London: Palgrave Macmillan: 101–119.

Kerasiotis, V. (2019). "Το χρονικό της μετατροπής της Μανωλάδας σε de facto Ειδική Οικονομική Ζώνη," ("The chronicle of the transformation of Manolada into a de facto Special Economic Zone"), *Σύγχρονα Θέματα*: 145 (in Greek).

Lerche, J. (2011). "The unfree labour category and unfree labour estimates: A continuum within low-end labour relations." https://eprints.soas.ac.uk/14855/1/Lerche_unfree_working_paper_2011.pdf.

Lewicka, M. (2011). "Place attachment: How far have we come in the last 40 years?" *Journal of environmental psychology* 31(3): 207–230.

Lewis, H., P. Dwyer, S. Hodkinson and L. Waite (2015a). "Hyper-precarious lives: Migrants, work and forced labour in the Global North," *Progress in Human Geography* 39(5): 580–600.

Lewis, H., P. Dwyer, S. Hodkinson and L. Waite (2015b). *Precarious lives: Forced labour, exploitation and asylum.* London: Policy Press.

Manolada Watch (2019). "Manolada Watch," *Generation 2.0 for Rights, Equality & Diversity.* https://g2red.org/el/manolada-watch/.

Mata-Codesal, D. (2018). "Is it simpler to leave or to stay put? Desired immobility in a Mexican village," *Population, Space and Place* 24(4): e2127.

McGrath, S. (2016). "Unfree Labor," *International Encyclopedia of Geography: People, the Earth, Environment and Technology: People, the Earth, Environment and Technology:* 1–8.

Mezzadra, S., and B. Neilson (2012). "Between inclusion and exclusion: On the topology of global space and borders," *Theory, Culture & Society* 29(4–5): 58–75.

Mountz, A. (2011). "Where asylum-seekers wait: feminist counter-topographies of sites between states," *Gender, Place & Culture* 18(3): 381–399.

Papadopoulos, A.G., L. Fratsea, and G. Mavrommatis (2018). "Governing migrant labour in an intensive agricultural area in Greece: Precarity, political mobilization and migrant agency in the fields of Manolada," *Journal of Rural Studies* 64: 200–209.

Phillips, N. (2013). "Unfree labour and adverse incorporation in the global economy: Comparative perspectives on Brazil and India," *Economy and Society* 42(2): 171–196.

Qu, S.Q., and J. Dumay (2011). "The qualitative research interview," *Qualitative research in accounting & management* 8(3): 238–264.

Schewel, K. (2019). "Understanding Immobility: Moving beyond the Mobility Bias in Migration Studies," *International Migration Review*: 0197918319831952. https://doi.org/10.1177/0197918319831952.

Schewel, K. (2015). *Understanding the aspiration to stay: a case study of young adults in Senegal.* International Migration Institute, University of Oxford.

Sheller, M., and J. Urry (2006). "The new mobilities paradigm," *Environment and planning A* 38(2): 207–226.

Sixsmith, J., M. Boneham, and J.E. Goldring (2003). "Accessing the community: Gaining insider perspectives from the outside," *Qualitative health research* 13(4): 578–589.

Skrivankova, K. (2010). "Between decent work and forced labour: examining the continuum of exploitation," *York: Joseph Rowntree Foundation.* https://www.jrf.org.uk/report/between-decent-work-and-forced-labour-examining-continuum-exploitation.

Stoyanova, V. (2018). "Sweet Taste with Bitter Roots: Forced Labour and Chowdury and Others v Greece," *European Human Rights Law Review*: 67–75.

Suter, B. (2013). "Untangling Immobility in Transit: Sub-Saharan Migrants in Istanbul," in Triulzi, A., and R. McKenzie (eds.). *Long Journeys. African Migrants on the Road.* Leiden: Brill: 93–112.

Tazzioli, M. (2018). "Containment through mobility: migrants' spatial disobediences and the reshaping of control through the hotspot system," *Journal of Ethnic and Migration Studies* 44(16): 2764–2779.

Triandafyllidou, A. et al. (2013). "Migration in Greece: people, policies and practices," *IRMA research project, ELIAMEP,* Athens. http://www.eliamep.gr/wp-content/uploads/2017/11/IRMA-Background-Report-Greece.pdf.

Triandafyllidou, A. (2014). "European Influences in Greece's Migration Policies: Between 'Hard' Impact and 'Soft' Influence," in Featherstone, K. (ed.). *Europe in Modern Greek History.* London: Hurst & Co.: 117–134.

Urry, J. (2000). "Mobile sociology," *The British journal of sociology* 51(1): 185–203.

Williams, C.C. (2016). "Diagnostic report on undeclared work in Greece," *International Labour Office, Geneva.* http://www.oit.org/wcmsp5/groups/public/---ed_emp/documents/projectdocumentation/wcms_531548.pdf.

CHAPTER 3

Constructing Immobility: Border Work and Coercion at the Hotspots of the Aegean

Vasileios Spyridon Vlassis

1 Introduction

This chapter sets out to present and discuss certain aspects of border work that has partially shaped the substrate on which the immobility of irregularized migrants has been constructed in the spatial and temporal context of the Hotspots located in the Greek islands of Lesvos and Chios during 2016 and 2017.

It draws from a critical reading and analysis of policy papers published during and shortly before that period, as well as ethnographic material gathered during field research visits in March 2016 and June 2017. The latter included non-participant observation of the registration process, and interviews with staff of the administrative personnel of the Hotspots, members of NGOs working there, as well as Greek Police and FRONTEX officers.

2 Some Ontological and Theoretical Admissions

Drawing from the Westphalia era, which is considered the point of departure for demarcating the nation-state in geographical terms (Zaiotti 2011), borders are primary institutions of nation states. They are traditionally considered to comprise an empirical-physical phenomena, well-defined, visible on a map as a line demarcating the end of territorial power of states and guarded by the state's armed forces (Paasi 2009). The idea of the border as a geopolitical frontier relates to the existence of the sovereign nation state in the post-Westphalian era, together with the idea of a nation of people sharing a national identity, a common history, language, religion, etc. (Cuttitta 2006). Dominant as they may be, borders, as clear demarcations between sovereign states, are not a-historical or inevitable. Different forms of separation have existed in the past, such as the *marches*, functioning more as buffer zones than clear demarcation lines, enabling a much less "monopolistic" exercise of power (Balibar 2009).

While in an abstract sense, borders are supposed to place each individual under a certain scrutiny in order to categorize them and act upon them accordingly, this 'universality' is not universal at all. Border guards and scholars alike know relatively well that not everyone is scrutinized in the same manner by any border apparatus. Balibar argues for the *polysemic nature* of the border. He shows that crossing the Croatia-Montenegro border can be a very different experience for a person with an Albanian passport, compared to someone with a German passport (Balibar 2009). On a similar note, Broeders (2011) discusses how anyone traveling to the EU who needs a visa is "by definition already suspect" and thus subjected to a different set of practices by border officials compared to e.g. a migrant from the USA. The list of examples is endless, clearly revealing that different individuals receive different treatment.

Again as Balibar puts it, every political border is "never the mere boundary between two states, but is always *over* determined and, in that sense, sanctioned, reduplicated and relativized by other geopolitical divisions" (Balibar 2002: 79). Thus, there is no linear pattern in the transformation of borders. They are "being both multiplied and reduced in their localization and their function, they are being thinned out and doubled" (Balibar 1998). In other words, both the intensity of e.g. control at border venues and in procedures, as well as their symbolic value is subject to radical and unpredicted changes enabled by factors that by far precede their locality.

An essentialist view of borders as a concept with stable content that only changes in terms of spatial shifting of a borderline, fails to encapsulate the plurality with which borders present themselves in contemporary societies. Building on that, border scholars have shifted from viewing borders as entities that exist in space and disrupt or facilitate mobility, to viewing them as "processes, practices, discourses, symbols, institutions or networks through which power works" (Johnson et al. 2011). Moreover, these processes themselves are considered to be in a constant process of becoming, in ways "that are neither linear nor unidirectional, but that are in many ways event-driven" (Kaiser 2012).

In the context of terminology, this shift has been materialized with the partial substitution of 'border' with the more inclusive 'bordering practices.' That accommodates the plurality of actors and processes at play in shaping the border, be they state or non-state actors, migrants or other forms of actors, as well as their distribution in geographical terms. De Genova calls for a focus on *bordering*, as a verb, an activity that "involves productive activity, a kind of *labor*" (De Genova 2016: 47).

This labor, these bordering practices despite being a largely (and increasingly) technologically mediated set of practices, legislated by complex and intertwined legal frameworks, is still largely performed by human agents who, are essentially "people who are informed in their practices by notions of what constitutes border, ..., and so their efforts might or might not turn out in the way intended" (Green 2010: 262). What Salter refers to as the formal performance of the border, namely the "description and defense of particular territorial borders," and its practical performance, including "the actual politics of enforcing the admission/expulsion and filtering process" (Johnson et al. 2011: 66) often do not coincide. Or as Wonders puts it, "state policies have little meaning until they are 'performed' by border agents" (Wonders 2006: 66). Without adopting a naïve position that would imply that state/border agents are free to perform the border in any way they find fit, we need to include in our analysis the way that prejudice, worldview and work ethics find their way into what *bordering* is and how it is performed.

These bordering practices have been analysed as having performative agency (Butler 2010) over their subjects. Although categories and dichotomies such as regular/irregular, or migrant/refugee, are presented as 'natural categories' existing in the wild, it is the bordering practices and their *performative* nature that shape and circulate said categories. It is through the construction of these categories, and the attribution of the subsequent identities, that "nation states legalize forms of belonging" (Mountz 2003). In this understanding of borders, registration of irregularized migrants, is more than the recording of personal data. It is the base on which a series of decisions through which "the border is augured into being" (Parsley 2003: 55) and an integral part of a continual state of exception (Salter 2008), that enforces different levels of exclusion and inclusion. The borderlands where these practices are materialized, in this case the Hotspots constitute zones of detention and uncertainty, and their geographies are geographies of coercion and repression.

3   The Centrality of Identification and Registration in the Context of the Migrant Crisis

Registration of irregularized migrants in the period before the EU–Turkey Statement cannot be discussed in uniform with regards to EU member states, as both the procedures as well as the discourse around them, would vary significantly. A North–South distinction, coinciding with the classification of borders, as internal/external seems to hold its analytical value in this case. On the one hand, for example in the case of Germany, registration was more related to the even distribution of asylum seekers among the different regions, and their classification as deserving asylum or not, as well as their subsequent enrolment in the relevant state sanctioned support in housing. A similar focus on the 'impact' of the populations on the move on the welfare state was present in the case of Sweden (Dahlstedt and Neergaard 2019).

On the other hand, and most notably for the Southern states of Greece and Italy, which were also the main geographical localisations of the Hotspot approach, things were different. As is discussed in further detail later, registration throughout 2015, and the first half of 2016, was less associated with the asylum procedure per se, and more with identifying and keeping track of the numbers of the incoming populations. Aside from the position of the two states as entry points to the EU, this was also directly related to the fact that during the 'summer of migration' and until the EU–Turkey Statement very few asylum applications would be lodged, as people could still continue their journey to the European North.

Both states have been criticized in the past by other member states on their failure or unwillingness to fully register incoming populations, a practice that has been argued to be a way of entry point member states to reduce the 'burden' of handling the asylum applications that migrants would subsequently lodge, if registered (den Heijer, Rijpma, and Spijkerboer 2016).

In the face of the 'migratory pressure' and the events occurring at border venues across the continent, on the 13th of May 2015, the European Commission published a 22-page text, entitled "A European Agenda on Migration" (European Commission 2015b). Without referring to a present 'crisis,' but with a view to 'EU's reaction to future crises,' the text presented a set of diverse measures for rescue at sea, 'targeting criminal smuggling networks' relocation and resettlement of refugees, 'tackling migration upstream' and more. These measures were under the general aim of Europe remaining "a safe haven for those fleeing persecution as well as an attractive destination for the talent and entrepreneurship of students, researchers and workers."

Many of the developments that shaped the realities of migrants' lives in the following years are outlined in the Agenda on Migration. The text hints towards the EU–Turkey Statement that followed just over a year later and has been a controversial issue for the years that followed to the day of writing of this chapter (October 2019). "Migrant smuggling networks" are discussed as clearly set, organized systems that function as operations. They are said to perform clear-cut risk and profit assessments and must be turned "from 'low risk, high return' operations for criminal into 'high risk, low return' ones." Finally, the Common European Asylum System is presented as a resource that needs to be in some way safeguarded against the very subject that it concerns, namely the migrants. The mere existence of a large number of asylum applications that are rejected, is seen by the European Commission as an "abuse" of the system, as it "hampers the capacity of Member States to provide swift protection to those in need." While acknowledging the denial of many Member States to accept refugees, as well as older, basic malfunctions of the Dublin system, the European Commission largely decides to attribute the 'blame' for the condition of the European Asylum System to the people who apply and are rejected. This approach paves the way for the radical reconceptualisation of the notion of asylum and the official practices associated with it that came just a year later, with the EU–Turkey Statement.

In communications and press releases following the publication of the Agenda on migration, *registration, identification* and *fingerprinting*, are three terms that come up very frequently with regards to migration flows as of April 2015 (European Council 2015a: European Council 2015b), often in relation to terror threats facing Europe (European Commission 2015c). After the initial 'shock.' and with tensions still rising at numerous border venues across Europe, and while political conflicts related to policies of relocation and reception are under full development, it seems that power centres at the core of the EU decided to place 'order' in the centre of a discussion that was previously dominated by a humanitarian undertone, where the focus of debate was that of 'saving lives' in the Mediterranean, and grassroots solidarity by citizens.

Characteristically, European Commission First Vice President Frans Timmermans's statements in February 2016 mention: "Getting back to an orderly management of flows is the most pressing priority today" (European Commission 2016). Official, bureaucratic and institutionalized 'European solidarity' is not unconditional and can only be manifested under a rationalizing frame that endorses and prioritizes 'order' as a value, and a specific form of 'responsibility' which struggles to legitimatize choices and actions "as both true to the European values of humanitarianism, solidarity, and asylum, meanwhile, taming the influx of newcomers that are feared to drain resources and destabilize social cohesion" (Triandafyllidou 2018). Along the same lines, European Commission President Jean-Claude Juncker after convening a Leaders' Meeting on 25 October to address refugee flows along the Western Balkans stated:

> The only way to restore the situation is to slow down the uncontrolled flows of people. The policy of waving through people to neighbouring countries has to stop. I want to be clear: people must be registered. No registration, no rights.
> JUNCKER 2015

Again, it is telling that in his official statement, Juncker did not mention the issue of relocation and its falling short in all expectations, and only superficially touched on the issue of living conditions along the Western Balkans route. However, he made a very strong point regarding the importance of registration, which taken at face value, annuls the main precondition for a person to have 'rights' which in the liberal democratic paradigm, is to be human. Two things are noteworthy regarding this statement in relation to the events that preceded it and followed it. First, as I shall discuss in the following section, there is no direct and constant correlation between registration and the attribution of 'rights' in the abstract way in which we usually refer to human rights. Instead, the registration process for thousands of migrants has been the entry point to a complex condition of uncertainty and limbo, lengthy bureaucratic procedures, detention and restriction of the right to move. Second, and equally important, is that the act of registration as the first stage of interaction with the EU's bureaucratic and administrative apparatus of migrant governance is a means of slowing down 'the uncontrolled flows of people,' a practice of coercion and restriction of mobility.

Of course, Juncker was referring to specific rights under the EU's asylum system. However, the fact remains that at a time when the EU was facing a 'humanitarian crisis' such a high-ranking official opted for this choice of words, which places human rights in a specific condition, one of a direct and even causal dependence on the wellness of a bureaucratic apparatus. Even more, Juncker does not directly mention a certain practice of non-cooperating on behalf of disobedient migrants, even though that is somehow implied in his statement. Instead, he reminds us of the power of EU and the Member States to withdraw from their moral and ethical responsibility of ensuring human rights if their organisational standards are not met. The 'inalienability' of human rights (Arendt 1973) is once again debunked. Instead, what prevails is the modern state and surpra-state mechanisms' fixation with rendering populations and individuals fit for future governance in the context of which their removal from EU territory is a very likely scenario.

Another context in which registration and the 'identity' of the incoming migrants would be often discussed was that of the association of migration and the 'terror threat' in Europe. The most notable case involve the Paris attacks on November 2015, where shootings and suicide bombings in the States de France during a football match, and a concert in the Bataclan theatre, left 130 people dead, and hundreds injured, in the second deadliest attack in Europe since the Madrid train bombings in 2004. Responsibility for the attack was claimed by the ISIL (Callimachi 2018). In the scene of the shootings, a Syrian passport was found, which in latter days was reported to have been used by a person that had entered Europe, through Greece. The Greek Minister of Migration, Giannis Mouzalas later confirmed this information, stating that "the owner of the passport (sic) passed through Leros, on the 3/10/2015 where he was identified according to the EU rules, as those were decided upon in the EU Summit on the refugee issue" (Antı 2015). Some voices in the international press, kept a dispassionate and cautious stance towards the finding of the said passport at the crime scene. Some, for example mentioned that given the status that Syrian passports had gained in the specific period, they were in high demand and an extensive illegal market had developed with them as a subject of contraband (Al Jazeera 2015), with networks that allegedly involved Syrian embassy officials (Hawramy, Dinic, and Kingsley 2015). Others noted that the passport could have been deliberately left in order to be found, in an effort to provoke tension focused on refugees fleeing Syria (Lichfield 2015; AFP 2015).

Overall, however, the presence of the passport fueled already existing associations between migration and 'terror threats' and was recruited by media and politicians working with an anti-migration agenda (Gallagher and Beckford 2015). The Polish Minister of European affairs, stated in the aftermath that "Poland must retain full control over its borders, asylum and immigration," (Traynor 2015). The Bavarian Finance Minister stated, "The days of uncontrolled immigration and illegal entry can't continue just like that. Paris changes everything" (Kingsley 2015). Even in the more remote context of the USA, governors from 31 states based their argument against the USA refugee resettlement program concerning Syrians, on the Paris attack (Healy and Bosman 2018). During this discourse, the EU's external borders between Greece and Turkey were attributed with new, safety-laden meanings, and were now even more seen as becoming "part of a different kind of front line, Europe's perimeter defense against possible infiltration by terrorists" (Lyman 2015).

3.1 *The Hotspot Approach*

While the Hotspot approach was introduced as a solution to the disorderly and incomplete registration of incoming populations, what is surprisingly in stark contrast with the European Commission's claim for a "consistent and clear policy" (European Commission 2015b), is the lack of a clear definition of what a Hotspot actually is and how it differs from the reception and registration centers already existing and functioning. This was clear in almost every discussion/interview that I conducted during my research trips to both islands, and has been a point of criticism among scholars and organizations (D'Angelo 2016; Statewatch 2015).

The European Commissioner for Migration and Home Affairs had to compose an "explanatory note" to the Home and Justice Affairs Ministers of the EU, in an effort to clarify what Hotspots would be and what their operational framework would be (Council of the European Union 2015). Again, a strict and clear definition is absent. Instead, a definition based on what the "Hotspots" aim at reads "to provide a platform for the agencies to intervene, rapidly and in an integrated manner, in frontline Member States when there is a crisis due to specific and disproportionate migratory pressure at their external borders, consisting of mixed flows and the Member State concerned might request support and assistance to better cope with that pressure."

The ad hoc definition is supplemented by an apposition of the actors that would be involved in the Hotspot, namely the aforementioned agencies that constitute the EU support mechanism: "the European Asylum Support Office, FRONTEX and Europol will work on the ground with frontline Member States *to swiftly identify, register and fingerprint incoming migrants.* The work of the agencies will be complementary to one another... Those claiming asylum will be immediately channeled into an asylum procedure where EASO (European Asylum Support Office) support teams will help to process asylum cases as quickly as possible. For those not in need of protection, FRONTEX (the EU agency responsible for guarding the borders) will help Member States by coordinating the return of irregular migrants. Europol (the EU's law enforcement agency) and Eurojust (the EU's juridical cooperation unit) will assist the host Member State with investigations to dismantle the smuggling and trafficking networks" (European Commission 2015a). Those functions have been the core of every reception center in Greece, and are, in themselves, nothing new. In that way, "in one sense, the hotspot is, then, already here" (Painter et al. 2016).

At face value, it seems there is not much in the "Hotspot approach" other than an increase of the involvement of EU agencies in the handling of the incoming populations. In the context of intra-EU tensions and antagonisms, there are some supplementary readings. The Greek and Italian states, two states of the European South, both under intense criticism regarding their management of migration throughout the past two decades, were now to have EU agencies take over basic functions of their bureaucratic apparatuses. Therefore, the Hotspot can be seen as a dual intensification of surveillance regarding migration. On the one hand, it signifies an enhanced and more thorough surveillance of migrant bodies who are now to be "datafied" and enrolled in the EU database assemblage. On the other, as an "enhanced mechanism of intra-governmental surveillance" (Garelli and Tazzioli 2016) that would discipline the states of Greece and Italy into fingerprinting all incoming migrants, in full accordance with the Dublin Regulation. In that way, the invigoration of EU agencies' presence through the Hotspot approach, both in terms of material apparatus, human workforces and upgraded role, can be seen as an intensification of center-periphery dynamics within the EU, which have been at play in a number of fields, no less in the implementation of the Dublin regulation. For some scholars, this raises issues of national independence under the emergence of an EU superstate (Painter et al. 2017). The fact that the Dublin Regulation has gone through various stages of inactiveness did not for a moment annul the biopolitical goal of a biometric and demographic archive of the populations on the move.

3.2   *Hotspots as Temporal Spaces of Exception*

Time and temporality are an essential element of the reality that migrants were subjected to after arriving in the Greek islands, and of the representation of this reality in media and political discourse. The "Hotspot approach" aimed at the "swift" identification and fingerprinting of incoming migrants. The dominant discourse around this "swiftness" has been one of a humanitarian "nature." It assumes that faster procedures would help cope with the bottleneck phenomenon that fingerprinting has been for a long time, and facilitate the mobility of migrants. However, this acceleration was not always smooth, and definitely did not always work in favor of the migrant subject interest. The "accelerated temporality of control" (Tazzioli 2016) imposed within the confined space of the Hotspot, but also stretching out well beyond its limits, was a complex set of dates and deadlines, waiting times, and "updates" on policies and practice protocols. This assemblage did not follow a linear "progress" model, and was subject to swift changes and transformations. Even the border guards had trouble staying updated, let alone understanding them. The EU–Turkey Statement signed in March 2016, stands out as the most important milestone in the "complex temporality" (Little 2015) that characterizes the border regime of the EU in this context. However in different periods, different procedures benefited migrants of different nationalities, and produced diverse dynamics in the populations (Kingsley and Domokos 2015). As Little puts it:

> [C]omplex temporality introduces elements of contingency that under-
> mine some of the normative certainty that borders have traditionally en-
> gendered... goes beyond the widely accepted notion that borders change
> over the course of time to focus on the nature and implications of that
> change across different bordering practices.
>   LITTLE 2015

The shifts in the protocol of migrant governance, the changes in criteria of selection, and the often-arbitrary practices of border guards, render the Hotspots a space of exception. The Italian Hotspots "have also been used for redistributing migrants already present on the national territory, and particularly for removing their unruly and contested presence from highly visible sites" (Tazzioli and Garelli 2018). In the Greek setting, and in the context of the implementation of the EU–Turkey Statement on behalf of the Greek state, the Greek Parliament voted for a law, that among other things, allowed for the detention of migrants in the Hotspots for a period of 25 days, leaving the decision to the authority of the Hotspot commander (Journal of the Government of the Hellenic Republic 2016: 1212).

The same law imposed a restriction on the right of migrants to move freely across the country of Greece, while their asylum applications were examined, thus turning the islands into capricious, large scale, detention centres for thousands of people who could not, for example, seek employment. The latter measure, almost two years later, was found by the Supreme Court of the country, to be insufficiently founded in the text of the law, and was cancelled (Mandrou 2018). However, its cancellation only concerned the migrants arriving at the islands after the Supreme Court's decision. Therefore, in practice it changed nothing for all those who were trapped on the islands in the meantime.

People arriving at a Hotspot would have little knowledge of what the outcome of their interaction with its mechanism would be. The infrastructure of the Hotspot "a technologically mediated, dynamic form that continuously produces and transforms socio-technical relations" would process the information, speech acts, and documents that migrant subjects would provide, and act upon them. However, the specific manner in which this act would unfold would very often be subject to change, as new directives were introduced at EU level, and new guidelines were introduced by the Greek Ministry of Migration. The Hotspot would not only impose temporalities (of detention, waiting for asylum claims to be processed, etc.), but as an infrastructure it was an entity subjected to temporalities itself. These temporalities, and the changes that brought, were of great importance for the migrants.

4   Border Work and the Construction of Irregularized Migrant (Im)mobility: The Case of the Screening Interviews

So far, I have discussed how the identification and registration of irregularized migrants arriving in EU territory through the Aegean has been invested with a range of meanings and values such as safety, order and deservedness. I will now go on to present an account of certain border guard practices that constitute identification and registration in the context of the Hotspot, stemming from my field work in the islands of Lesvos and Chios. More specifically, I will discuss the screening interview, which is carried out by Greek Police and FRONTEX officers, under the goal of assessing a person's nationality and country of origin.

The screening process, in both the Hotspots, is the part of the registration in which FRONTEX is involved the most and has the most dominant position. FRONTEX officers are in constant training mode, providing information and know-how to Greek Police officers who had undergone screening training in the past. The principle goal of the screening process is to "establish a presumed nationality," as well as to confirm or denounce other claims they might be making about themselves, such as age and family relationships. As FRONTEX themselves put it:

> As the vast majority of migrants arrive undocumented, screening activities are essential to properly verify their declaration of nationality. False declarations of nationality are rife among nationals who are unlikely to obtain asylum in the EU, are liable to be returned to their country of origin or transit, or just want to speed up their journey. With a large number of persons arriving with false or no identification documents or raising concerns over the validity of their claimed nationality – with no thorough check or penalties in place for those making such false declarations, there is a risk that some persons representing a security threat to the EU may be taking advantage of this situation.
>
> FRONTEX 2016

It easily becomes clear that this is an important instance of the border work that we meet in the Hotspot – one that also produces very persistent outcomes. While the assessment of the screening committee can be appealed, in the reality of the Hotspot, such an appeal is a highly time-consuming process that also depends on other forms of 'social capital' that the migrant may or may not bear.

In principle, the rationale under which screening is conducted is that the border guards examine and assess an individual's familiarity with cultural, linguistic, political and economic 'standards' of the claimed country of origin. This includes the person's dialect and accent, but also their ability to recognize currency, street names, locations, figures of politicians and singers, vehicle license plates and so on. Towards that goal, FRONTEX officers have compiled a paper dossier whose pages contain the above-mentioned pictures, which they ask migrants to point out. In addition, they have developed a set of around 110 questions that they pose to migrants to indicate familiarity with the claimed country of origin. The questions are mixed up and circulated to avoid the emergence of 'routine tests.' While this is the 'protocol' for the process, some officers often function outside that, as they consider it to be an outdated method. Screeners that I interviewed for example believed that there were organized "schools in Turkey where they (the smugglers) train them (the migrants) how to pass as different nationalities than their actual ones" (Interview with Greek Police/FRONTEX screener, June 2017, VIAL, Chios). They resort to other similar methods like checking the spelling that migrants used when writing their names, and using this as evidence of the migrant's origin.

In addition, screeners show a reliance on the use of Google Maps, as a means to assess a person's familiarity with a claimed place of origin.

> Everything has changed with the internet. Now you can ask someone their address, and immediately see what exists next to their house and ask them about it. For that reason, I make sure I always have data on my phone, because sometimes the connection here might go down. With Google Maps, even if they are e.g. from a village with no street names and such, you can ask them about neighbouring villages, mountains, and rivers.
>
> Interview with Greek Police/FRONTEX screener, June 2017, VIAL, Chios

However, beyond the methods used, it is worth noting that screening and nationality assessment is to a large extent based on instinct and intuition. Other than numerous field reports of such reliance, instinct as a resource is present in official institutional testimonies by FRONTEX itself. "You develop a kind of sixth sense for when people are not telling you the truth," said a "policewoman with 20 years' experience from Denmark" (FRONTEX and Fergusson 2014: 34).

It becomes clear from the above that screening as an identification process and as border work does not happen in an epistemological vacuum. Instead, the screener's work is saturated with epistemological and ontological presuppositions. First of all, the process of identifying' a person, and the necessity of this action, presupposes the eventuality of the person lying about their identity. In a universe where there would be a certainty that nobody is willing or able to lie about their identity, there would be no need for identification measures and equipment in the first place. Here on the other hand, the motivation for a person to lie about their identity is more than present, it is the norm and it is supported by a widespread discourse around bogus refugees that far exceeds the limits of the Hotspot. The culture of disbelief' (Anderson, Hollaus, and Williamson 2014), depends heavily on the stereotypes cultivated by border guards, shaping their criteria and decisions (Jubany 2011). Immigration officers, like all humans, inhabit worlds where rumors, stories and personal experiences, interact with other people's similar accounts, often within the context of bureaucratic work and shape their 'thought worlds' (Heyman 1995: 271–273). These 'thought worlds' can be very specific, extending well beyond the general notion of disbelief, as illustrated by my informant screener's belief in the existence of training schools for ambitious bogus refugees in Turkey. Furthermore, such beliefs, regardless of their truth value, shape not only the manner in which a border guard sees and considers a migrant standing in front of his office but are also in a position to shape their practices. In the present case, it affected my informant to the extent of him discarding the 'traditional' method of the dossier and questions and relying on Google maps instead, thus conceiving new standards of geographical literacy and habitude in the screening process.

It is worth noting that even though the outcome of the screening process in the form of a nationality assessment is a potent factor of the migrant's mobility (or lack of), and it is quite hard to challenge within the institutional framework of the Hotspot, screeners as well as higher ranked FRONTEX officers are open to the fact that it cannot be accounted as a 'scientific' method, or as a method of high accuracy. Instead they refer to it as "a working hypothesis, the best we can do and what we will work with" (interview with FRONTEX Operational coordinator, Lesvos, March 2016). While this testimony coming from a high-ranking field officer may seem to conflict with FRONTEX's self-declared task of "properly verifying" a migrant's declaration of nationality, one can meet the same general attitude in FRONTEX's operational handbook from 2014, where a screener is described as "an officer of a competent authority of an MS who interviews and establishes assumptions on the nationality of an undocumented person" (FRONTEX 2014) and the whole process of screening as being "carried out to establish a presumed nationality" (FRONTEX 2014: 22).

The screening process and its outcomes have been criticized as being prone to problematic decisions in the past, before the emergence of the 'migrant crisis' and the Hotspots. Many of the denouncements revolve around the (apparently not always guaranteed) presence of an interpreter who can speak the language of the interviewee, the extent to which the interviewee is properly informed (PROASYL 2012), cases of mistaken assessments, (Migreurop, FIDH, and EMHRN 2014), the unclear role that the interpreters play in decision-making (Keller et al. 2011), and the distribution of tasks among Member-State officials and FRONTEX officials (Maniar 2016). Other denouncements concern the inappropriateness of the screening material "for illiterate people or for those who have lived for long periods as refugees in other countries, thus not being able to give the proper answer to geographical, political and cultural questions" (PROASYL 2012: 21).

Other points of critique exceed issues of the proper execution of the script of the process, and to the realities enacted by the possible outcomes available to the screeners. A report from Migreurop from 2014, based on a research visit conducted in October 2013, examined the category of 'stateless person' and its implications in the context of the Greek border work. More specifically, it mentions cases where Palestinian refugees from Syria, carrying Syrian travel documents were recorded as 'stateless' from Greek Police and FRONTEX "despite the fact that they had been living in Syria, they were unable to benefit from the specific regime applicable to Syrian refugees (obligation to leave the territory within 6 months) and were given an order to leave the territory within 30 days" (Migreurop, FIDH, and EMHRN 2014: 36).

The testimonies of the screeners and other FRONTEX officers can be analysed and discussed as a part of the performative agency of the border. The interviewed person is called to back up their identity claim, and more specifically their nationality claim, through a satisfactory performance of a script that the screeners set before them. The flow of their speech, their accent and their spelling are all seen as elements of this performance, evaluated and compared by the expertise of officials, each of whom "has his (sic) own method, his own measure" (Interview with Anonymous Greek Police officer, screener, Lesvos (August 2017)). They are called to 'do themselves with words' to paraphrase Austin. However, the performance is not solely verbal, but includes non-verbal cues, such as the apparel that the person examined is wearing, as well as the vigour with which they support their claim.

It has been impossible for me to dig deeper into the content of the screening process, as the precise content of the questions would of course consist of classified material. In any case, attending an interview was out of the question and would have raised significant ethical concerns. However, from the screener's approach to spelling, it is clear that the interviewed person is expected to perform specific modes of literal existence, to satisfy criteria that shape the understanding of nationality for the screener. It is also through these criteria that the individual being interviewed is being performed, shaped as a specific kind of subject, worthy or less worthy, allowed to remain in the territory, and deserving of compassion and access to institutionalized support or not.

At the same time, and through the same process, it is the border as a filter that is being performed. Through the actions of the border guards, and "as a judgment is performed on an interviewee, so the border is augured into being" (Parsley 2003: 55). In this interaction of the border guards' presumptions and methods with the answers that migrants provide, borders are constituted not geographically as lines in the sand, but as sets of social processes, as the outcome of human labor.

One final point on the construct of the screening outcome, comes from positioning the screening process and its conceptualisation by the screening officers in the institutional context of the Hotspot. It is beyond the scope of this paper to account for the institutional relationships between FRONTEX, Greek Police and other actors active in the Hotspot. However, it is worth noting that when screeners make their decisions, they do so also taking into account the existence and agency of other actors, such as the Asylum Service. Again, drawing from my field work, I will quote a Greek Police screener:

> Here we have 20 minutes maximum to make decisions, people are tired, scared, babies are crying in their mothers' arms. After a few days, they have rested, they have been told their rights and the Asylum Service officers have more time to do their job. So, if we make a mistake, it can be fixed. That makes me feel safer, and I think it works the same for my colleagues. We are not gods you know... So, if people protest my decision, they may do it for a thousand reasons, but I won't change it, because I know that there is a second procedure.

In this quote, it is clear that the screener is convinced that a different agency and set of actors, in this case the Asylum Service and the asylum operators, will be in a position to address and correct a possibly flawed assessment stemming from the screener. This conviction actively shapes the screener's own perception of his actions and their consequences. More precisely, it distributes decisions on the nationality assessment across a wider set of actors active at the Hotspots. This distribution of accountability has two effects. Firstly, it lightens the moral burden of a possible false assessment, as the latter is now distributed to a vaguely interconnected system that is the Hotspot. However, and perhaps more importantly, it makes it easier for the screener to discard a person's objections and protests, and enforce his initial decision, as the screener is assured that if he makes a mistake, others are in a position to fix it. This sharing of the moral burden allows screeners to act as "petty sovereigns" (Butler 2006), inside the general context of an institution which they do not fully control or understand. Being part of such an apparatus of governmentality and enjoying the moral relief of functional backdrops allows for decisions to be made.

While the Hotspot approach has been introduced as an effort on behalf of the EU to enhance the reception procedures, and thus facilitate the further mobility of 'deserving' migrants, in practice Hotspots in the Greek islands have functioned as de facto spaces of coercion. In the period between 2015 and March 2016, the Reception and Identification Centres (RIC), some of which later became Hotspots were places that migrants would cross through after a short stay, as moving on towards the European North was still a viable option. With the gradual closure of European borders throughout 2016, and more significantly with the publishing of the EU–Turkey Statement, the temporal character of the Hotspot changed, through the implementation of the Statement by the Greek state.

The construction of migrant immobility in the context of the Hotspot can be seen as the combined effect of a series of several factors which in the policy level include but are not limited to the systematic neglect of advertised measures such as the relocation and resettlement programs that by far missed their goals, the radical changes in the asylum procedures also introduced with the implementation of the EU–Turkey Statement, the ban of movement from the islands towards the Greek mainland. In combination with the dire conditions of living in the camps, the documented arbitrary and violent practices of the Greek Police, and the institutionalized uncertainty of everyday life for thousands of migrants, the Hotspots of the Aegean have functioned as zones of coercion, immobility and lack of freedom.

Apart from the critical examination of the policy decisions that give rise to these conditions, it is important to investigate the everyday mundane practices of border guards that materialize said policies and bring them into being in the field. The screening process, as part of the 'identification and registration' of irregularized migrants, is an instance of the performativity of the border in a twofold way. Through it, the border as a filtering and sorting mechanism is materialized, rendering the migrant subject known and governable for the EU's apparatus of migration governance. At the same time, it is a practice of coercion, where the migrant is called to persuasively and effectively perform their identity, and more specifically their claim about the their country of origin through the successful conduction of an examination/confession faced with trained border guards that inhabit their own 'thought world' and act as 'petty sovereigns' within the infrastructure of the Hotspot.

References

AFP (2015). "Islamic State May Be Trying to Exploit Refugee Debate: German Minister," *The Express Tribune.* November 16, 2015. https://tribune.com.pk/story/992533/islamic-state-may-be-trying-to-exploit-refugee-debate-german-minister/.

Al Jazeera (2015). "How Easy Is It to Obtain a Fake Syrian Passport?," November 23, 2015. https://www.aljazeera.com/news/2015/11/easy-buy-syrian-passport-facebook-151121124233394.html.

Anderson, J., J. Hollaus, and C. Williamson (2014). "The Culture of Disbelief," WORK-ING PAPER SERIES NO. 102. https://www.rsc.ox.ac.uk/files/files-1/wp102-culture-of-disbelief-2014.pdf.

Antı (2015). "Από την Λέρο πέρασε ο ένας τζιχαντιστής που αιματοκύλησε το Παρίσι," antenna.gr. November 14, 2015. http://www.antınews.gr//news/Politics/article/428234/apo-tin-lero-perase-o-enas-tzixantistis-poy-aimatokylise-to-parisi.

Arendt, H. (1973). *The Origins of Totalitarianism*. First edition. New York: Harcourt, Brace, Jovanovich.

Balibar, E. (1998). "The Borders of Europe," in P. Cheah, and B. Robbins (eds.). *Cosmopolitics: Thinking and Feeling Beyond the Nation*. Minneapolis: University of Minnesota Press.

Balibar, E. (2002). *Politics and the Other Scene*. Reprint edition. London: Verso.

Balibar, E. (2009). "Europe as Borderland," *Environment and Planning D: Society and Space* 27(2): 190–215.

Broeders, D. (2011). "A European 'Border' Surveillance System under Construction," in H. Dijstelbloem, A. Meijer, and M. Besters (eds.). *The Migration Machine*. London: Palgrave Macmillan: 40–67.

Butler, J. (2006). *Precarious Life: The Powers of Mourning and Violence*. London: Verso.

Callimachi, R. (2018). "ISIS Claims Responsibility, Calling Paris Attacks 'First of the Storm,'" *The New York Times*, January 19, 2018, sec. World. https://www.nytimes.com/2015/11/15/world/europe/isis-claims-responsibility-for-paris-attacks-calling-them-miracles.html.

Council of the European Union (2015). "Explanatory Note on the 'Hotspot' Approach-10962/15." http://www.epgencms.europarl.europa.eu/cmsdata/upload/0dcf8b85-5e3d-42ae-aa4c-ebf9fd4bf3ba/Session_1_-_Explanatory_note_on_the_Hotspot_approach.pdf.

Dahlstedt, M., and A. Neergaard (2019). "Crisis of Solidarity? Changing Welfare and Migration Regimes in Sweden," *Critical Sociology* 45(1): 121–135.

D'Angelo, A. (2016). "Migrant Crisis? The Italian Hotspot Approach Is Not a Solution, but It Has Been Politically Effective," *Middlesex Minds* (blog). February 26, 2016. https://mdxminds.com/2016/02/26/migrant-crisis-the-italian-hotspot-approach-is-not-a-solution-but-its-politically-effective/.

De Genova, N. (2016). "The 'Crisis' of the European Border Regime: Towards a Marxist Theory of Borders," *International Socialism* 150: 31–54.

European Commission (2015a). "The Hotspot Approach to Managing Exceptional Migratory Flows." https://ec.europa.eu/home-affairs/e-library/multimedia/publications/the-hotspot-approach-to-managing-exceptional-migratory-flows_en.

European Commission (2015b). "Communication from The Commission to the European Parliament, the Council, the European Economic and Social Committee and the Committee of the Regions a European Agenda on Migration." https://eur-lex .europa.eu/legal-content/EN/TXT/?uri=CELEX%3A52015DC0240.

European Commission (2015c). "Communication from the Commission to the European Parliament and the Council Eighth Biannual Report on the Functioning of the Schengen Area 1 May – 10 December 2015," Koninklijke Brill NV. https://doi .org/10.1163/2210-7975_HRD-4679-0058.

European Commission (2016). "Implementing the European Agenda on Migration: Progress on Priority Actions." https://ec.europa.eu/commission/presscorner/detail/ en/IP_16_271.

European Council (2015a). "Draft European Council Statement." https://www. consilium.europa.eu/en/press/press-releases/2015/04/23/special-euco-statement/.

European Council (2015b). "European Council Meeting (25 and 26 June 2015) – Conclusions EUCO 22/15." https://www.consilium.europa.eu/media/21717/euco-conclusions-25-26-june-2015.pdf.

FRONTEX (2014). "FRONTEX Document Challenge II." https://euagenda.eu/upload/ publications/untitled-6372-ea.pdf.

FRONTEX (2016). "FRONTEX Annual Risk Analysis 2016." https://data.europa.eu/ euodp/en/data/dataset/ara-2016.

FRONTEX, and J. Fergusson (2014). "12 Seconds to Decide." https://op.europa.eu/en/ publication-detail/-/publication/961ce343-be1d-469f-b200-44000e784797.

Gallagher, I., and M. Beckford (2015). "French Attacker Identified as Being from Paris," *Daily Mail Online.* November 14, 2015. https://www.dailymail.co.uk/news/article-3318379/Hunt-Isis-killers-Syrian-passport-body-suicide-bomber-Stade-France. html.

Garelli, G., and M. Tazzioli (2016). "The EU Hotspot Approach at Lampedusa," *OpenDemocracy.* February 23, 2016. https://www.opendemocracy.net/can-europe-make-it/ glenda-garelli-martina-tazzioli/eu-hotspot-approach-at-lampedusa.

Green, S. (2010). "Performing Border in the Aegean: On Relocating Political, Economic and Social Relations," *Journal of Cultural Economy* 3(2): 261–278.

Hawramy, F., M. Dinic, and P. Kingsley (2015). "How Easy Is It to Buy a Fake Syrian Passport?," *The Guardian,* November 17, 2015, sec. World news. https://www.theguardian .com/world/2015/nov/17/how-easy-is-it-to-buy-a-fake-syrian-passport.

Healy, P., and J. Bosman (2018). "G.O.P. Governors Vow to Close Doors to Syrian Refugees," *The New York Times,* January 19, 2018, sec. U.S. https://www.nytimes.com/2015/11/17/ us/politics/gop-governors-vow-to-close-doors-to-syrian-refugees.html.

Heijer, M. den, J.J. Rijpma, and T. Spijkerboer (2016). "Coercion, Prohibition, and Great Expectations: The Continuing Failure of the Common European Asylum System," *SSRN Scholarly Paper ID 2756709.* Rochester, NY: Social Science Research Network. https://papers.ssrn.com/abstract=2756709.

Heyman, J. (1995). "Putting Power in the Anthropology of Bureaucracy: The Immigration and Naturalization Service at the Mexico-United States Border," *Current Anthropology* 36(2): 261–287.

Johnson, C., R. Jones, A. Paasi, L. Amoore, A. Mountz, M. Salter, and C. Rumford (2011). "Interventions on Rethinking 'the Border' in Border Studies," *Political Geography* 30(February): 61–69.

Journal of the Government of the Hellenic Republic (2016). "ΝΟΜΟΣ ΥΠ' ΑΡΙΘΜ. 4375."KANhttps://www.kodiko.gr/nomologia/document_navigation/183712/nomos-4375-2016.

Jubany, O. (2011). "Constructing Truths in a Culture of Disbelief: Understanding Asylum Screening from Within," *International Sociology* 26(1): 74–94.

Juncker, J. (2015). "European Commission – Press releases – Press Release – Speaking Points of President Juncker – Press Conference on Western Balkans Route Leaders' Meeting," October 26, 2015. http://europa.eu/rapid/press-release_SPEECH-15-5905_en.htm.

Kaiser, R.J. (2012). "Performativity and the Eventfulness of Bordering Practices," in *Companion to Border Studies, A*: 522–537.

Keller, S., U. Lunacek, B. Lochbihler, and H. Flautre (2011). "Frontex Agency: Which Guarantees for Human Rights," *Brussels, Greens/EFA in European Parliament.* http://www.migreurop.org/IMG/pdf/Frontex-PE-Mig-ENG.pdf.

Kingsley, P. (2015). "Why Syrian Refugee Passport Found at Paris Attack Scene Must Be Treated with Caution," *The Guardian*, November 15, 2015, sec. World news. http://www.theguardian.com/world/2015/nov/15/why-syrian-refugee-passport-found-at-paris-attack-scene-must-be-treated-with-caution.

Kingsley, P., and J. Domokos (2015). "Chaos on Greek Islands as Refugee Registration System Favours Syrians," *The Guardian*, November 21, 2015, sec. World news. http://www.theguardian.com/world/2015/nov/21/chaos-greek-islands-three-tier-refugee-registration-system-syria-lesbos.

Lichfield, J. (2015). "Why the Passport Found near a Paris Suicide Bomber Is Intriguing French Investigators," *The Independent*, November 15, 2015. http://www.independent.co.uk/news/world/europe/paris-terror-attacks-ahmed-almuhameds-passport-may-have-been-planted-by-terrorists-a6735476.html.

Little, A. (2015). "The Complex Temporality of Borders: Contingency and Normativity," *European Journal of Political Theory* 14(4): 429–447.

Lyman, R. (2015). "Regulating Flow of Refugees Gains Urgency in Greece and Rest of Europe," *The New York Times*, November 25, 2015. http://www.nytimes.com/2015/11/26/world/europe/regulating-flow-of-refugees-gains-urgency-in-greece-and-rest-of-europe.html.

Mandrou, I. (2018). "ΣτΕ: Οι πρόσφυγες από εδώ και στο εξής θα κυκλοφορούν ελεύθερα," April 17, 2018. http://www.skai.gr/news/greece/article/371437/to-ste-ekrine-oti-oi-prosfuges-apo-edo-kai-sto-exis-tha-kukloforoun-eleuthera/.

Maniar, A. (2016). "(Language) Policing at Europe's Borders," June 23, 2016. http://www.irr.org.uk/news/language-policing-at-europes-borders/.

Migreurop, FIDH, and EMHRN (2014). "Migreurop at the Border of Denial." http://www.migreurop.org/IMG/pdf/rapport_en_web-2.pdf.

Mountz, A. (2003). "Human Smuggling, the Transnational Imaginary, and Everyday Geographies of the Nation-State," *Antipode* 35(3): 622–644.

Paasi, A. (2009). "Bounded Spaces in a 'Borderless World': Border Studies, Power and the Anatomy of Territory," *Journal of Power* 2(2): 213–234.

Painter, J., E. Papada, A. Papoutsi, and A. Vradis (2017). "Hotspot Politics—or, When the EU State Gets Real," *Political Geography*, January. https://doi.org/10.1016/j.polgeo.2017.02.012.

Painter, J., E. Papada, A. Papoutsi, and A. Vradis (2016). "Flags Flying up a Trial Mast: Reflections on the Hotspot Mechanism in Mytilene," *Society & Space* (blog). November 8, 2016. http://societyandspace.org/2016/11/08/flags-flying-up-a-trial-mast-reflections-on-the-hotspot-mechanism-in-mytilene/.

Parsley, C. (2003). "Performing the Border: Australia's Judgment of 'Unauthorised Arrivals' at the Airport," *Australian Feminist Law Journal* 18(1): 55–75.

PROASYL (2012). "Walls of Shame. Accounts from the Inside: The Detetnion Centres of Evros." https://www.proasyl.de/wp-content/uploads/2013/11/12_04_10_BHP_Evros.pdf.

Salter, M.B. (2008). "When the Exception Becomes the Rule: Borders, Sovereignty, and Citizenship," *Citizenship Studies* 12(4): 365–380.

Statewatch (2015). "Explanatory Note on the 'Hotspot' Approach." https://www.statewatch.org/news/2015/jul/eu-com-hotsposts.pdf.

Tazzioli, M. (2016). "The Migration Hotspot: Accelerated Temporality of Control and Temporal Borders." https://www.academia.edu/28003369/The_migration_hotspot_accelerated_temporality_of_control_and_temporal_borders.

Tazzioli, M, and G. Garelli (2018). "Containment beyond Detention: The Hotspot System and Disrupted Migration Movements across Europe," *Environment and Planning D: Society and Space*, February, 0263775818759335. https://doi.org/10.1177/0263775818759335.

Traynor, I. (2015). "Germany 'May Have Foiled Plot to Supply Arms to Paris Attackers,'" *The Guardian*, November 14, 2015, sec. World news. https://www.theguardian.com/world/2015/nov/14/germany-may-have-foiled-plot-to-supply-arms-to-paris-attackers.

Triandafyllidou, A. (2018). "A 'Refugee Crisis' Unfolding: 'Real' Events and Their Interpretation in Media and Political Debates," *Journal of Immigrant & Refugee Studies* 16(1–2): 198–216.

Wonders, N.A. (2006). "Global Flows, Semi-Permeable Borders and New Channels of Inequality," *Borders, Mobility and Technologies of Control*: 63–86.

Zaiotti, R. (2011). *Cultures of Border Control: Schengen and the Evolution of European Frontiers*. Chicago and London: University of Chicago Press.

CHAPTER 4

"Cyprus Is a Big Prison": Reflections on Mobility and Racialization in a Border Society

Leandros Fischer

1   Introduction: Liberating Mobility from Neoliberalism

Global market integration from the late 1970s onwards was widely understood to be the catalyst for increased geographical, and by implication social mobility. The deepening of EU integration and the bloc's expansion was one of the political developments reflective of this optimism. Boundaries disappeared, giving citizens the right to live, work and even vote in other member-states. In the aftermath of the 2008 global economic meltdown, this optimism has faded away. 'Freedom of movement for EU nationals' has emerged as a contentious political issue in Brexit Britain. The so-called 'refugee crisis' of 2015, the partial suspension of the Schengen agreement by EU states, as well as the ongoing deaths by drowning in the Mediterranean Sea have exposed the limits of geographical permissiveness. Globally, new walls are being erected, such as in Palestine and along the US–Mexico border, while bordering practices are being steadily externalized (Casa-Cortes, Cobarrubias, and Pickles 2016).

A consensus in public discourse dictates that a borderless liberal world order, so carefully crafted for half a century, is under threat by populists who engage in trade wars, appeal to racist instincts, reject cosmopolitanism, and preach isolation. Conversely, the pre-populist era has come to be associated with 'mobility,' understood as an expression of a yearning for self-fulfilment against the allegedly collectivist impulses of the populists. Thus, anti-Brexit imagery in Britain and elsewhere places heavy emphasis on positive experiences of once having been an ERASMUS student, striking friendships in other European countries, or even finding romantic love there. Mobility becomes detached from the social structures affecting it on a daily basis, while being reduced to a colorblind experience of individuals participating in society primarily as consumers, or 'market citizens' (Streeck 2016). Nevertheless, by disassociating mobility from structure, the former inevitably converges with 'expatriate,' a figure deriving from the colonial past, who is individualistic, skilled, cosmopolitan, adaptable, and more often than not white (Kunz 2016; Cranston 2017).

As Quinn Slobodian (2018) has aptly shown, no fundamental conflict between right-wing populism and neoliberal globalisation exists. Whereas today's right-wing populists want to suspend the movement of (some) peoples,
their objections to the free movement of goods, capitals and services are infi-
nitely less. More importantly though – and aided by the interplay of various
legal and institutional factors – the expansion of mobility rights for some
groups of workers in the context of neoliberal regimes like the EU is often concomitant to the geographical confinement of others, sometimes leading to a
blurring of distinctions between 'free' and 'unfree' labor for the latter. It is thus
important to disassociate the idea of neoliberal economic integration from the
idea of 'free movement,' while recognizing that the ways in which mobility is
guaranteed for some, presuppose the discrimination of others based on
racialization – understood here as the attribution of innate characteristics to
certain groups of people based on their perceived common features such as
skin colour, religion, culture, or language.

This chapter examines the mechanisms by which migrants are confined in
Cyprus – a divided island at the border between Europe and the Middle East –
often forcing them to accept worse working conditions, challenging notions of
'free labor.' Through filtering, legal classification, work restrictions, and racialization, migrants – such as refugees fleeing recent wars in Syria, Iraq and elsewhere – find themselves 'stuck,' becoming an overexploited and deportable
segment of the labor force, lacking any civic rights. I argue that a combination
of legal, political, historical, and physical factors renders Cyprus a prime example of a coercive geography. The chapter is structured along five segments.
First, I present an overview of critical approaches in migration studies dealing
with the logic behind bordering practices, mobility, and stuckedness. In the
second part, a historical overview of Cyprus as a place of migration and confinement is presented, aimed at tracing the origins of current state strategies.
By interrogating these historical lineages, the contours of contemporary confinement are examined in the third part. I then focus on the perceptions of
migrants themselves.[1] Concluding, I reflect on the question of mobility as a
contested element within contemporary capitalism, structured along the lines
of class and race.

---

1   Insights for this article derive from ethnographic fieldwork in Cyprus in the first half of 2018
    for a project on Cyprus as a place of exile and asylum in the Middle East. Qualitative inter-
    views were conducted with Syrian Kurdish, Palestinian, and Syrian Arab migrants. All the
    informants' names have been altered.

2   Borders, Mobility, Stuckedness

There is a consensus that the disappearance of borders within the EU has gone in tandem with a reinforcement of external frontiers, in a process known as 'Fortress Europe.' Indeed, the early 1990s not only witnessed the rapid deepening of European integration, but also the abandonment of (relatively) generous asylum systems in countries such as Germany in 1991. The signing of the three Dublin Regulations on asylum (1990, 2003 and 2017) aimed at combating 'asylum tourism,' also heralded a shift in perceptions of migration, now seen as a burden on the welfare state. Looking further back, the end of mass recruitment of foreign workers in many countries in the 1970s signalled a shift towards the management of migratory flows as fundamentally a problem of handpicking deserving persecuted refugees and harnessing the creativity of skilled migrants. This development coincided with the twin triumph of neoliberalism and an individual rights-based humanitarian discourse oblivious – and often subservient – to dominant economic and political interests (Harvey 2019; Weizman 2017). Conversely, a tendency of securitizing mass migration as a potential threat to public order and social cohesion (Huysmans 2000) accelerated after the 'war on terror' since 2001, leading to a racialization of Muslim migration in particular (Fredette 2014), as well as moral panics in the aftermath of the 'summer of migration' of 2015 (Weber 2016).

However, a belief in omnipotent borders fails to account for two important realities. On the one hand, the strand known as the 'autonomy of migration' approach has emphasized the many ways in which the autonomous practices of migrants on the move subvert border regimes and the selective mechanisms they entail, forcing the latter to continuously reconfigure themselves (Bojadžijev and Karakayali 2010; Papadopoulos and Tsianos 2013). On the other hand, the notion of borders as primarily aimed at stopping migrants has been challenged. The ongoing proliferation of borders, whether physical or legal, must be seen more as an exercise of synchronizing population flows with the needs of labor markets through a process of filtering (Mezzadra 2013). In other words, the coercive geographies behind the current confinement of populations in reception and deportation centres are not solely intended to deter further migratory flows but to classify migrants and regulate their entry into local economies.

Furthermore, 'autonomists' encourage us to view migration as a social movement in itself, yet one refraining from making institutional demands. This occurs through the participation of migrants in the 'mobile commons' (Parsanoglou, Trimikliniotis, and Tsianos 2016). Described as 'the organizational ontology of migrant life beyond sovereign control' (Papadopoulos and

Tsianos 2013: 191–192), the mobile commons encompass elements such as autonomous solidarity practices, infrastructures of connectivity, knowledge on migratory routes, as well as informal economies. These lie beyond sovereign control, thus challenging bordering practices and attempts of classification and control by the state.

For other theorists, migration not only denotes a relocation in geographical terms, but also a "class journey" (Pedersen 2012), where some achieve upward social mobility through migration, while the movement of others though space is accompanied by a relegation on the social scale. More often than not, migration-induced social trajectories are conditioned by an intersection of class, race, religion, ethnicity and/or gender, where a dichotomy between downwardly mobile racialized migrants on the one hand, and cosmopolitan expatriates possessing "the class consciousness of frequent travellers" (Calhoun 2008: 11) on the other, becomes conspicuous. It becomes tempting to think of mobility in the quantitative terms of Bourdieu's sociology (2010), as a form of capital that can be converted from economic capital. This resonates, considering the existence of a global hierarchy of citizenship that views some citizenships as more powerful than others do, since they allow entry and social benefits in more countries and thus more mobility, both physical and social.

Complementing social mobility, we can also add the parameter of what Ghassan Hage (2009: 97) refers to as "existential mobility," a "sense that someone is going somewhere" in life. Accordingly, some people migrate because they sense a restriction on their existential mobility, or a sense of "stuckedness." The concept has been further developed into the notion of "racial stuckedness" (Alloul 2020), translating into a push factor for some migrants, who migrate out of a sense of going nowhere due to racial stigmatisation. It may appear that existential mobility is merely an expression of social mobility and indeed, both notions are used interchangeably. However, they are not identical, as according to Hage (2009: 99), "[o]ne can be in a job and climbing the social ladder within that job yet still feel stuck in it." The conditions of ongoing crisis mean that on the subjective level, an increasing number of people feel that they are living in a "society of descent" (Nachtwey 2018). They do not only feel relegated on the socioeconomic scale, but also a loss of status and therefore the individual horizons this status implies. Although Hage does not mention this, I believe that a key difference between social and existential mobility concerns the range of strategies available to those experiencing a decrease in the case of the former. Under certain conditions, people experiencing downward mobility can organize and fight for better conditions. In that sense, they can be seen as still collectively 'going somewhere' in purely existential terms, in this case by challenging the structures responsible for their predicament. If, however, conditions are such that individuals feel powerless due to perceived atomization, a sense of stuckedness can prevail. Indeed, Hage asserts that feelings of being stuck are the norm rather than the exception in conditions of permanent crisis. He nevertheless asserts that this feeling is dealt with ambivalently, not only as a situation "one needs to get out at any cost" (Hage 2009: 97), but as a condition to wither in almost heroic fashion. The latter strategy can be seen as essential to a neoliberal ethos, forming part of a "new form of governmentality that invites and indeed valorizes self-control in times of crisis" (ibid.: 105).

Many migrants today face both a class journey of downward social mobility, as well as a sense of existential stuckedness. While downward mobility may result from processes along the intersection of particular features such as race and class, it is also the product of state practices that seek to regulate the flow of migration, not only through the reception and the deportation center, but also through legal measures like working restrictions. Migrants can feel stuck, and may decide that the best survival strategy might be to 'wait out the crisis' (Hage 2009). However, this waiting out can include an acquiescence to worsened living condition, effectively leading to an internalization of coercive structures and the blurring of distinctions between what constitutes free and unfree labor. While theoretically free to choose, migrants nevertheless become the object of engineering practices by the state intended to confine them into certain labor niches through a complex set of legal mechanisms. As migration often coincides with a relegation on the social scale, migrants see their capacity to withstand this predicament dwindle. Coercive geographical confinement can also exacerbate a prevailing sense of stuckedness and loss of possible escape routes, often dealt with by 'waiting it out.'

The geographical position of Cyprus as an insular borderland along major migratory routes, its politically ambiguous status, as well as its character as a crisis-hit peripheral European society, make it an ideal case study for the interrogating the multiple links between migrant autonomy and austerity. Such an interrogation cannot only occur through an examination of existing structures, but also through exploring the subjective experience of migrants themselves.

3 Migration to Cyprus: Location Is Everything

Migration to Cyprus is affected by three variables following their own autonomous logics, as well as their mutual interactions. The first one concerns the perceived economic benefits of migration that produce a bias for well-off migrants considered beneficial for 'development' (*anaptyxi*). The second pertains to demographic concerns that are closely related to the ongoing Cyprus dispute. For instance, the arrival of Armenians to Cyprus after the 1915 Genocide and the parallel limits to Greek refugees from Asia Minor, sowed suspicion among Greek Cypriots who suspected a British ploy to subvert the Greek desire for union with Greece, or *enosis*. The British drafted the constitution of the independent Republic of Cyprus in 1960, making citizenship conditional on either the Greek or the Turkish community, which were in turn declared mutually exclusive components of the new state. Religious affiliation, already nationalized by the British (Constantinou 2007), became a component of communal belonging, making Greeks out of Armenian, Maronite and Catholic Christian minorities, and Turks out of Muslim Roma Cypriots. Due to this colonial legacy, migration to Cyprus inevitably became entangled with demographic concerns, with the two ethnic communities viewing migration as a zero-sum game towards their respective national aspirations. This continued after independence with the organized mass migration of Turks to Northern Cyprus after 1974, referred to by Turkey as 'economic migrants' and by Greek Cypriots as 'illegal settlers' (cf. Demetriou 2018).

Furthermore, the position of Cyprus as a geopolitical borderland between Europe and the Middle East, with all the inherent ambiguities of borderland societies, must be considered. Strategically located in the Eastern Mediterranean, the island was historically contested between rival empires. At times, the island was a neutral zone, as during the 300-year period of the Byzantine–Arab condominium, when the Caliphate and the Byzantines jointly ruled Cyprus, while both empires were at war elsewhere. In 1878, the British effectively took control of Cyprus, while it formally belonged to the Ottoman Empire until the outbreak of World War I. In 1960, Cypriot gained an independence supervised by three NATO states, Greece, Turkey and the United Kingdom, with the latter retaining important military facilities on the island. Nevertheless, Cyprus also joined the Non-Aligned Movement and cultivated close ties with the Eastern Bloc and neighbouring Arab countries. Even after EU accession, the island maintains close financial links to Russia, while expanding its ties to China (Panayiotou 2012).

In modern times, Cyprus also became a place of exile and transit for groups of persecuted peoples in a region marked by colonialism, emerging nationalism, and ethnic cleansing (Chatty 2010). Circassians fled to the island from the Caucasus after the 1870 Russian–Turkish War, Armenians after the 1915 Genocide, as well as European Jews fleeing Nazism and transiting on their way to Palestine from the 1930s onwards. In the latter case, Cyprus became an experiment for the application of imperial technologies in the classification of people on the move (Rappas 2019). In British considerations, the island's geography converged with demography and economic concerns. In an attempt to regain legitimacy after the crackdown of an anticolonial revolt in 1931, authorities evoked local demographic concerns over immigration to only allow the entry of affluent Jews considered 'refugees' and seen as beneficial to the local economy. In contrast, the aftermath of World War II Cyprus became a detention centre for destitute Jews trying to reach Palestine, who were labelled 'illegal migrants' since their movement conflicted with British policy at that time and was unpopular with the local population.

The British inherited to the Cypriot state these mechanisms for the management of populations, both desired and undesired. The bicommunal state collapsed just three years after its establishment, as the majority's vision for *enosis* and the minority's vision of partition (*taksim*) proved irreconcilable. Following armed clashes and reacting to proposed constitutional amendments stripping them of their role as politically equal partners in the new state, the Turkish Cypriots who made up 18 percent of the population, withdrew to enclaves scattered across the island that only made up five percent of the state's territory (Papadakis 2005). While the Turkish Cypriots began establishing proto-state structures within these enclaves, the situation primarily benefited the Greek Cypriots, who monopolized the state and reaped the benefits of an economic boom. Turkish Cypriots were internally colonized, with the now Greek-controlled government setting up checkpoints around them and controlling the flow of people, goods, and services like water and electricity, while Turkish Cypriots were forced to rely on UN escorts to move from one enclave to the other. The situation was dramatically reversed in 1974. Following a Greek-sponsored coup against the democratically elected (Greek) Cypriot government, Turkish forces landed on the island and ended up permanently occupying its northern half. Turkey used its military advantage to force a population exchange, which saw Turkish Cypriots in the South moving north, while around 200,000 Greek Cypriots were ethnically cleansed from the North. Small groups from both communities, who stayed put, were placed under house arrest or under the surveillance of intelligence services (Trimikliniotis 2009).

Nevertheless, Greek refugees from the North provided a pool of cheap labor, especially for the construction and tourism industries. In the face of what was perceived as a state of exception in the face of national disaster, social standards were lowered, enabling the economy's rapid growth to levels surpassing those before the Turkish invasion. Following a shortage of manual labor in the early 1990s, the Cypriot government also began issuing working visas to female domestic workers, mostly from Sri Lanka and the Philippines, as well as to male unskilled workers from Eastern Europe and the Middle East. The program was characterized as the "importation of foreign labour" (*eisagogi ksenou ergatikou dynamikou*) and often involved severe restrictions in the movement of female domestic workers, often leading to slave-like conditions and arbitrary deportations (Trimikliniotis 1999). At the same time, the demand for cheap, non-unionized labor encouraged irregular migration to the island, mostly from Syria, literally producing a "spectacle of migrant illegality" (De Genova 2013) exemplified by televized police ambushes on landing boats. In addition, women from Eastern Europe were trafficked under "artists' visas" to Cyprus, often under false pretences, and forced into prostitution. Cyprus became a "multidiasporic space" (Teerling and King 2012) composed of a plurality of nationalities and social trajectories, and typical of the "southern European model of migration" (King and Thomson 2008), characterized, among others, by a location along main migratory routes, gendered and racialized labor niches, as well as the absence of any official policy of integration.

4 Contemporary Migration between Racialization, Austerity, and Mobility Privilege

The legal environment of migration to Cyprus changed significantly with EU entry in 2004, as the country joined the common European framework on asylum and migration. Responsibility for non-Cypriot refugees was transferred from UNHCR to the government, while the island became a destination for those fleeing new wars and persecution in the Middle East. Whereas in the past, employers' demand for cheap labor, the perceived economic advantage of affluent migration, or political expediency[2] dictated migration policies, Cyprus now became obliged to offer the prospect for asylum for victims of war and persecution as a matter of principle.

Nevertheless, some local factors prevailed. The ongoing harsh treatment after EU accession, not only of migrants and asylum applicants from third countries, but also of EU nationals nominally entitled to the same rights as Cypriots, has been attributed to the lingering Cyprus question (Trimikliniotis 2013). The continuation of the Republic after the withdrawal of its Turkish constituent component in 1963 was legally justified by the 'doctrine of necessity' giving wide discretion to the executive. According to Constantinou (2008), this particular state of exception was bound generate more states of exception, in this case leading to aberrations of Cypriot migration policy from the European framework it is nominally obliged to uphold. Indeed, government officials

---

2 In the latter case, the government gave preferential treatment to a group of Kurdish political refugees from Turkey in the early 1990s.

mention the island's small size and conflict-related demographic concerns as the main reasons for Cyprus's restrictive migration policy. The non-participation of Cyprus in the Schengen Agreement is also related to the island's division, as the government fears the erection of a hard border along the UN-monitored buffer zone, which separates the Republic from the internationally unrecognized Turkish Republic of Northern Cyprus (TRNC), something considered politically unacceptable across the political spectrum. For many migrants, this – along with the absence of a ferry link to Greece, the nearest EU state – precludes the usage of Cyprus as a transit stop towards other EU countries.

However, the role of European policies in shaping the Cypriot migration regime should also be emphasized. An infrastructure of reception and deportation centers forms the material manifestation of EU bordering practices on the island. Furthermore, the Dublin regulations require migrants to apply for asylum in the first EU country they set foot it. Coupled with geography and the non-participation in Schengen, this means that irregularized migrants coming across the buffer zone on foot or rescued from shipwrecks have the choice either to remain undocumented or to apply for asylum. In the latter case and if accepted, they will most likely not receive refugee status, but 'subsidiary protection.' This status provides for no travel documents, bars family reunifications and does not protect against eventual forced repatriation. For these reasons, Cyprus is generally avoided by migrants fleeing was in Syria and elsewhere, while many of those forced to come to Cyprus opt to remain invisible to the authorities and try to reach Turkey via the TRNC and from there on other European countries. European legal classifications thus merge with the local context to produce a particularly coercive form of geography for migrants.

Also, not to be overlooked, is the nexus between migration and austerity policies. Cyprus was indirectly hit by the Eurozone crisis in Greece, leading to the collapse of its bloated banking sector in 2012 and the latter's bailout by the state, which transformed the banking crisis overnight into a fiscal crisis. In early 2013, the government agreed to an EU 'bail in,' a somewhat innovative way to repay the debt by forcing ordinary depositors to 'chip in.' Thus, a haircut was imposed on bank deposits over 100,000 Euro.[3] The panic that ensued following the closure of ATMs fitted neatly with what Naomi Klein (2008) defines as the "shock doctrine," the promotion of neoliberal shock therapies aimed at eradicating any potential resistance through feelings of disorientation. Indeed, what followed was a wholesale reengineering of Cypriot society along

---

3   The measure was intended for all bank depositors but was amended following a massive outcry in the days following the closure of ATMs.

neoliberal principles, which included massive privatisations, the slashing of welfare benefits and public sector cutbacks (Ioannou 2014). However, the paralysis inflicted on the populace translated to a marked absence of the social resistance against austerity seen in other countries like Greece, Portugal or Spain.

In a measure aimed at normalizing austerity, the government introduced a so-called living wage, the EEE (*Elachisto Eggyimeno Eisodima*, or 'Minimum Guaranteed Income'), to which recipients of subsidiary protection are entitled, making undesired migrants dependent on scarce welfare benefits in the process. Confirming the idea that border regimes do not intend to keep migrants out but to filter them according to the needs of labor markets, migrants – just like Greek Cypriot refugees after 1974 – are being utilized as a pool of cheap labor in a neoliberalized economy. Yet the use of migrant labor is tightly regulated by the state, which confines migrants to certain labor niches, irrespective of their actual qualifications. For example, a law amendment in 2014 allowed migrants receiving the EEE allowance to work only in construction, sanitation and farming. On other hand, a 2019 amendment granted subsidiary protection recipients full access to the labor market, whereas those with pending applications were given access to low-skilled professions, including construction, processing, waste management, and agriculture. Evident here is an attempt by the state to confine certain migrants into specific niches, thus generating a series of downward social trajectories.[4]

Furthermore, this disadvantageous position of migrants in the labor market is predicated on, and perpetuated by their racialization. While undocumented workers were cast as 'illegals' in the 1990s, processes of contested solidarities (Della Porta 2018) in the wake of the 'refugee crisis' have transformed the image of undeserving 'asylum seekers' to that of people in need of solidarity and material assistance, a framing deriving in part from discursive juxtapositions of the fate of Syrian refugees with that of Greek Cypriots after 1974 (UNHCR 2019). Yet, and in accordance to the autonomy of migration of approach, the state response to these interactions between migrants and local solidarians has been to reconfigure bordering practices and discourses, specifically by emphasizing the recent migrants' background as Muslims. Accordingly, the Home Affairs minister stated in 2015 that Cyprus would accept only 300 refugees from Syria, but would prefer that they are Orthodox Christians (Kambas 2015). Media

---

4 A local solidarian recalled the case of an Iranian nuclear physicist who applied for asylum on the island. While his qualifications could theoretically land him an academic position, he was granted 'subsidiary protection' and sent to work in the fields.

discourses frequently cast irregularized migrants as pawns infiltrated by Turkey to increase the number of Muslims on the island and shift the demographic balance to the disadvantage of Greek Cypriots. Conflict-related concerns merge with European right-wing populist discourses, over-determining the status of migrants as a racialized segment of the Cypriot labor force. In this, they resemble migrants in other postcolonial states riddled with demographic concerns, such as low-wage Syrian workers in Lebanon (Chalcraft 2007), both racialized and perceived in the 1990s as instruments of Syrian domination over the country.

The racialization of migrant workers becomes more pronounced, when contrasted to actions the Cypriot government has undertaken in recent years. In parallel to austerity measures, it announced a citizenship-by-investment program as a way of exiting the crisis, aimed at non-EU citizens – primarily Russian and Chinese nationals – who are in turn encouraged to purchase luxury real estate on the island. Cypriot citizenship thus is commodified as an entry ticket to Europe, conceived as a privileged space in a global hierarchy of mobility regimes. According to EUROSTAT (2019), even 205 Syrians were registered as Cypriot citizens in 2017, the overwhelming majority most likely through participation in the "golden visa" scheme. The dialectics of mobility and immobility are thus ultimately structured by class; while irregularized migrants face racialization, geographical confinement and labor restrictions, those able to procure citizenship can experience the island as 'expats.' In the second case, a continuity is observable with the past – colonial policies vis-à-vis affluent Jewish refugees in the 1930s, the accommodation of the Lebanese banking sector in the 1980s, as well as the entry of capital from the former Soviet Union since the early 1990s, which solidified the Cyprus's character as an offshore banking hub.

The legal exceptionalism engendered by the Cyprus dispute explains authoritarian practices towards migrants only up to a certain point. The ethnic conflict is not the cause but rather the symptom of modes of domination inherited from colonialism. These are in turn determined by geography. In this case, the spatial location of Cyprus between Europe and the Middle East, as well the temporal location of its social structure between Balkan late nation-state formation and Middle Eastern postcoloniality, which privileges demographic concerns over any practical commitment to civic equality. On the other hand, crisis and austerity are the factors significantly amplifying a promiscuous mobility policy towards those able to afford it, and a policy of racializing and warehousing contemporary migrants deemed a surplus population.

5 Navigating Immobility: Three Snapshots

In the following segment, I present three ethnographic snapshots to highlight the subjective ways by which migrants deal with a predicament of immobility. These are drawn from fieldwork and qualitative interviews conducted in 2018 with three of the most visible groups of migrants from the Middle East: Palestinians formerly residing in Iraq, stateless Kurds from Syria, as well as refugees from Syria's ongoing civil war.

5.1 *Stuck in Larnaca*

Palestinians from Iraq began arriving in Cyprus around 2006. While living in Iraq for decades, Sunni Muslim Palestinians became targets of violent attacks by Shia militias following the US invasion in 2003. Based on prior knowledge of it as a tourist destination, the formerly affluent Palestinians made their way to Cyprus, requesting asylum. During its peak, the community numbered around 3,000 persons, overwhelmingly living in the coastal city of Larnaca. Their presence led to growing tensions, far-right street mobilisation, and stories in the press about huge sums allegedly collected by them from welfare services. Their relatively large numbers and the fact that most had crossed over to Republic through the buffer zone, generated conspiracy theories about Turkish policies of 'flooding' the island with Muslims to alter the demographic balance. Eventually, many left Cyprus for other destinations, such as Scandinavia, Canada, or Malaysia and Indonesia, from where they attempted deadly sea crossing to Australia.[5] Meanwhile, following protests by the Palestinians against their treatment by the authorities, the state dispersed the community to other cities on the island. Today, around 500 remain, mostly in Larnaca.

In a café on the Larnaca sea front late on a March afternoon, I interviewed a group of five middle-aged Palestinians, while airplanes flew overhead towards the city's airport nearby. All of them received the EEE welfare allowance, alternating between chronic unemployment and occasional menial jobs. Their case is typical for a class journey of downward social mobility giving way to a lack of existential mobility. Most of the conversation was directed by the men to the past of living in Iraq, where the community was prosperous, or to visits in Larnaca in the 1980s as well-off tourists, when Cyprus was an *ersatz* hub for wealthy and middle-class Arabs following the Israeli invasion of Lebanon and the destruction of Beirut.

---

5 https://electronicintifada.net/blogs/ali-abunimah/palestinian-refugees-forced-out-iraq-feared-lost-sea-en-route-australia.

While men tended to downplay incidents of racism and discrimination in Cyprus, women were much more vocal and tended to steer the conversation towards the issue of welfare allowances such as the EEE. At a group interview some weeks later, Palestinian women from Iraq recounted stories of arbitrary discrimination and verbal abuse at welfare services, or of labor department officials referring *hijab*-wearing women to work in bars serving alcohol. Because of anti-Muslim prejudices in the labor market, most women – many of them in possession of university diplomas – stay at home, indicating a restriction of both social and existential mobility. Nevertheless, they perceive living in Cyprus in conditions of crisis and austerity as an endurance test: "We endure the financial crisis together [with the Cypriots]. Anything that is good for them is also good for us (Issam, Palestinian, subsidiary protection)." Endurance, or "steadfastness" (*sumud*), occupies a prominent role in the Palestinian predicament of struggle and exile. Dire conditions are thus rationalized as part of an ongoing political struggle, with Palestinians mentioning feeling lucky to be closer to Palestine in Cyprus, compared to living in Australia, Europe, or North America. Yet this steadfastness also dovetails with neoliberalism's endurance test in times of austerity, hence the Palestinians have little difficulty to relate to other crisis-hit Cypriots. Feelings of existential stuckedness are compounded by the lack of citizenship, permanent residency, or refugee status, which translates to geographical isolation, and a sense of going nowhere. The Palestinians thus make a claim to citizenship, not so much out of a drive to integration, but out of a desire to be mobile, seen as a perquisite to normality: "We would like to have [Cypriot] citizenship. To be able to travel, to visit Arab countries. To become and feel like normal citizens. We lived our entire lives as refugees, without citizenship, without nothing" (Reem, Palestinian, subsidiary protection). The right to citizenship is in the case the right to be mobile, a right granted to those migrants with the money to pay for it, but denied to those experiencing a downward class journey.

5.2   Camping outside the Ministry of Interior

In front of the Ministry of Interior in Nicosia, a Kurdish family from Syria regularly camps out, engaging in hunger strikes and making claims to citizenship. The family's predicament is tied to that of tens of thousands of Kurds, who were denationalized by the Syrian state in 1962 for refusing to assimilate. Following anti-regime riots in North-eastern Syria in 2005, individual family members began making their way to the Republic through Turkey and then through the TRNC. Assisted by a local advocacy group, they demand the right to be recognized as refugees or citizens through a process of naturalisation. Their status of 'subsidiary protection' does not provide them with any travel documents. The family was eager to proclaim their 'allegiance' to Cyprus, claiming to even have forgotten some Kurdish words to the advantage of their Greek equivalents, pointing out to friendships made, contributions to social security paid, and feeling closer to Cyprus than anywhere else:

> I was 19 when I came here. And I feel like a part of it, a Cypriot citizen but without any papers. [...] We struck roots here, we grew up here. And even if things in Syria were ok, it would be a very difficult decision for us to go back.
>
> HAWAR, Kurd, subsidiary protection

In their placards, the Kurds make use of a universalist right-based discourse: "Everyone has the right to citizenship – United Nations." Experienced in activism after so many years, the three brothers camped outside government buildings were eager to show me the rejection letters sent out to their elderly parents. In them, an 'unwillingness to integrate' is mentioned as a reason to deny them the citizenship they never possessed back in Syria. The contrast with other foreigners purchasing EU passports becomes obvious, as many – if not most – 'golden visa' citizens reside on the island only nominally, leaving their luxury apartments idle. Economics trumps universalism in this case. Nevertheless, the Kurds' protests have been partially successful, as the government conceded citizenship in some cases. But it's not only a blatant sense of injustice that drives these protests:

> We have been living in Cyprus for 12 years and for us Cyprus is really a big prison. You cannot travel abroad or have a change of scenery. Let's say you have friends in Germany who are getting married. Or my brother wanted to study abroad; he couldn't. Because he doesn't have any travel documents.
>
> AHMED, Kurd, subsidiary protection

Evident here is a sense of racial stuckedness related to being geographically confined to an island and unable to 'have a change of scenery.' The Kurds are going nowhere, neither geographically, nor socially, for instance by not being able to study abroad like a significant percentage of Cypriots. Denationalized and discriminated against in Syria, the Kurds consciously came to Cyprus, believing it to be a democratic country were they would be accepted. Yet due to their low-income status, their Muslim background, as well as their entry through the heavily securitized buffer zone, often constructed as a playground of illicit practices (Papadakis 2018), the Kurds have been racialized, securitized and classified as second-class refugees, undeserving of international protection.

5.3 *Zainab, a Palestinian Refugee from Syria*

Zainab personifies many of the experiences associated with both the European border regime, as well as the European regime of austerity. A schoolteacher from the Palestinian refugee camp of Yarmouk near Damascus, she first relocated to the Shatila Palestinian refugee camp in Beirut, Lebanon following the outbreak of armed hostilities in the Syrian capital. The dire condition of Palestinian and Syrian refugees in Lebanon, prompted her to pay smugglers to take her and her daughter by boat to Greece in 2014. Like many before her, she hoped to eventually reach friends in Germany through the Balkan Route. Nevertheless, the boat she was travelling in soon encountered difficulties due to a malfunctioning GPS device and was lost at sea. There, they were intercepted by the Cypriot coast guard and brought to the island. She and her fellow travellers were given the option of applying for asylum. Based on circulated knowledge about conditions in Cyprus, she was sceptical:

> I did not want to sign any asylum papers after we saw the situation in the reception centre. But I saw many families that came on their own to welcome us. One time, while the centre was closed, me and my daughter were standing by the door when a family of Cypriots came by. They stopped and we talked in English and they gave my daughter a small present. This was four or five days after we arrived. This act made me change my mind and I decided to apply.

An act of autonomous solidarity, largely framed through the experience of Greek Cypriot refugeehood, contributed to Zainab's decision to stay on the island. The failure of the restrictive policies of the Cypriot government, which actively try to deter migration through exemplary harsh treatment, is evident here. However, this was not the end of the story. Upon applying for asylum, Zainab did not receive refugee status but the highly precarious status of 'subsidiary protection.' Consequently, she was filtered into the labor market and streamlined in the Cypriot austerity-welfare complex by applying for the EEE benefit:

> In reality, I work, I clean houses illegally, but I am willing to admit that. Why do the Arabs work illegally? Because they do not give us any other opportunity. I get 800 Euro from EEE but my rent is 400 Euro. I pay 300 for

food, water and electricity and I also have to pay 300 Euro for my daughter's expenses. Why should I have my allowance cut? How will I live?

Unable to sustain herself and her daughter with her meagre welfare allowance, Zainab was forced to join the expanding informal economy, a vital part of the migrant 'mobile commons' referred to earlier. The self-perception as 'Arab' in the labor market points to a process of racialization. Despite the abstract legal categories bestowed upon all migrants once their asylum applications are processed, migrants feel relegated to the lower echelons of the social hierarchy due to their ethnicity. Furthermore, while the non-unionized informal economy might lie beyond sovereign control, its effects nevertheless contribute to the normalization of austerity, by creating in this case a substratum of overexploited racialized workers. Zainab's story is exemplary of the possibilities as well as the limits of migrant autonomy. The Cypriot state might have preferred she moved somewhere else, but non-state local solidarity convinced her otherwise. On the other hand, she might work 'illegally' beyond the reach of the state, but this decision is not so much an unintended consequence of welfare policy; it can be seen as its logical and perhaps intended outcome. In this case, a dialectic between bordering practices and racialization is on display, which in the end helps to perpetuate a regime of austerity.

6   Conclusion: mobility as a Site of Contestation in Contemporary Capitalism

To what extent does geography constitute a factor in the formation of coercive and highly exploitative labor relations? In the case of Cyprus, this complex question can be answered in two ways. Cyprus is a border society at the edge of Europe. Its insular character and historic geopolitical ambivalence make it a mobility hub within the world system. Not only capital, goods, and services pass through Cyprus but people as well. However, the latter are highly stratified along class lines. Cyprus is the ideal hub of the individualist expat who wants to consume unlimited European mobility. To paraphrase Bourdieu, wealthy, or at least upwardly mobile non-Europeans can purchase Cypriot citizenship and thus transform their economic capital into mobility capital. At the same time, Cyprus represents a transit stop (at least) for migrants fleeing war and persecution, mostly from the Middle East to Europe, but sometimes the other way around, as in the case of Jewish migration in the 1930s. While the movement of privileged expats is concomitant to the rise of their social mobility, less privileged migrants discover that their migration to Cyprus has been accompanied by a downward social trajectory. Unable to return but also unable to move further, they are stuck, both socially and existentially. Their low economic capital leads to an almost complete disappearance of their mobility capital. This process, however, is mediated by another important factor: racialization.

It is in this sense that geography matters in another way: Cyprus lies at a historical-geographical nexus between late arrival of nationalism in the Balkans on the one hand, and the postcolonial space of the Near and Middle East on the other. Arriving in a post-Ottoman environment of cultural pluralism, Greek and Turkish nationalisms sought homogeneity and, therefore, viewed migration to the island as a zero-sum game respective to their aspirations. Nonetheless, British colonialism did not remain an innocent bystander. By institutionalizing a governmentality of classifications along ethnic lines – while managing migration flows based on political, geopolitical and demographic grounds – colonialism thwarted the formation of any civic identity after independence, making the collapse of the bicommunal state a foregone conclusion. Today, this legacy translates into an exceptionally restrictive migration policy that views migrants as suspicious elements aimed at undermining regimes of ethnic supremacy. Seen from this perspective, Cyprus shares more similarities with neighbouring countries like Israel and Lebanon, than with other EU states.

The inclusion of Cyprus into the borderless European space did not replace already existing modes of governing along ethnic lines. The EU border regime has rather supplemented the latter with its own technology of classifications along the lines of 'EU citizenship,' 'refugee status,' and 'subsidiary protection.' Furthermore, European integration did not displace particularisms but has transformed them to a certain extent. In convergence with contemporary European discourses, migrants in Cyprus are racialized and securitized as threatening Muslims, while being assigned a precarious legal status aimed at preventing them from striking roots on the island. In addition, the ongoing postcolonial Cyprus dispute keeps the island out of Schengen, leading to a loss of possible escape routes for migrants.

Nevertheless, it would be mistaken to view the geographical factor fatalistically, by assuming that migrants become the object of total control by the state. It is indeed the historical-geographical location of Cyprus within Middle Eastern postcoloniality, with its history of ethnic cleansing and refugeehood, which enables some locals to relate to migrants and form relations of solidarity escaping sovereign control. These relations subvert the border regime, which is not only manifested in infrastructure, but also in legal categories, as well as racializing discourses. However, the current regime of crisis prevents migrant autonomy from unfolding its subversive potential any further. By being incorporated into a disciplinary rather than empowering welfare system, migrants are deprived of their existential mobility. In conjunction with historical factors, as in the case of the downwardly mobile Palestinians, they come to view their immobility as an endurance test. Others are forced to seek out work in the precarious informal sector. In doing so, migrants constitute a racialized and overexploited segment of the local workforce. Both state practices and geography circumscribe migrant agency in this case, generating labor relations that are free only in name. The general lack of resistance to austerity in Cyprus forms the general enabling framework in this case.

Not all migrants, however, decide to wait out the crisis. Since the most obvious expression of this confinement is the lack of movement, some migrants like the Syrian Kurds make militant claims to citizenship, seen as synonymous with mobility. The right to be mobile is one that racialized subjects at the bottom of the social scale have to actively contest, in contrast to those affluent migrants who can simply convert their economic capital to mobility capital. Contesting the right to be mobile is not only about the free movement through space. Migrants want to be able to experience education, leisure, or simply have the feeling that they are going somewhere. As a border space, Cyprus presents a microcosm of global landscape of crisis, characterized by the dialectics of physical, social, and existential mobility.

References

Alloul, J. (2020). "Leaving Europe, Aspiring Access: Racial Capital and Its Spatial Discontents among the Euro-Maghrebi Minority," *Journal of Immigrant & Refugee Studies* 18(3): 313–325. doi: 10.1080/15562948.2020.1761504.

Bojadžijev, M., and S. Karakayali (2010). "Recuperating the Sideshows of Capitalism: The Autonomy of Migration Today," *e-flux journal* 17: 1–9.

Bourdieu, P. (2010). *Distinction*. London: Routledge.

Calhoun, C. (2008). "Cosmopolitanism in the Modern Social Imaginary," *Daedalus* 137(3): 105–114.

Casas-Cortes, M., S. Cobarrubias, and J. Pickles (2016). "'Good neighbours make good fences': Seahorse Operations, Border Externalization and Extra-Territoriality," *European Urban and Regional Studies* 23(3): 231–251.

Chalcraft, J. (2007). "Labour in the Levant," *New Left Review* 45: 27–47.

Chatty, D. (2010). *Displacement and Dispossession in the Modern Middle East*. Cambridge: Cambridge University Press.

Constantinou, C.M. (2007). "Aporias of Identity: Bicommunalism, Hybridity and the 'Cyprus Problem.'" *Cooperation and Conflict* 42(3): 247–270.

Constantinou, C.M. (2008). "On the Cypriot States of Exception," *International Political Sociology* 2(2): 145–164.

Cranston, S. (2017). "Expatriate as a 'Good' Migrant: Thinking through Skilled International Migrant Categories," *Population, Space, and Place.* Published online 29 March 2017 in Wiley Online Library. Accessed July 28 2019. https://doi.org/10.1002/psp.2058.

De Genova, N. (2013). "Spectacles of Migrant 'Illegality': The Scene of Exclusion, the Obscene of Inclusion," *Ethnic & Racial Studies* 36(7): 1180–1198.

Della Porta, D. (2018). *Solidarity Mobilizations in the 'Refugee Crisis.'* Basingstoke: Palgrave Macmillan.

Demetriou, O. (2018). *Refugeehood and the Post-Conflict Subject: Reconsidering Minor Losses.* Albany: State University of New York Press.

EUROSTAT (2019). "Acquisition of citizenship by age group, sex and former citizenship, 2017," . http://appsso.eurostat.ec.europa.eu/nui/submitViewTableAction.do.

Fredette, J. (2014). *Constructing Muslims in France: Discourse, Public Identity, and the Politics of Citizenship.* Chicago, IL: Temple University Press.

Hage, G. (2009). "Waiting Out the Crisis: On Stuckedness and Governmentality," in G. Hage (ed.). *Waiting.* Carlton: Melbourne University Press: 97–106.

Harvey, D. (2019). *Spaces of Global Capitalism.* London: Verso.

Huysmans, J. (2000). "The European Union and the Securitization of Migration," *JCMS: Journal of Common Market Studies* 38(5): 751–777.

Ioannou, G. (2014). "Employment in Crisis: Cyprus 2010–2013," *The Cyprus Review* 26(1): 107–126.

Kambas, M. (2015). "Cyprus says it could take up to 300 preferably Christian refugees," *Reuters.* September 7. https://www.reuters.com/article/us-europe-migrants-cyprus/cyprus-says-it-could-take-up-to-300-preferably-christian-refugees-idUSKCN0R711220150907.

King, R., and M. Thomson (2008). "The Southern European Model of Immigration: Do the Cases of Malta, Cyprus and Slovenia fit?," *Journal of Southern Europe and the Balkans* 10(3): 265–291.

Klein, N. (2008). *The Shock Doctrine: The Rise of Disaster Capitalism.* London: Penguin.

Kunz, S. (2016). "Privileged Mobilities: Locating the Expatriate in Migration Scholarship," *Geography Compass* 10(3): 89–101.

Mezzadra, S., and B. Neilson (2013). *Border as Method or, the Multiplication of Labor.* Durham, NC: Duke University Press.

Nachtwey, O. (2018). *Germany's Hidden Crisis: Social Decline in the Heart of Europe.* London: Verso.

Papadakis, Y. (2005). *Echoes from the Dead Zone: Across the Cyprus Divide.* London: I.B. Tauris.

Papadakis, Y. (2018). "Borders, Paradox and Power," *Ethnic & Racial Studies* 41(2): 285–302.

Papadopoulos, D., and V.S. Tsianos (2013). "After Citizenship: Autonomy of Migration, Organisational Ontology and Mobile Commons," *Citizenship Studies* 17(2): 178–196.

Panayiotou, A. (2012). "Border Dialectics: Cypriot Social and Historical Movements in a World Systemic Context," in N. Trimikliniotis and U. Bozkurt (eds.). *Beyond a Divided Cyprus: A State and Society in Transformation.* London: Palgrave Macmillan: 67–82.

Pedersen, M.H. (2012). "Going on a Class Journey: The Inclusion and Exclusion of Iraqi Refugees in Denmark," *Journal of Ethnic and Migration Studies,* 38(7): 1101–1117.

Rappas, Al. (2019). "Jewish Refugees in Cyprus and British Imperial Sovereignty in the Eastern Mediterranean, 1933–1949," *Journal of imperial and Commonwealth History* 47(1): 1–29.

Slobodian, Q. (2018). *Globalists: The End of Empire and the Birth of Neoliberalism.* Cambridge, MA: Harvard University Press.

Streeck, W. (2016). *How Will Capitalism End? Essays on a Failing System.* London: Verso.

Teerling, J., and R. King (2012). "Of Hubs and Hinterlands: Cyprus as an Insular Space of Overlapping Diasporas," *Island Studies* 7(1): 19–48.

Trimikliniotis, N. (1999). "Racism and New Migration to Cyprus: The Racialisation of Migrant Workers," in F. Anthias and G. Lazarides (eds.). *Into the Margins: Exclusion and Migration in Southern Europe.* Burlington, VT: Ashgate. http://www.rednetwork.eu/resources/toolip/doc/2011/11/16/nt-racialisation-of-migrant-workers-in-cyprus.pdf.

Trimikliniotis, N. (2009). "Nationality and citizenship in Cyprus since 1945: Communal Citizenship, Gendered Nationality and the Adventures of a Post-Colonial Subject in a Divided Country," in R. Bauböck and B. Perchinig (eds.). *Citizenship Policies in the New Europe: Expanded and Updated Edition.* Amsterdam: Amsterdam University Press: 389–418.

Trimikliniotis, N. (2013). "Migration and Freedom of Movement of Workers: EU Law, Crisis and the Cypriot States of Exception," *Laws* 2: 440–468.

Trimikliniotis, N., D. Parsanoglou, and V.S. Tsianos. (2016). "Mobile Commons and/in Precarious Spaces: Mapping Migrant Struggles and Social Resistance," *Critical Sociology* 42(7–8): 1035–1049.

UNHCR Cyprus (2019). *Perceptions of Cypriots about Refugees and Migrants.* Nicosia: UNHCR.

Weber, B. (2016). "'We Must Talk about Cologne': Race, Gender, and Reconfigurations of 'Europe,'" *German Politics and Society* 34(4): 68–86.

Weizman, E. (2017). *The Least of All Possible Evils. A Short History of Humanitarian Violence.* London: Verso.

CHAPTER 5

"When the Snow Falls, They Have All Left": Infrastructures of Seasonal Labor in Migration Corridors

Karin Krifors

1 Introduction

In the fiction epos "The Iron Tracks" by influential Swedish author Sara Lidman, Didrik, a young man in the late 19th century, attaches hopes and fantasies of a different future to the construction of a railway to the North West of Sweden. This region, inhabited by indigenous Sami people and settlers who have escaped from poverty or hierarchical family structures elsewhere, is peripheral to the Swedish national project yet exploited for its resources. Here, where "the forest was too large, too empty of people. The few cottages in the region on the contrary too small, too crowded" (Lidman 1979: 122), Lidman portrays a geographical imbalance and the dreams of how links and connections to other places can change the precarious lives of people who suffer through 'weak years' or the endless labor of ditching for fertile soil. The novel suite illustrates the emergence of new economic, religious, social, technological and political infrastructures that affect how different settlers live in this particular place. Some live on hard work and prayers, others trust the chance of the moment and the occasional poached ermine and yet others are convinced by technology and progress. Encounters with soldiers deserted from Russian armies who hide in forest caves and the tales about them mirrors the own fear, curiosity or altruism. Contempt from officials of the South or people from the more connected coast line evokes feelings of powerlessness, isolation and desire, but also loyalty that transcends the different ways in which people deal with both unpredictability and monotony in the villages that depend on snow for transportation. This text deals with how, at certain points in time, the fundamentals of the everyday change in ways that are difficult to bypass, for instance through the attachment to iron tracks. The railway constitutes a strong image of an infrastructure that connects places in particular ways and adds a spatial layer that make mobilities appear as possible or not. This chapter aims to discuss other less obvious infrastructures that affect how certain movements come to be understood as ordinary and, in other words, applies an infrastructural perspective on what both facilitates mobility and structures immobility (Lin et al. 2017).

This region of the Swedish North-West, illustrated in Lidman's portrayal of generations who navigate precarities of class relations, modernisation and intimacy, is also one of the centres for a commerce that has received much attention in media and Nordic research over the last two decades, namely the presence of a new migrant workforce. Thousands of people arrive from Thailand to pick wild forest berries; cloud berries, blue berries and lingon berries, that grow on the slopes, forests and fens during a couple of months every summer. By providing a container for a flow of seasonally returning migrant workers and by offering links between two different localities across continents, the arrangements of the wild berry industry can be understood as a migration corridor. This metaphor has also been used by Hedberg, Axelsson and Abella (2019) in a report on the conditions of the industry. This particular migration corridor, though often thought of as peculiar in its coupling of two very distant places, springs from the emergence of a Thai diaspora in these Swedish regions that have hosted a 'surplus' of unmarried men with the opportunity to meet women from a different continent through travelling, technology and, increasingly, a transnational social network. This chapter begins with a discussion on how precarity is an important dimension of migrant labor in the wild berry industry and how this relates to coercive geographies. I will illustrate how the formation of a migration corridor is supported by arrangements between specific buyers, suppliers and employers and by a liberal lenience of state policy and controls. Following this, the chapter makes use of infrastructures as an analytical concept to consider alternative mobilities and immobilities in and around this migration corridor, as well as how these different ways of working and living in transnational spaces affect precarity. With reference to the precarisation of labor that this book examines, this chapter aims to discuss whether the migration corridor makes a horizon of opportunities in a distant Sweden accessible, or whether the shape of the corridor itself obstructs the vision for someone who is weighing their options to escape precarious conditions of life in Thailand.

The transnational space of the wild berry industry has been portrayed as something close to a forced situation for migrant workers: there have been news reports about workers who were cheated off wages or forced to live in crowded and unhealthy conditions during their stay in Sweden and workers who were indebted because of the migration costs. There has also been critique against a failure of Swedish labor market policy, which is characterized by an exceptionally liberal labor migration policy since 2008, to protect migrant berry pickers against forced labor. Although precarity and transnational inequalities are a prerequisite for the migration corridor between these places in Sweden and Thailand, however, the everyday experience of this precarity is not that berry picking in Sweden is its cause. Understanding this transnational space as a coercive geography therefore requires the analysis to let go of a Eurocentric imagination of a non-precarious past that is only now being consumed by deteriorating social and economic conditions, because, as the introduction to this volume emphasizes, such conceptions risk reproducing particular Western standards as the normal state of people's work and life situations.

The organisation of the wild berry industry today is a morass of different suppliers and brokers, but normally consist of larger wholesale companies, Swedish owned berry companies who organize the harvest and living arrangements in Sweden and Thai recruitment agencies that are the formal employers of the pickers whose earnings therefore can be exempted from Swedish taxes. The part of the berry industry that employs Thai workers has collaborated in battling hyper-exploitation and very few incidents have been reported during recent years (Wingborg 2014). Unpredictability in terms of work and wages has for instance been addressed by an implementation of minimum wages as complementary to the piece rate of berries per kilo, which has decreased the risk of migration costs that exceed what workers earn. These industry actions have also led to a correspondence between how these transnational arrangements are understood and dominant notions of a win-win-win situation of circular migration that are being brought forward by many international organizations (OSCE 2006; Commission 2007). There is a strong narrative about the positive opportunities for the berry industry in Northern Sweden and for economically marginalized farmers in Thailand that the transnational 'match' represents (Krifors 2017). The ambitions of this book to discuss precarity as a constitutive and functional element of global neoliberalism is helpful in terms of unsettling such notions of aligned global success in specific patterns of transnational migration. Understanding precarity as situations where migrant rights and entitlements are both present and absent in different constellations (Goldring, Berinstein, and Bernhard 2009: 240) brings out the ambivalent tensions between optimism and hopes of transnational economic opportunities and its tendency to lock people in precarious everyday lives. Precarity references both specific conditions of labor and life under neoliberalism and vulnerability that, widening the historical and geographical gaze, also constitutes a norm (Neilson and Rossiter 2008) and an ontology of human vulnerability (Butler 2006). In this text, I understand Thai berry pickers as conditioned by precarity, because in the relative terms of the concept (Sanchez 2018) these workers are precarious enough to perform work that is too difficult to recruit for in places that would require far less migration costs. The question is rather how this precarity is navigated and understood in the context of circular migration.

Precarity is the condition of vulnerability and risk that characterizes people's lives, but is distinct as a concept because it is also conceived as possible points of mobilisation (Waite 2009). Though this chapter does not deal explicitly with labor conflicts, or protests that form a collective resistance towards the moral conditions of poverty and exploitation (Scott 1977; Thompson 1971), I pay attention to ways of navigating precarity through a particular form of short-term labor migration. Paret and Gleeson argue that the value of precarity as a rather loose concept is how it connects micro and macro by "situating experiences of insecurity and vulnerability within historically and geographically specific contexts" (Paret and Gleeson 2016: 280). In this chapter the connections between micro and macro are done through the discussions of a particular migration corridor and the infrastructures that shape it. Although opportunities of social mobility through circular migration are actively reflected in migrant strategies, social policy and corporate initiatives, the transnational context of repeated migration also links different aspects of precarity in people's lives, what Silvey and Parreñas call precarity chains (2019). I use the term infrastructures not because it is specific or precise, but because it opens up to the analytical possibility that the design of policy, new communication technologies or social networks can exist both as structures that normalize precarity and as tools of living in these unpredictable and vulnerable socioeconomic conditions. The examples, through which this chapter approaches coercive geographies pay attention to infrastructures of social networks, professionalized commercial relations and established expectations on how to invest for future returns. The analysis pays attention to two main dimensions: how these infrastructures support labor uniformity and circularity in different ways. I discuss this in the context of adapting to social and economic unpredictability and how the migration corridor can therefore be understood as a coercive geography.

2   Understanding Precarity – Institutional Ethnography as Inspiration

The design of the study has been inspired by Institutional Ethnography that highlights how the everyday experience of people is essential in order to understand relations of ruling (Smith 2005), or, in this case, the circumstances that structure how precarity is lived in this migration corridor of circular mobility. I have been especially inspired by the insistence on maintaining a contextualisation of people's experience, asking 'how is it that people are saying what they are saying?' (DeVault and McCoy 2001: 769). The data for the study on the organization of Thai migrant labor in the wild berry industry (Krifors 2017) consisted of participant observations and interviews with entrepreneurs, experts and berry pickers. Longer interviews with experts and entrepreneurs were generally recorded. During two main field trips I have documented conversations and interviews with approximately 40 berry pickers, most of these through fieldnotes because of ethical considerations to make sure that conversations were not overheard and for convenience in the crowded camps and difficult forest terrain. Data about Thai berry pickers in Sweden was collected mainly between 2011–2015, whilst some interviews with experts and entrepreneurs were performed as late as 2019.

In the analysis, I use accounts from berry pickers to illustrate different situations of precarity, as well as how the Swedish wild berry industry has provided an opportunity for the informants to 'get somewhere.' Some quotes are chosen because they illustrate a general statement or situation that returned throughout my fieldwork, which will be conveyed in the text. Yet, some situations that I report are not representative of a 'majority,' but are instead used to illustrate the diversity of experiences that I found, which also contrasts to how the background of berry pickers is often portrayed in media and reports. I therefore do not claim to invalidate research on how berry pickers in general calculate their earning or experience the working conditions, but rather show how a diversity of strategies tend to be hidden behind a main story of the type of social and economic precarity that berry pickers face.

Although I maintain that transnational sites are important in order to understand the migrant experience of precarity (Paret and Gleeson 2016: 278), I have only met berry pickers during their time in Sweden. This, naturally, excludes many possible insights to how they make decisions about their labor and migration, although it also provides opportunities to talk to people who might have been difficult to find in Thailand because they live at different places and work with different things. Skews and biases in ethnographic research are sometimes difficult to communicate or compare to other interview studies. Yet, some of these aspects that concern this study can be declared in a rather straight forward way. Because it was easier for me to reach a situation of trust and mutuality with female berry pickers, I have talked to more women than is representative of a general sample. I have also connected easier to people who knew a few words in English, though longer conversations and interviews have been done with an interpreter. It is my guess that many of the people that have approached me or been comfortable enough to share dinners, days in the forest or evening conversations with me have a social and lingual habitus that is affected by having experiences of different kinds of work, perhaps in more urban areas, or more often than others have previous experience of working abroad.

3   Infrastructures of Transnational Space and the Everyday Migration Corridor

Physical and organisational architectures are generative of migrant mobilities (Lin et al. 2017: 169), both because they shape migrant decisions and because they are themselves reshaped by the different ways that migrants move. An important infrastructural disposition of the wild berry industry is that Sweden has a unique law of right to public access of nature and to the wild berries that grow on private land. Yet, seasonal migration has come to reshape the general notion of this right to public access in relation to the transnational precarities that it makes visible. Picking berries has traditionally been a way to support the household economy and can therefore be thought of as a local practice, something, which is done in familiar forests. Many people have however travelled far in search of the desirable cloudberries or to increase the supply of blueberries, which in this wild form is also called bilberries, or lingonberries for household use. During the First World War, unemployed women from the south of Sweden were recruited to the north to pick berries and contribute to the national food provision (Sténs and Sandström 2013). Seasonal mobility across national borders came to define labor during the last decades of the 20th century as the industry grew. From the 1980s and onwards, Polish pickers were increasingly mobilized in systematic ways through recruitment campaigns and chartered busses, though many also arranged their own seasonal work. Pawel who now works with logistics in the wild berry industry came to Sweden for the first time as a berry picker and thinks that the attention that the Thai berry pickers have received is curious:

> Me and my wife had just met and we came up here with a small group of people. I think we saw an ad somewhere with information. Me and [my wife] picked many berries that year. The others couldn't handle it, they just gave up and sat by the tent and told stories. But I wanted to build a house for her. It's the same thing, some of these people [the Thai berry pickers] are great at it and then it can get you somewhere. We have our house here now, anything can happen.

As signalled in this quote by Pawel, there is an experienced ordinariness to transnational arrangements of the seasonal harvesting in Swedish forests.

During one of my visits I walk with the Swedish entrepreneur David, owner of a berry company, to the local shop to buy lunch: "The store is here because of the refugee centre they set up here, it would have been closed down otherwise," he tells me as we walk past a line of parked walkers and talk about the aging villagers and depopulation of many parts of northern Sweden.

> People in this village don't vote for the Swedish democrats, you know. We are happy that people want to live here. It's the same thing with the pickers, that people see it as a nice thing that they come here year after year. We also buy berries from some of the guys at the [refugee] centre. They don't pick very much but it's great if they can get some pocket money and something to do.

David emphasizes a need for local attitudes that make this business easier for him. I also interpret this as the existence of cultural and social infrastructures: what David sees as a particular openness to different people and opportunities that can be *performed* (Pelizza 2016) commercially. Descriptions like that of Pawel and David furthermore illustrate a multitude of different histories and infrastructures that link the wild berries in North-western Sweden to labor from other places. Yet, today the dominant link is characterized by transnational business relations, political agreements, serial migration and a top position of statistics on issued working visas in Sweden linking this region *specifically* to Thailand in what can be called a migration corridor. What contrasts this migration corridor to other arrangements of seasonal berry picking is the dominance of particular infrastructures that serve to professionalize labor and business relations, which I will return to below. First, it is important to mention that the ordinariness of seasonal labor away from home, which Pawel speaks of above, is also maintained by many people in the wild berry industry today. They do not consider the specificity of the migration corridor between the North of Sweden and Chaiyaphum in Thailand as neither surprising nor exotic, but rather as space that is based in local histories and a succession of social networks. This specific transnational space can even be observed in the geographical landscape, for instance because the world's most Northern Buddhist temple is planned in the Swedish village Fredrika. The potential of integration and expansion beyond its immediate locality is a central feature of infrastructures (Star and Ruhleder 1996). Emotional or social infrastructures of kinship, marriage or religion are such examples of infrastructures that extend the locality of the north-west of Sweden, as well as of regions in Thailand. There are also other local material infrastructures that affect the possibilities of transnational mobilities, for

instance schools abandoned through depopulation, which now accommodate Thai berry pickers.

The commercial infrastructures that dominate the image of the wild berry
industry today, such as the tight communication and supply-chain relations
between Swedish berry companies and Thai recruitment agencies (Hedberg
2013; Krifors 2017) are layered on the social infrastructure of a Thai diaspora,
which has emerged primarily through partner migration. The emergence of
this transnational industry and how it is portrayed is however conflictual.
A description that returned during my fieldwork was that Thai berry pickers
who were tied to a Thai woman living with a foreign (Swedish) husband, called
a 'madam,' were often suffering under abusive and informal arrangements that
lacked transparency. I have met several berry pickers who witness that they
were previously tied to forced employer relations characterized by a madam's
monopoly on the knowledge and transnational networks that made berry
picking in Sweden possible. Hedberg (2016) recognizes a masculinisation of
the industry during the 1990's, when business became increasingly dominated
by male entrepreneurs with Swedish origin. During my fieldwork, the notion of
a 'madam' was still present as a representation of someone who, because of
their knowledge of the business and the Thai language, could ask berry pickers
who were formally employed by other companies to sell their berries through
her. While the right to public access is a prerequisite for the professionalized
wild berry industry, these infrastructures of a right to roam are layered with
commercial infrastructures of large businesses, the scope of which makes visible how difficult it is to supervise large forests. During my fieldwork I came
across discussions, often jokingly jargoned with an undertone of seriousness,
querying whether any independent berry buyers had been spotted out on the
roads and I saw signs designed in warning letters saying 'no madam,' which
could be used by groups of berry pickers who wanted to dodge unwanted
confrontations.

Thinking about this as the infrastructural geography of berry picking allows
us to see the alternative economic and social relations that are currently over-
shadowed by the professionalized supply chains and efficient large-scale recruitment. Because there are also traces of countering meanings to these gendered infrastructures of wild berry picking. Preeda, a woman who moved from
Thailand to Sweden in the 1980's, described how she herself started picking
berries and, amazed by the economic opportunities, wanted to extend this to
others that she knew 'at home.' Similarly, the research by Erika Sörensen (2015)
has described how Thai women who have migrated to Sweden see these entrepreneurial initiatives as opportunities to be economically independent, as well
as acts of solidarity that provide support for relatives and friends in Thailand

and as an act of love tied to their practices of saving and sending remittances. Also, not all berry pickers with whom I spoke experienced the previous engagement with a madam as exploitative. Today, many women from Thailand who have settled in Sweden act as brokers for larger companies (Axelsson and Hedberg 2018). These conflictual representations of what constitutes abuse can also be understood as symptomatic of an ambivalence towards precarious migrant labor. The vulnerability of migrant workers is what makes them valuable to western economies (Bauder 2006), yet this precarity needs to have limits in order to be acceptable. In other words, the continuous precarity of the South (Munck 2013) is a prerequisite for this transnational labor exchange, but it also needs to be regulated. Yet, measures to regulate and professionalize this mobility may affect migrants' migratory capabilities (Xiang and Lindquist 2014) to navigate their vulnerable life situations. In contrast to the kinship and diaspora that initiated this transnational industry, the composition of today's commercial actors are symptomatic of supply chain capitalism (Krifors 2017; Eriksson, Tollefsen and Lundgren 2019). The most characteristic traits of this professionalisation are the scale, the logistics and the regulations of business and labor relations. The industry, mainly governed by large wholesale companies in Sweden, partly caters for needs of bilberry antioxidants in the beauty industry and engages Swedish berry companies and recruitment companies in Thailand with increasingly standardized agreements. The most important dimension of worker protection has been the enforcement of minimum wages. Despite indications that workers are often denied, or fail to claim, minimum wages as a complement to the piece rate salary (Hedberg et al. 2019) these regulations have proven to decrease the risk that workers, who themselves pay for travelling, administration and accommodation along with other costs, are left indebted. These regulations have been initiated by the industry (Wingborg 2013) and an active engagement by the Swedish trade union, LO (interviews with three officials of the LO trade union, 2011–2015). In this transnational setting, the responsibilities for regulation and control of labor standards is highly decentralized but carries a mutual commitment to battling abuse and forced labor. One of the explanations for the diffusion of regulations and responsibilities is the difficulty to standardize the labor of wild berry picking. Migration in the wild berry industry is essentially (de-)regulated in similar ways as labor migration across the Swedish labor market, following liberalisations in 2008 (Calleman and Herzfeld Olsson 2015). Although failures to control that labor conditions follow standards of collective agreements are common also in other sectors (ibid.), berry picking is difficult to control due to the lack of a specific workplace and a particular bypassing of taxation. The deviations in terms of labor standards are mostly explained with reference to the exceptional nature of working in wild forests and the desire of migrants to work as much as possible on piece rate because they want more than what the minimum salaries can grant them. In the literature on precarious migrant labor we can find similar examples of seasonal work that is deemed 'exceptional' with references to its conditions, with the effect that they are exempted from regulative and moral norms of worker protections (see e.g. Horton 2016: 63). In the wild berry industry, the evasion of taxation is both a result of the posted worker arrangement, recruitment agencies abroad acting as formal employers, and an older regulative infrastructure that grants everyone a right to sell berries up to 1300 euro tax free (though this sum is often exceeded by professional berry pickers).[1] The situation in the wild berry industry is not representative of a withdrawal of the state and a de-regulation of what was previously regulated. State involvement does not actively support Thai-Swedish recruitment specifically, but silently agrees to a situation in which a majority of workers seem to accept the conditions. I therefore consider this a state lenience that creates an infrastructure of support for this specific migration corridor.

This chapter asks: what is precarious about the migration corridor? Silvey and Parreñas (2019) argue that serial labor migration requires a perspective on interlinking aspects of precarity in labor, migration and the future, which connects an understanding of migrants' work, the ways in which they can and cannot move and their possibilities of social mobility over time (2019). Precarity of labor can be many things but picking wild forest berries is indisputably hard work. The days in the northern hemisphere are long during the summer months and unhindered by darkness the pickers leave their camps early and return late. The hills are steep, the bags are heavy and most of the pickers experience a significant pressure to pick as much berries as possible to return to Thailand with earnings that can make a difference. The earnings that can be brought back home, and what they can be used for, represents the category of the future in Silvey's and Parreñas's conceptualisation (2019). The im/mobility of the Thai migrant workers is, for instance, represented by the visas they receive that are specifically issued for seasonal berry picking, and their stays that are planned and controlled by recruitment agencies and berry companies. The circular migration of these berry pickers is however often seen as unproblematic, like one berry company manager told me during an interview:

> They harvest their own crops in Thailand later in the year and I think that
> they can arrange to be away without problems, with children and so on

---

1   These circumstances may however change in 2020 as a general taxation is suggested and the
    future of the current design of the industry is highly uncertain.

because the time is so short. They don't all arrive at the same time, there is a plan. Some arrive for the first ripe berries and only a few stay for the last lingon berries. And then, when the first snow falls, they have all left.

Somchai, a berry picker who had returned to Sweden seven times when I met him confirms this way of moving and working. "I travel with my son," he explained and pointed at a young man who were carrying boxes of blueberries from their car to the weighing station at the camp. "We work the fields together at home too and this is the first year that he gets to come here with me. We hope to make enough money to make better farming at home." In many ways Somchai seems 'typical' to the majority of berry pickers who are male, middle-aged, without higher education, from the rural regions of Chaiyaphum and returning over the course of several years, which Hedberg, Axelsson and Abello have found in a larger study (2019). Still, the methodological difficulties of mapping berry-pickers, their earnings and their social mobility are significant (ibid.). Therefore, there is a risk of reproducing a notion of social mobility through circular or serial migration as one of a win-win-win situation if the contexts of precarious migrant labor are not taken into account (Silvey and Parreñas 2019).

Knowledge about the everyday experiences of the typical workers within this typical migration corridor can be completed with experiences that contradict these images in order to find the important nuances of precarious labor and mobility. In the next section I will turn the attention towards infrastructures that conflict with boundaries of the professionalized mobilities between places in Sweden and Thailand. This discussion of a lenience towards the specific arrangements of Thai migration and wild berry picking, as well as the monitoring of its particularities of worker identities, points out a need to adjust the notion of a migration corridor as neatly delimited and detached from other precarious conditions of life.

4   Monitoring the Migration Corridor and Labor Uniformity

Writing about the precarity chain of serial migration in domestic work, Silvey and Parreñas argue that although programme agreements within the industry and policies have reduced migrant insecurities and can be life-saving on an individual level, they also "'serve to legitimate the sending and receiving states' ongoing trade" (2019: 12) with workers who are often stuck in precarious situations. To exemplify this dynamic I will discuss two dimensions that I see as particularly characteristic of the wild berry migration corridor, what I call infrastructures of uniformity and infrastructures of circularity. I have previously presented infrastructural explanations to why Thai workers dominate the wild berry industry. Yet, the conflictual infrastructures of this uniformity of labor needs to be further attended because the ethnic, national and local constitution of the labor force is important to how precarity is understood in this migration corridor. Links of kinship have, for instance, been described as sources of potential abuse, as in the cases of 'madams' that I described above. Kinship is, however, also unquestionably important to migrant mobilisation to control their labor and their migration. Both pickers and managers have told me that friends and family members in Thailand who meet others with relatives who work in Sweden, for example at the marketplace, influence the transnational situation. They get information about spots where blue berries are particularly easy to pick, or about buyers who are prepared to pay a higher price per kilo. This information is passed on to berry pickers who, despite being in Sweden, are less connected because of the long working days and the distances between camps and companies. The information can be used to get transferred or to mobilize for getting more money per kilo blueberries. Xiang and Lindquist have observed that such dynamics of knowing and navigating transnational networks, what they call migrant capabilities, can be negatively impacted by the professionalisation and involvement of more actors who govern the mobility and work process (2014). Although both a professionalized supply chain arrangement and social networks build on a certain uniformity or similarity among the Thai workforce, it may have very different consequences for the industry and for the workers.

The dominant notion of a transnational migration corridor also creates a notion of a seamless exchange of experience, which would make Thai workers more suitable because they can better receive information through social networks. One Swedish berry entrepreneur told me that the biggest problem of working with other 'Asian groups,' like Vietnamese workers, was that it was difficult to make sure that they knew what the work was about. One group that came to Sweden thought the berries would be big like golf balls, the entrepreneur told me with reference to how blueberries are normally around a centimetre in diameter. Yet, despite local brokers in Thailand who are seen as knowledgeable, along with strategies to find "strong and healthy pickers that want to do this job," as the same entrepreneur said, the recruitment in a migration corridor is not a guarantee against unexpected situations. In fact, health must be considered an essential aspect seasonal migrant labor and the risks associated to their possibilities of making a living (Holmes 2013). One berry picker that I met, a man who was in Sweden for the first time, had to go to the local medical centre for a pain in his chest. He told the nurse that he felt terrified when he was alone on the mountains and that his medication against anxiety had stopped working. "He has a case of lappsjuka," the nurse said, using the term 'lappsjuka'[2] that signifies existential discomfort caused by being alone in desolate places. The conditions in the Swedish forests are difficult for individual Thai migrants to plan for in the context of migration. These difficulties of prediction and risk reduction on an individual level seem, at least in part, related to the distance and the dramatic differences between Thailand and Sweden that migrants experience. Both distance and difference are downplayed as risks within the framework of the well-trodden migration corridor and the emphasis on its social networks and supply chain relations. Yet, as these examples show, this precarity persists. In addition to studying the main tracks of migration corridors the importance of diverse situations that deviate from an imagined standard therefore need to be systematically attended to in research about precarity.

Migrant capabilities can be, yet are not necessarily, dependent on ethnicity or local social networks. The homogeneity of berry pickers with regard to these traits does not seem to be the result of Thai workers who protect a migration corridor, but rather the effect of complex transnational links that I have presented above. A state lenience towards this migration corridor depends in part on how it bypasses claims on social rights or issues of citizenship. Such bypassing and lenience can be compared to the situation of Roma berry pickers that constitute a significant labor force in more southern parts of the forest rich regions of Sweden. Compared to Thai workers their presence as workers has been more controversial (Mešić and Woolfson 2015), and Roma migrants are often linked to discourses of 'social tourism' rather than professional identities of berry pickers. Fear of social tourism and its impact on how Roma berry pickers are understood as migrants rather than workers demonstrates how different constellations of presences and absences of rights and entitlements affect precarity (Goldring et al. 2009).

A different example of how the migration corridor of Thai berry pickers contrast to other infrastructures of migration and labor can be found in a public comment made by the Social democratic party together with the trade union confederation in a critical article against the liberal labor migration system (Dagens Nyheter 2017). They propose that the Swedish labor market make use of newly arrived migrants for simple work such as berry picking. If followed through this position would challenge the conditions of the migration corridor for Thai workers, such as the lenience towards labor standards and

---

2   combines an outdated term for Sami ('lapp'), seen as derogatory, with a word for decease (sjuka).

taxes that currently supports it. The statement also illustrates how the industry around Thai migrant workers avoids difficult issues of conditioned citizenship because their rights and entitlement are present only in terms of work. The scenario of assigning berry picking as work for newly arrived refugees as a condition for social rights would bring other dimensions of forced labor and coercive geographies for refugees to the fore. In contrast to migrants who are publicly known to desire permanent residence permits, the homogeneity of the Thai–Sweden migration corridor is, at least in part, a result of claims that are *not* made. This leads us to the second infrastructure that I discuss in this chapter, namely that of circularity.

5   Infrastructures of Circulation

As I talked to Boonrit about his time in Sweden, being here for the third time, he told me that he would like to work in a factory. "But there are only trees here and no work to find," he said. Almost all of the pickers I talked to said that they found the season for wild berries to be too short, a fact of nature that is perhaps difficult to challenge and an infrastructural foundation if you will. However, what Boonrit's statement primarily displays is how there is not enough time to make money that escapes precarity and achieves social mobility. This addresses other infrastructural circumstances of the migration corridor, such as the migration costs, the salaries and the difficulty of moving from berry picking to other work because of migration regulations and language barriers. The system may be more transparent in terms of what to expect from the working conditions and the migration regulations following the professionalisation of the industry. Repeated attempts to reach social mobility through this short-term migration and failure to do so, however, are also increasingly difficult to evaluate as results of any single factors. Instead, migrants move within the smooth walls of the migration corridor. There is a strong narrative around the 'perfect match' between harvest seasons that decrease the risks and losses of incomes in Thailand during seasonal migration, notions of workers who are especially skilful at this labor (Krifors 2017) and a strong imperative of success stories from top pickers (Hedberg, Axelsson, and Abella 2019). Though earnings are often significantly higher than incomes from farming in Thailand (ibid.), these narratives may affect how earnings can be evaluated. One of these top pickers, Thanason, had been to Sweden over 20 years when we met. "Before I was nobody. Now everybody wants to be my friend," Thanason said and emphasized the change that it has made in his life to 'know something' and, now a broker for a large recruitment agency, be allowed to 'lead others.'

Very few berry pickers that I have talked to described working one job. Pick-ing berries in Sweden was one amongst many different ways to get by through-out the year. Still, much hope and longing for a better life was ascribed to this opportunity. Sirada, who was in Sweden for the second time when we met, told me that she did not think she would come home with any earnings to speak of this year, just like the year before. "What will you do if you don't make money this year either?," I asked. "I will come back of course," she said, "if they will have me I will come back next year and the year after that and the year after that." I would say that Sirada contradicts a dominant idea that the positive or negative sides of specific labor migration can be evaluated in relation to how migrants choose to return and invest in these particular mobilities, though this is not to say that Sirada's own judgement is not valuable to the analysis. Here, I return to the question posed by institutional ethnographers: "how is it that people are saying what they are saying?" (DeVault and McCoy 2001: 769). From a position of working many jobs and experiencing a frustrating social immobil-ity, returning despite previous failure to earn enough money is not an irratio-nal or naïve standpoint. Analyses of coercive geographies of migrant labor re-quire a nuanced understanding of the alternatives that people see and calls for a critical examination of what migrants understand that they have to lose or to gain from undertaking this type of short-term migration. The multitude of practices involved in making a living in a 'wageless life' (Denning 2010) make it difficult to determine what such alternatives to an investment in a berry sea-son in Sweden can be or whether any skills or networks gained in this very specific migration corridor can be transferred to future opportunities. Hence, the repeated investments in mobility also constitute a risk of being stuck in a chain of precarity (Silvey and Parreñas 2019). Living with the uncertainties of a new precarity, Narotzky and Besnier argue, 'affects people's ability to repro-duce materially and emotionally, creating difficulties in forming new families, maintaining existing ones, forming caring relations, and feeling respected' (Narotzky and Besnier 2014: 8). Circular migration in the wild berry industry is often understood as a practice that is planned within a family that control a structured calculation of social mobility over time, which is supported by a majority of berry pickers being middle-aged fathers who often state that they will invest in the future, for instance the children's schooling or farming equip-ment (Hedberg, Axelsson, and Abella 2019). This is also how the possibilities of circular migration are portrayed by the IOM (OSCE 2006). Linking this discus-sion back to the impact of success stories as infrastructures in this migration corridor, however, shows that precarious conditions do not always allow the discrepancy between hopes and an everyday disarray of problems and strate-gies to be expressed. For instance, although indebtedness because of high migration costs have been prevented to the most part during recent years in the migration corridor where Thai workers move, precarity is also related to a feeling of failure to move away from unpredictable social and economic lives (Allison 2014). This is reflected in the story of Yuwasak, a berry picker who told me that he had decided to come to Sweden after a divorce that left him 'without a life and without money' whilst David, a renowned boxer, had decided to try his luck as a berry picker in Sweden after falling deep into a gambling debt.

6   Conclusion

When the snow falls at one end of the migration corridor, in the north of Sweden, all workers have returned to their lives at the other end, in Thailand. This transfer seems straight forward and delimited. Yet, migrants do not live in a static structure of opportunities in the sending region, neither do they work abroad in a vacuum, which is why precarity must be understood as a dynamic process across transnational sites. Precarity is situated in a need to re-invent social or economic situations and to creatively navigate new risks and pitfalls. In this text I have analysed mobility across these places as a possible strategy to *navigate* precarity. Although seasonal berry picking in Sweden may rarely cause precarious life situations for those who were previously better off, this text has discussed how it can neither be understood as a benign opportunity without negative consequences for social mobility in the future. Circular migration in the structure of a corridor bring about advantages of a relatively homogenous workforce that grants a certain level of predictability for both migrants and industry. The corridor, however, also risks locking people up in a precarious economy with a due date and disarm migrant capabilities to re-invent this work and this transnational migration from below. I have analysed the migration corridor where Thai workers become berry pickers in Sweden as a result of complex infrastructures of diaspora and social networks, commercialisation and professionalisation, as well as a state lenience where no claims on social rights are made. I have furthermore argued that the delimited and bounded space of a migration corridor is a misconception, which can be confronted if we pay attention to conflicting ways that berry picking could be organized or to alternative possibilities for Thai workers to make a living. Precarity is not bounded to specific places outside this migration corridor, such as working for a Thai 'madam' or being a Roma migrant in the hands or a smuggler. Like Ettlinger (2007) argues, precarity inhabits small spaces of the everyday life though people disengage from its stress and disillusions by imagining certainty and stability.

In the story about the iron tracks in the inland of the Swedish north, Sara Lidman captures the complex intersections of emotional obligations and privileges in light of new economic and social demands and opportunities. This novel suite reaches across generations where a multitude of everyday strategies are equally rational, in its own context of love, poverty or financial investment. Yet, some infrastructural reconfigurations also come to dominate the horizon of possibilities, illustrated by how the dream of a railway seduces Didrik to imagine a certain future of progress and social mobility that spans across differences between people that inhabit his native soils. Ethnographies provide good tools for discussing these complex dimensions of precarity and can capture aspects of the multitude of fragmented life situations that it entails. Yet, there are also difficulties of analysing precarities of the future or querying how people relate to challenges such as 'sustaining life across generations' (Narotsky and Besnier 2014: 6). These difficulties of determining what constitutes precarity need to be increasingly acknowledged in research about social mobility through circular migration. Such a nuanced understanding of precarity that extends into the future of migrants' lives also requires a perspective on situations of precarity in the past, which other contributions in this volume address.

References

Allison, A. (2014). *Precarious Japan*. Durham, NC: Duke University Press.

Axelsson, L., and C. Hedberg. 2018. "Emerging topologies of transnational employment: 'Posting'Thai workers in Sweden's wild berry industry beyond regulatory reach," *Geoforum* 89: 1–10.

Bauder, H. (2006). *Labor movement: How migration regulates labor markets*. Oxford: Oxford University Press.

Butler, J. (2006). *Precarious life: The powers of mourning and violence*. London: Verso.

Calleman, C., and P. Herzfeld Olsson (2015). *Arbetskraft från hela världen*. Stockholm: Delmi.

Denning, M. (2010). "Wageless life," *New left review* 66 (November–December): 79–97.

DeVault, M.L., and L. McCoy (2001). "Institutional Ethnography: Using Interviews to Investigate Ruling," in J.F. Gubrium and J.A. Holstein, eds. *Handbook of Interview Research: Context & Method*, pp. 751–776. London: Sage.

DN (2017). "Vi vill ha nya regler för arbetskraftsinvandring," DN 2017-02-12.

Eriksson, M., A. Tollefsen, and A.S. Lundgren (2019). "From blueberry cakes to labor strikes: Negotiating "legitimate labor" and "ethical food" in supply chains," *Geoforum* 105: 43–53.

Ettlinger, N. (2007). "Precarity unbound," *Alternatives* 32(3): 319–340.

European Commission (2007). *On Circular Migration and Mobility Partnerships between the European Union and Third Countries.* European Commission Brussels.

Goldring, L., C. Berinstein, and J.K. Bernhard (2009). "Institutionalizing precarious migratory status in Canada," *Citizenship studies* 13(3): 239–265.

Hedberg, C. (2013). "'Grapes of wrath'? Power spatialities and aspects of labour in the wild berry global commodity Chain," *Competition & change* 17(1): 57–74.

Hedberg, C. (2016). "'Doing gender'in the wild berry industry: Transforming the role of Thai women in rural Sweden 1980–2012," *European Journal of Women's Studies* 23(2): 169–184.

Hedberg, C., L. Axelsson, and M. Abella (2019). "Thai berry pickers in Sweden: A migration corridor to a low-wage sector." https://www.researchgate.net/publication/335219805_Thai_Berry_Pickers_in_Sweden_A_Migration_Corridor_to_Low_Wage_Sector.

Holmes, S. (2013). *Fresh fruit, broken bodies: Migrant farmworkers in the United States.* Vol. 27. Berkeley, CA: Univ of California Press.

Horton, S.B. (2016). *They leave their kidneys in the fields: illness, injury, and illegality among US farmworkers.* Vol. 40. Berkeley, CA: Univ of California Press.

Krifors, K. (2017). "Managing Migrant Workers: moral economies of temporary labour in the Swedish IT and wild berry industries," Linköping University Electronic Press. https://liu.diva-portal.org/smash/get/diva2:1095730/FULLTEXT01.pdf.

Lidman, S. (1979). *Vredens Barn.* Stockholm: Albert Bonniers Förlag.

Lin, W., J. Lindquist, B. Xiang, and B.S.A. Yeoh (2017). "Migration infrastructures and the production of migrant mobilities," *Mobilities* 12(2): 167–174.

Mešić, N., and C. Woolfson (2015). "Roma berry pickers in Sweden: Economic crisis and new contingents of the austeriat," *Transfer: European Review of Labour and Research* 21(1): 37–50.

Munck, R. (2013). "The Precariat: a view from the South," *Third World Quarterly* 34(5): 747–762.

Narotzky, S., and N. Besnier (2014). "Crisis, value, and hope: rethinking the economy: an introduction to supplement 9," *Current Anthropology* 55(S9): S4–S16.

Neilson, B., and N. Rossiter (2008). "Precarity as a political concept, or, Fordism as exception," *Theory, Culture & Society* 25(7–8): 51–72.

OSCE, OMI (2006). "OIT: Handbook on establishing effective labour migration policies in countries of origin and destination," Vienne: OSCE. https://www.ilo.org/global/docs/WCMS_203851/lang--en/index.htm.

Paret, M., and S. Gleeson (2016). "Precarity and agency through a migration lens," *Citizenship Studies* 20(3–4): 277–294.

Pelizza, A. (2016). "Developing the Vectorial Glance: Infrastructural Inversion for the New Agenda on Government Information Systems," *Science, Technology, & Human Values* 41(2): 298–321.

Sanchez, A. (2018). "Relative Precarity," *Industrial Labor on the Margins of Capitalism: Precarity, Class, and the Neoliberal Subject* 4: 218.

Scott, J.C. (1977). *The moral economy of the peasant: Rebellion and subsistence in Southeast Asia.* New Haven, CT: Yale University Press.

Silvey, R., and R. Parreñas (2019). "Precarity chains: cycles of domestic worker migration from Southeast Asia to the Middle East," *Journal of Ethnic and Migration Studies*: 1–15.

Smith, D.E. (2005). *Institutional ethnography: A sociology for people.* Lanham, ML: Rowman Altamira.

Star, S. Leigh, and K. Ruhleder (1996). "Steps toward an ecology of infrastructure: Design and access for large information spaces," *Information systems research* 7(1): 111–134.

Sténs, A., and C. Sandström (2013). "Divergent interests and ideas around property rights: The case of berry harvesting in Sweden," *Forest Policy and Economics* 33: 56–62.

Sörensson, E. (2015). "When Your Child Gets Easy Money, It Feels Good Being A Mom," *Nordic Journal of Migration Research* 5(4): 207–214.

Thompson, E.P. (1971). "The moral economy of the English crowd in the eighteenth century," *Past & present* 50: 76–136.

Waite, L. (2009). "A place and space for a critical geography of precarity?," *Geography Compass* 3(1): 412–433.

Wingborg, M. (2013). "Bärbranschen tar krafttag för bättre villkor i blåbärsskogen," *Swedwatch report* 60. https://docplayer.se/361484-Barbranschen-tar-krafttag-for-battre-villkor-i-blabarsskogen.html.

Wingborg, M. (2014). *Villkoren för utländska bärplockare säsongen 2014.* Stockholm: Arena idé.

Xiang, B., and J. Lindquist (2014). "Migration infrastructure," *International Migration Review* 48(1_suppl): 122–148.

CHAPTER 6

Turning Migrants into Slaves: Labor Exploitation and *Caporalato* Practices in the Italian Agricultural Sector

Susi Meret and Irina Aguiari

I am currently in Italy in a town called Boreano 2. Here I am picking tomatoes in a tomato field. They pay me 4 euros per crate. A crate weights 300 kg average; this means they are making money out of this, while I get nothing.

DAISE BI LÀ-BAS in BUKOWSKI 2016

• • •

I left Rome to go to the fields and save some money to study [law at the university]. I found the fields worse because I had never done such work. The first time I arrived I saw people working...I was practically in shock. I found 150 people working on a field. The closest cities are at least 20 km far away: you cannot go by bike there.

MUSSE SILIMAN

• •
•

0   Preamble

Under the burning sun, from sunrise until late afternoon, the farmworkers are bending down to pick up the red ripe tomatoes from the plants. Their salary is based on the number of crates they can finish off within their working day. A filled-up crate weights about 375 kg and its pay is in average 5 euros per unit, often less than this. The tomatoes are transported to the processing factories, where they get packed in cans and sold on the supermarket shelves. They are then ready to end in our shopping bags. Yet, the conditions of harvesting, production and distribution are something we very seldom think about when doing our shopping. This shows the ambivalence inherent in a tomato tin can when transformed into a commodity. The red fruit is one of the core ingredients of the Mediterranean diet but also one of the main Italian export agro-products, whose economic value constitutes an important source of profit for the Italian agro-business. As a finished consumption item, the tomato tin can conceal the conditions of labor exploitation and oppression, the modern forms of coerced labor and the illicit practices that permeate and characterize this production field.

The investigation of the *caporalato* system and of the way this profits the neoliberal economy, finds space in this volume as it well-illustrates how the convergence of spatial coercion, ethnic segregation, and the geographical organisation and dispersion of a dispossessed workforce (through the intersection of class, gender, and racial oppressions) are made indispensable to maintain and reproduce the profits within the contemporary agri-business sector.

1   Introduction

Our contribution is an analysis of the *caporalato* system in Italy, understood as the regulation of underpaid and overexploited labor force within the agricultural sector, which is today predominately (but not only) provided by migrant workers. The definition *caporalato* originates from the role played by the *caporale*, a sort of middleman and 'gangmaster' at the same time. The *caporale* is vested by the agricultural entrepreneurs with the power and responsibility of selecting, hiring, transporting and organizing the workforce at given payment conditions. In this way, the *caporale* – oftentimes a former worker himself, acts as the intermediator between the farmer and the workers, matching labor demand and offer. Yet the power of the *caporale* is only part of a bigger and more wide-ranging system that exploits opportunities of labor precarisation and the vulnerability and deprivation of groups of workers within the productive phase, but whose activities today control also sectors of the big distribution chain. The *caporalato* system can thus affect decisions as to how much to produce, where to distribute the product in the retail market and at what conditions and costs (Fanizza 2018: 12–13).

In this sense, it is perhaps more correct today to speak about the *caporalato* system understood as the process of illicit control and managing of all phases of the production, which also includes the distribution through the networks of the large-scale retail trade. The overall impact of the *caporalato* system on the Italian agro-industry economy is substantial, and it reveals the broader implications and extensiveness of this system of labor coercion and exploitation within neoliberal capitalism. We argue this latter has become dependent on the availability of a right-less, extremely pauperized and segregated labor force.

Our chapter contributes to the literature on the *caporalato*'s structural embeddedness within contemporary neoliberal economy. The *caporalato* system reaches today beyond the Italian borders (Omizzolo 2019: 81–109) and it affects also other sectors of production than agriculture. This chapter emphasizes some of the historical patterns of development that reflect what we consider being the continuities and ruptures between today's ethnic and racially based forms of landless peasantry exploitation and past ones, mainly involving the use of the landless poor in the Italian South. The historical comparison allows to understand the deep-rooted structural function of this form of exploitation, as well as the multiple and historically adaptive patterns of oppression. Within this framework, the social and physical marginalisation and segregation of the migrant poor is exacerbated by stricter immigration laws. The criminalisation of immigration (Stumpf 2006) has over the past decades made increasingly difficult for migrants in Italy to get (and to maintain) papers and a regular permit to stay, making their social and economic situation more and more critical and precarious. This contributed to increase the overall number of those people willing to accept poor labour conditions and exploitation. Immigration laws turn them into a deprived, right-less and physically segregated migrant underclass. Towards the end of the chapter, the interviews with workers' collectives and associations describe some of their experiences within these coercive geographies of labor. At the same time, while on the one side these voices speak of the physical and structural conditions that create, sustain and reproduce enslavement, oppression and confinement, they also configure the emergence of spaces of diffuse resistance and the creation of alternative solidarity-based practices of production.

2   The Italian Agricultural Sector's Own Spoon River

On August 6th, 2018 the Italian newspapers' chronicle section (Bellizzi and Zanni 06-08-2018) reads:

> Yet another tragedy on the road in the Foggia district. Twelve people, all with immigrant background, died in the car accident that occurred on Monday, August 6th afternoon along the main province road SP16 at the Ripalta junction, in the Lesigna countryside. A van with a Bulgarian number plate and transporting non-EU passengers frontally collided with a truck loaded with starchy foods.

Two days earlier, on August 4th, 2018, three other migrant farmworkers had lost their lives in yet another car accident. In both cases they were workers on their way back from the tomato fields. In 2019, the registered deaths at work were more than 1,000 (National Institute for Insurance against Accidents at Work INAIL 2020). About 200 were registered in the agricultural sector, which according to the Independent Observatory of Bologna, represent with 29 pct. of the deaths the most dangerous sector (Osservatorio Indipendente di Bologna 2020). These figures include several workers with immigrant background, although official statistics are seldom complete. For instance, they do not include the names of Becky Moses, Mamadou Konate and Nouhou Doumbia, who lost their lives in the fire that raged through the unauthorized working slump of San Ferdinando in the Calabrian region and in the so-called Ghetto di Rignano, Apulia. Nor do figures count Sacko Soumayla, the twenty-nine years old trade union activist, who was shot dead on June 3rd, 2018, while he was searching for metal plates to repair his self-made shack put up in an abandoned field nearby the San Ferdinando camp. All of them were agricultural workers living in desperate conditions of deprivation and segregation: without money and without a place to stay, but working on the fields for more than seven hours a day (Meret and Goffredo 2017a). These conditions turn migrants in similar situations into an agricultural reserve army of labor that can provide cheap, non-unionized and easy to recruit and exploit agricultural manual work. This shapes both the preconditions and the opportunity for the *caporalato* to continue to thrive, particularly within those Italian regions where the agro-economy represents one of the main economic revenues.

3   The *Caporalato* System in the Italian Economy – between Informality and Forced Labor

The term *caporalato* is usually referred to the illegal "system of intermediation of labor, recruitment and organisation" (Salvia 2015: 147). Traditionally, it affects the agricultural sector, but in recent decades it has spread to several other productive environs such as to the construction and the service[1] sector

---

1   While writing, the food delivery services are under judicial investigation in Milan charged for highly exploitative labor intermediation practices, whereby undocumented migrants are subcontracted as riders. https://www.corriere.it/video-articoli/2019/09/18/caporalato-digitale-rider-account-italiani-venduti-migranti-irregolari-dammi-20percento-ti-cedo-account/1b4db12c-d9db-11e9-a5d9-ff444289a2e0.shtml.

(Perrotta and Sacchetto 2014: 80). In all these cases, the *caporalato* is to be understood as the aggregate of various practices of illegal intermediation of workforce, based on informal/illegal working relationships defined either as grey or black work. In the first case, partial contracts strategically cover only a minimum share of the established minimum wage. More often, however, the contract is fictitious and stipulated only to avoid the control of the authorities. This means that it only partially registers the number of effective worked days, while the unregistered work is given 'under the table' (Liberti and Ciconte 2018). In the case of black work, the laborers' employment and working conditions are completely deregulated. The worker is deprived of even the most obvious basic rights, such as a minimum pay, decent housing and a healthcare insurance in the case of injury or sickness. Black and grey work are widely diffused in the agricultural sector, partly due to its productive features such as the seasonality of the work, the fluctuating market costs of the agricultural product, the difficulties of the authorities to conduct extensive controls and a contract agreement allowing to register the worked days up to three months after. These factors have heavy consequences on society and on economy at large, besides of course the direct wide-ranging implications experienced by the worker.

Estimated in numbers, the hidden economy in Italy amounted to about €211 billion in 2017. Of this, €192 billion referred to the informal economy and about €19 billion to illegal activities. Overall, the informal economy makes up to 12 pct. of the total GDP (ISTAT 2019).

Within the agricultural sector only, the share of irregular work corresponds to about 39 pct. of the employed workforce. In the past years, the Italian Institute of Statistics registered an increasing percentage of the irregularly employed: it rose from 36 pct. in 2012 to 37.7 pct. in 2014. This figure translates to 400,000–430,000 farmworkers, whose work is irregularly intermediated and who thus are to be considered as the potential victims of the *caporalato* (CGIL-FLAI 2018). Besides, more than 132,000 laborers are estimated to live in conditions of high social and economic vulnerability. 300,000 of the agricultural workers (about 30 pct. of the total) work less than fifty days per year. According to the Istituto Nazionale della Previdenza Sociale (INPS, the national social welfare institute) in 2017, on a basis of about 1 million agricultural workers with a regular contract, 28 pct. were migrants (286,940 people): 53 pct. came from another EU country (151,706 people) and the remaining 47% from outside the EU (135,234 people). Including the irregular workers, the number of migrants employed in agriculture makes up to 405,000 of the working force, with an estimated 16.5 pct. employed through informal contracts (67,000 workers) and 39 pct. receiving much lower wages than the contract regulated (157,000 workers). The Italian regions with higher numbers of migrant agricultural workers are the Centre-Northern districts: Lazio,

Lombardia, Emilia Romagna. In some of these districts, the immigrant communities are segmented in particular agricultural production fields, for instance the Indians Sikh in Lombardia and Emilia Romagna work for the milk production sector, or in the Agro Pontino (Lazio region), the Tunisians in Sicily within the fishing industry, the Africans and Eastern Europeans with the tomato harvesting in Apulia.

For most of these people, the working conditions are extremely precarious and encompass:
– the lack of legal protection and of basic labor rights (working hours, healthcare, decent housing);
– a daily wage of about 20–30€;
– a medium of 8 to 12 working hours per day;
– a piecework rate salary of 3/4€ in exchange for 375kg of product;
– a salary which generally is 50 pct. lower than the amount established by the national and regional contract agreements;
– a gender-gap remuneration reaching the 20 pct.;
– several examples of high exploitation, where the salary drops to 1€ per hour.
Besides this, the agricultural worker is additionally charged for the service that is directly provided by the caporale, whose costs often include:
– about 5€ for the transport to/from the fieldwork;
– 1.5€ for a bottle of water and 3€ for a sandwich.
The fourth report on *Agromafie e Caporalato* (CGIL-FLAI 2018) estimates that there are about 30,000 farms which make use of the services provided by the caporale. This counts up to 25 pct. of their total number at the national level. In Italy, the *caporalato* is commonly practiced in about eighty Italian agricultural districts. Thirty-three of these districts have working conditions designated as 'indecorous,' while twenty-two register severe forms of labor exploitation. In the Italian fields, more than 100,000 agricultural workers live under work, health and housing conditions that violate the most basic human, working and health rights (MEDU 2018). 62 pct. of the agro-seasonal migrant workers do not have access to basic needs, such as fresh water and sewage. Many get sick with work related pathologies such as respiratory and digestive illnesses provoked by the extreme conditions of deprivation. High are the reported osteo-articular disorders due to the physically demanding work in the fields. Several of the workers bear signs and symptoms of past experiences of torture and of inhumane and degrading treatment. Many deal with psychological distress. Nonetheless, even among the regularly registered workers, the percentage of those assigned to a local practitioner is very low (MEDU 2018).

The stories and personal experiences of the people we interviewed substantiate the conditions illustrated above: they describe experiences that turn statistics into a tangible and ferocious reality. Grazia and Vita (interview

10-03-2019) both living in Ceglie Messapica, a small town located in the province of Brindisi, Apulia. They have been working in the fields since they were just teenagers together with the other women of their families. Through their memories, they describe a reality of exploitation where informal and underpaid work was the norm (Argentiero, Ciccarone and Urgesi 2018). Although in the 1980s the minimum wage was officially fixed at 28.000 Italian lire (about 15€) by the national contract, they only received a maximum of 17,000 lire (about 9€). Grazia and Vita were paid half of the due salary and still, it was not only the money that the *caporalato* system and the thirst for profit took from them. Respectively their mum and sister died in a car accident in 1980. Women were often crammed in dangerous means of transport to reach the fields:

> [T]hat day they went off with a different van than the usual because that one had been seized the day before. But it was the last day of work so the owner [*il padrone*] in order to finish with the harvesting, and the *caporale* they put them [the women] on that van […].

Nowadays, working conditions in the fields are even worse. Abu (interview 07-04-2019) originally from Ghana, but currently living in Bari and collaborating with local political collectives, has in the past three summer seasons worked in the fields of Foggia harvesting tomatoes. His wage was paid per piecework; the piecework salary is a mechanism, which forces the worker to work faster to earn more, albeit the daily wage is always lower than what would be the case if remunerated per worked hour. Also, Abu is paid per crate – 3€ for each crate he fills up (375 kg). He can fill-up up to fifteen crates per day, whilst other workers stop at five or ten, depending on their physical strength. Yet for each crate collected he has to give 1.5€ and a supplementary 3€ to his *caporale*. He also has to pay 5€ for the transport. After a rapid calculation, if Abu collects everyday 15 crates, he earns less than 15€ per day.

> The capo they have a furgone, you pay 5€ to go everyday with your pocket money. When you work each cassetta [crate] you have to give him one cassetta free. Now, a day if I have 10 cassetta I have to try to get 11 – I give him one and I get 10 cassetta and even each cassetta, I have to give him 1.50€.

The remittance in cash required by the *caporale* (Mancini 2018: 72; Perrotta 2015: 18) is a fundamental characteristic of the *caporalato* system. This is made possible since the *caporale* stays in between the employees and the employer. Control and discretion on the division of the labor and of the money to be distributed among the workers is entirely transferred to the *caporale* (Abu, interview 07-04-2019):

In Foggia we are facing a lot of difficulties because you cannot meet the farmer by yourself, you have to meet someone they call capo and the capo has to connect you to the farmland for you to work in the field. Before they pay you, they have to pay the capo, the capo then pays you. You cannot meet the farmer by yourself. Sometimes when you finish the job, my boss refused to pay, and you have to go. When they pay, I will call you, that's the end of it. We cannot meet the farmer by ourselves. So, we discover that we are being used every time... (...) What I discovered about Foggia is like this: here is the farmer, then he will find someone here and then the immigrants are here [moving objects to symbolize that the capo stands between the farmer and the workers].

The stories of Grazia, Vita, and Abu testify how labor exploitation and intermediation represent a constant in the Apulian agriculture through decades. In the past, the seasonal workforce required for agriculture was recruited among the poor and dispossessed peasantry at local level or within the region, eventually from the rest of the country (Colucci 2012: vii–ix). Moving to find work was part of the historical patterns that have defined Italy's internal migrations in the modern times (XIX and XX centuries). The agricultural work is in this sense a form of 'migration practice' which drives people from place to place. This also determined the rise of conflicts and struggles between local workers and the *forestieri* (strangers), who back in history were the Italians coming from outside the region. These situations contributed to the rise of the workers' mobilisations and organisation, which gave rise to the early *leghe contadine*/the peasant leagues (Colucci 2012). Most of the exploited agricultural workforce that in the past was hired among the Italian landless poor is today provided by the migrants implying a structural reorganisation of the entire *caporalato* system.

4   *Caporalato* – **Past and Present**

The most recent developments in the practices of intermediation within the agricultural labor may mistakenly suggest we are facing a completely new phenomenon. In turn, the emergence and consolidation of the intermediaries as professional figures within the agricultural sector can be traced back to the XIX century. Under the Bourbon ruling of the Kingdom of the Two Sicilies (ca. 1816–1849) in the South of Italy, the concentration of large estates in the hands of a few rich local families favoured the consolidation of the role of the so-called *antiniere*. Similarly, to the *caporale*, the *antiniere* had to balance labor demand and offer to guarantee the agricultural production. The encounter between the *antinieri* and the workforce was not only social in terms of creating labor relationships, but foremost physical. The principal task of the *antiniere* was to transport the laborers from their place of residence to the fields. Labor mobility and the need to move workforce from one property to another can thus be considered at the origins of the emergence of the figure of the middleman, first the *antiniere* and later the *caporale* (Alò 2010: 50). The seasonal migrations of farmworkers determined the spreading of the practice of illicit intermediation of labor and characterized the *caporalato* beginnings as mainly involving the recruitment, control and transport of the farmworkers. Towards the end of the XIX and the beginning of the XX century, the position of the *antiniere* gradually disappeared and another figure emerged: the *sovrastante* (Leogrande 2016: 104). In the Apulian region, the so-called *cafoni* worked the land of the local counts or barons who detained wealth and power. They were controlled by the *sovrastante* – a former laborer, who in exchange for small personal favours, performed the tasks of the owner and overlooked the other workers becoming *de facto* an intermediator.

These figures of the past can be considered as the ancestors of the contemporary *caporali*; similarly to the *antiniere*, the *caporale* represented the gate to access to the agricultural work for the dispossessed laborers (Alò 2010: 36). They progressively gained a position of privilege through which they exerted a stronger control and surveillance on the farmworkers; they managed the productive process by matching agricultural job offer and demand and by bridging the fragmentation and geographical distance among the landowners and the workforce. A fragmentation that continued up to the 1950s and which determined the consolidation of the *caporalato* system, transforming it into a recruitment strategy, where the work logistics are illegally managed and organized.

The practice of intermediation of labor as we know it today is also rooted into, and encouraged by the dynamics of seasonal mobility of the workforce, by the wish of ascendant social mobility of the intermediators and by normative and legal conditions that until now have proven rather ineffective in halting the practice. Through time, the structure of the *caporalato* itself has in fact adapted to the changing demographics of the workforce, in order to keep exploiting different vulnerabilities to grant growing illicit profits in return. In the aftermaths of WW2, partly due to the emigration of the men to the North, the *caporali* started recruiting local female laborers. The intermediators profited of the women's precarious economic conditions and of their exclusion from other labor market activities, which forced them to accept irregular forms of employment in the fields and to work subjugated to the *caporale* (Curci 2008). At the end of the 1970s, with the increasing opportunities of large-scale profits derived from the activity of intermediation, but also from the control of the whole chain of production and distribution, we witnessed an increasing involvement of the criminal organisations in the agro-business sector (Fanizza 2018: 12):

> The ability to influence [...] and penetrate the dynamics that govern many areas of the sector represents an evolution due to the effects of the organized criminality in agriculture. Whereas in the past the illegal activity of the *caporali* mainly consisted of organizing the transport of the laborers from the camps where they lived to the fields, today [they] condition [all] phases of the agricultural manufacturing.

This of course had serious effects not only on the exploited workers, but also on the socioeconomic development at large: it impoverished the living conditions in the involved societies, engendering a negative spiral of socioeconomic inequality and dependency on the system.

5   Exploiting Migrant Workers – the Ethnic *Caporalato*

With globalisation and the intensification of international migratory and mobility patterns (since 2004 in particular from the EEC) within and outside Europe, the illegal intermediation of labor has developed methods and practices that profit from these circumstances. While in the past the agricultural labor force was hired from nearby local districts or from the other regions of the country, it is now mainly recruited transnationally. The replacement of the local labor force has transformed the *caporalato* system into an international agro-mafia regime that exploits the migrant and dispossessed poor, besides creating a new rural landless lumpenproletariat. It is the *ethnic caporalato* (BSA 2012: 5; Botte 2015: 119) where the farmer and landowner relies on the local *caporale,* who then engages a migrant *capo* to recruit labor. Migrants are often employed by the so-called *capo nero* – black *capo*, another migrant who ascended to the rank of local *caporale*, recalling some of the functions played in the past by the *sovrastante*. On his turn, the *capo nero* is tied to an Italian intermediator, who is under the direct ruling of the landowner. In practice the power chain has broadened and intensified by including more players, while at the same time it expanded geographically, since the workers can be moved from one place to another, and also from region to region. Yet, the availability and the continuity of the work, as Zakaria explains (interview 14-03-2017), depend on the relationship between the worker and the *caporale*:

> Z.: The *caporali* know other *caporali* in other regions, so you can be hired to do other works if it is necessary.
> Q.: Thus the more the *caporale* trust you, the more likely it is you get a job?
> Z.: Sure, but not just that. If you get in a good relationship with your *caporale*, if you don't make troubles, and if you do a "neat" job, you can also aspire to get a contract.
> Q.: You mean, also the 151 working days necessary to get the unemployment benefit?
> Z.: Noo, never those. They are reserved to the friends of the Italian farmer.
> Q.: And as for the work in the fields, how often do you work with people from other countries? I think of the Bulgarians living nearby here, but also the Italians.
> Z.: The Italians are more and more. This summer I have seen many of them who arrived in front of the CARA, waiting for someone to pick them up in a van. But most of them do not have a *caporale*. The Bulgarians work a little more South, from *Cerignola* downwards. Here nearby Foggia the owners (*i padroni*) prefer the black people, they say we do the job more neatly.

The recruitment of a migrant labor force is to be seen in relation to the decline of the family-based management of the rural production, and to the shrinking of the available local labor force, due to patters of internal emigration and to the development and organisation of the labor market. Hiring migrants (and women) allows the labor exploitation of vulnerable, deprived and very often poorly unionized subjects. This reduces the costs of labor and it allows the producers to continue making their profit and to remain competitive on the neoliberal agro-market business (Colloca and Corrado 2013 as cited in Olivieri 2015: 56).

In the Apulian region, where we conducted most of our interviews and observations in the years 2017–2019, the first important immigration in contemporary times dates back to the early 1970s. In 1973, the gross migratory balance of the region registered positive values after decades of demographic decline (SVIMEZ 2011). A positive trend that continued over time, registering a remarkable increase in the years 2006 and 2007, when the (registered) immigration to the region went from 4,558 to the 14,110 units (SVIMEZ 2011). To begin with, the Tunisian diaspora was the largest, but it was soon topped by migrants coming from the Maghreb and the sub-Saharan Africa. From the 2000s, groups of immigrants from Eastern Europe (Poles, Bulgarians, and Romanians especially) started populating the agricultural fields of the South (Leogrande 2016; Perrotta and Sacchetto 2012: 11). In recent years, the so-called North African Emergency programme (2011) created by the Arab Spring and the Syrian war intensified the arrivals of new and potentially exploitable migrants. Nowadays, the migrants employed in agricultural sector are an indispensable component of the Italian agri-business (Pisacane 2018: 49).

6   In the Ghetto – The Spatial Organization of the *Caporalato*

In Apulia the migrant farmworkers live a paradoxical double condition of hypervisibility and invisibility. Their hypervisibility is caused by the constant attention of the media and by a political debate that often builds on diffuse stereotypes and on racially based fears, but which hides the brutal reality of their living and working conditions (Curci 2008: 162). At the same time, invisibility and vulnerability are achieved through diverse forms of segregation and physical displacement that include (Perrotta and Sacchetto 2014: 78):

- Spatial segregation: migrants live in remote settlements far away from the rest of the population and from the main urban centres;
- Economic segregation: since the job centres have been privatized, they no longer provide an efficient contractual intermediation between workers and employers. In particular, the agricultural contracts register the work retroactively (one to three months after the completion of the work), which can induce cheating both the system and the authorities' controls (a lower amount of registered working days; poorly controlled applications for unemployment benefit);
- Cultural segregation: the migrant workers live often in ghettos, which allow them to maintain some form of networks, but keeps them physically segregated from the rest of society;
- Political segregation: the migrant workers are considered as people with no legal rights. Employers maintain they are doing the worker a favour by taking him/her at work, while the local institutions and voluntary associations intervene only on humanitarian, or 'emergency' grounds.

The convergence of these different forms of segregation is maintained through the ghettos, which are "concentrations of several hundred workers living in self built shacks, abandoned houses, factories and other derelict buildings" (Perrotta and Sacchetto 2014: 78). The ghettos represent in this sense concrete geographies of urban marginality for the reproduction of the *caporalato* itself, as they guarantee an all-inclusive and unchallenged control on the labor force (Perrotta and Sacchetto 2014: 97). People are, so to say, 'stuck in place' and living in places hidden away from the rest of society. A list of ghettos of this kind includes: San Ferdinando and Rosarno in Calabria, the ghettos of Nardò (until 2009), Rignano Garganico and Borgo Mezzanone in Apulia, Palazzo San Gervasio in Basilicata, Foro Boario in Saluzzo, Piedmont. These are only the most renowned spaces of confinement, segregation and exploitation. Some of them are or were attempted closed by local authorities; others were raged by fires and later rebuilt. As observed by Sagnet and Palmisano in their book *Ghetto Italia* (2015):

> This of the ghettoes is the most telling phenomenon of the whole story because – no matter if they are made of shacks, tents, sheds, or open-air camp beds – the housing condition always reveals the brutality of the life of these workers.

The ghettos constitute a fundamental spatio-geographical component for the economy of exploitation. The 'ghetto economy' (Mangano 2014) not only allows to keep the exploitable labor force confined within a delimited and remote space, but it also generates another potential internal market demand, produced by the needs of the people living in the place: food, electricity, transport, sex, to name a few. As Angelo Cleaopazzo (interview 01-02-2017), activist in the solidarity network Diritti A Sud/*Rights to the South*[2] described us:

> The ghetto [in Nardò, Lecce] was here where we are now. That summer [2009] between 350–400 people lived here. All this space was cramped with shacks; a ghetto through and through, which included a range of inner services: food catering, a job centre, prostitution, a market for the selling of stolen goods and car plate numbers. You could find virtually everything. There was a thriving black market, although everything costed more than outside. This is to say that to live in the ghetto means to have to pay more for services that would cost you much less in the city; and I say this also to dispel the conventional myth reciting that by living amongst themselves and in a deplorable situation, the migrants spend nothing and save lots. Instead, here they spend all what they earn and for basically everything they might need. Their money goes straight into the pockets of those hierarchically above them in this chain of command (...)

---

2   https://www.dirittiasud.org/.

everything is smuggled in, and (...) everything costs more, notwithstanding the already tough conditions of these places where they must stay.

The recruitment of migrants from the ghettos gives their recruiters the chance to hire at lower and much poorer wage and conditions, besides providing them the opportunity to control an already spatially contained workforce and to keep their living environments away from the eye of the society.

The ghetto problem is portrayed by the people we have interviewed as one of the most pressing issues to be taken care of in order to undermine some of the structural basis supporting the *caporalato* system. Pietro Fragasso (interview 24-04-2019), of the social cooperative Pietra di Scarto,[3] which harvests and transforms fresh tomatoes through the regular employment of migrant farmworkers, defines the system of the ghettos as a "functional social exclusion." In his words, migrants in the ghettoes are physically and socially excluded from the spaces and life of the local communities, thus preventing forms of mutual exchange and integration. Yet they also represent an indispensable source of cheap labor force to the local agricultural business. Angelo Cleopazzo (interview 01-02-2017; 03-05-2019), and the solidarity collective *SfruttaZero*,[4] which auto-produces tomato bottles, observed that the lack of housing alternatives is the result of the unholy alliance between the representatives of the institutions and the farmers, who want to turn workers into ghosts and in this way allow their exploitation at work, which awards more and more profits to the agro business.

In agriculture these geographies of coercion and segregation have reproduced a labor division along ethnic and racial lines (see also above). The African migrant in Apulia is for instance almost certainly to be found in the tomato fields, but not in the olive fields. Angelo Cleopazzo (interview 03-05-2019) observes for instance how in *Nardò* the migrant workers from the area of the Maghreb are traditionally employed for the watermelons' harvesting, whilst those from the Sub-Saharan Africa tomatoes "which is physically [a] tougher [job], certainly paid per piecework, and characterized by longer working days than the watermelon harvesting."

The ghettos also function as informal recruitment centres. Abu (interview 07-04-2019) explains how things work in the ghetto of Borgo Mezzanone. Borgo Mezzanone is located nearby the city of Foggia in Northern Apulia and established nearby one of Italy's biggest and most populated CARA, centre for the reception of asylum applicants (Meret and Goffredo 2017b). It is worth noting how the geographies of the ghettos and the state structures for the reception of the migratory flows interact in a vicious circle of segregation and labor

---

3   https://www.pietradiscarto.it/.
4   http://www.fuorimercato.com/rimaflow/categorie-di-prodotti/sfruttazero.html.

exploitation. Abu lived in Libya until 2011, when a NATO bomb hit his house and he decided to flee and reach Europe via Lampedusa. Upon his arrival on the isle, he was transferred to the CARA in *Bari,* where he lived for about two years. When he obtained the humanitarian protection, he had to leave the centre, but he had nowhere else to go:

> So, they finally give us, they say one-year humanitarian [permit] and they called it emergency North Africa. That's where we started, from the one year. Later, they gave us two years document. After giving us the one year, they asked us to leave the camp. No house, no money, we don't have anywhere else to go, so we end up on the street. We ask for help, where can we go? They don't care. We have to hit on the streets and face the life ourselves. So, in this Bari, some of us sleep in the station, in the churches, under bridges. It is not easy; life is very difficult for us. So, we don't have other options.

Many of his friends were in the same situation and they also lived on the streets. When the tomato season started, they all moved to *Foggia,* to the ghetto Borgo Mezzanone, where they knew some people. There, they met a *capo,* who found a job for them in the fields. The ghetto economy, as well as the inefficient system of first and second reception of the migrants, are both functional to the maintenance and reproduction of the irregularisation and later recruitment of the migrants in the agricultural sector.

The ghetto can be described as a seclusionary space, whereby seclusion is to be understood as the "spatial arrangement that reinforces the overlap of work, leisure, rest and more generally all aspects of daily reproduction of an individual or a group in one place, from which they are formally free to leave" (Perrotta and Sacchetto 2014: 78). Musse Siliman (interview 03-05-2019) who lived close to the Ghetto of *Nardò* (Lecce) before joining *SfruttaZero*, describes his surprise at the sight of a restaurant in the ghetto, organized by the *caporali* to feed the 150 workers that were living there. The reality of the ghettos is well known by the local populations. Carolina (interview 08-04-2019) a member of the *Bari* based university students' organisation Link[5] refers to the concept of seclusion when observing that the Gran Ghetto of Rignano (13 km from Foggia) 'offers' everything that can be exploited: labor force for the harvesting of tomatoes, prostitution,[6] drugs. As a consequence, the living conditions in the most deprived ghettos are particularly challenging.

---

5   https://it-it.facebook.com/linkbari/.

6   The women often succumb to a "double exploitation" (Sciurba 2013): "They are exploited in the fields thru exhausting and underpaid working rhythms and sexually abused by the farmer, the caporale or the men."

This picture draws an overall context of coercion, deprivation and subalternity characterizing the work and the life of the migrant workers. In the *caporalato* system, the organisation of the spaces of life, work and recreation of the migrant workers represents the way this system sustains and reproduces itself on a daily basis. These major evolutions in the system of the illicit intermediation of labor in agriculture are embedded in the global restructuring of the neoliberal economy.

7   The Neoliberal Turn in the *Caporalato* System

After the workers' movements of the XX century and the achievements obtained by the workers' struggles for the recognition of their basic labor rights and for the consolidation of minimum welfare guarantees, the counter-response of neoliberalism was to transform and adapt its model of production, shifting from Fordist to post-Fordist models of production (Alò 2010). The relation between the markets and the productive sectors was reversed – whilst the Fordist production was virtually unrestricted with the aim of stocking huge quantities of goods and reducing its costs through scale economies, post-Fordism inverted this process (Alò 2010: 113). In agriculture, the global restructuring of the neoliberal economy prioritizes the ability of the producers to place their products on the markets pushing production time and costs down to the minimum (Alò 2010: 38). These dynamics shifted the balance of the agri-food sector from a producer-driven towards a supplier-driven paradigm. This means that the agri-food industry is no longer determined by the seasonality, by the periods of sowing and harvesting and by the availability of the agricultural product. Now the big retailer chain, the huge supermarkets and in particular the major distribution are those determining the conditions of the fruit and the vegetables' production by imposing higher working speed and lower prices based on their margin of profit (Perrotta 2015: 27). The Italian Fresh Fruit and Vegetables production represents an integral sector in this trend, wherein the global production chains reorganize labor relations to experiment new ways of extracting surplus value under more and more precarious conditions of work (Salvia 2015: 146). Specifically, the pressure exerted by the international economic competition curtails the prices that the big distribution companies are willing to pay to the agricultural producers. In the case of tomatoes, but without this being an exception, the supermarkets impose low selling prices to the transformative industries. In short, the pressure exerted by the international economic competition curtails the prices that the big distribution companies bid to the producers. To absorb this potential loss, the factories try to buy the raw material from the farmers at an even lower price to accumulate value. The farmers on their turn unload this pressure on the workforce by exploiting the workers and relying on the system of intermediation to find cheap but effective manpower (Ciconte and Liberti 2019). The *caporalato* thus enters this scenario with the function of satisfying the producers' needs of labor force in a renovated and even more interdependent social and economic business context (Alò 2010: 84) often relying on the recruitment of migrant workers to profit of a cheaper and non-unionized labor (BSA 2012: 12). As USB trade unionist Aboubakar Soumahoro (interview 18-02-2017) observes:

> Out there on the fields they do not ask for charity, they want labor and social rights. There is no such thing that a man must live out there in the countryside, far away from the rest of the world: before and after the work there something called a life, namely a social life.

In his book *Humanity in Revolt* (2019: 22) Soumahoro explains how both his own personal experience and his engagement as a USB[7] trade union activist were an eye opener to understand different forms of exploitation and how these relate to the more general transformations of the labor market:

> The trade union experience has learned me about the different conditions within the various productive sectors and it has shown me how complex the model of exploitation is, besides what we see practiced in certain areas. That model [of exploitation] has today become ingrained in the normative plan: the immigrants are only arms for work and their rights are in fact subordinated to their capacity to work and to the labor market demand...What makes the life of the migrant worker so precarious and 'for sale' [*ricattabile*] is only the most extreme manifestation of the transformations that are affecting the life of us all.

In this sense, the trade unions need again to become central players in the struggles for the workers' rights, by providing not only support, but also creating a network of activities at the local level which can push towards the achievement of rights, that can then be extended to other areas and sectors.

---

7   Unione Sindacale di Base, USB (Base Union Trade) was formed in 2010 from the merging of different locally based trade unions. The USB has today a regular national structure and it counts about 250,000 members. It is especially active in the public sector and in struggles, such as the struggle for the right to housing (through the tenants' union ASIA USB) and for migrants' rights. https://www.usb.it/.

The ethnic *caporalato* or migrant *caporalato* profits of the precarisation of the labor force, which results from globalisation trends, relationships and transformations and from economic deregulation (BSA 2012: 91). Decades of stricter and tougher citizenship and immigration laws have contributed to the creation of an ethnic-based underclass. These include the 1998 Turco-Napolitano law, which launched the first Centres of Temporary Permanence, beginning to criminalize immigrants without documents. In 2002, the Bossi-Fini law made migrants reliant on a working contract to obtain and maintain their residence permit. In more recent years the so-called 'security package' have introduced the illegal migration crime (*reato di clandestinità*) and broadened the power of the authorities to safeguard the national security by introducing anti-immigration measures. Matteo Salvini's (Lega) *Decreto Sicurezza*/Security Decree is perhaps the most paradigmatic in this sense, as it abolished the right of asylum on humanitarian basis, thus exponentially increasing the number of 'deportables' while at the same time it criminalizes acts of pro-migrant solidarity.

Within all this, the strategies of hyper-flexibilisation and precarisation of the work that include the Treu market reform and Matteo Renzi's Jobs Act operated broadly and not only within the agricultural sector. In Italy, the globalisation process goes hand in hand with the de-regulation and precarisation of labor (Fana 2017: 103). In relation to this, the analysis of the *caporalato* system brings forward further considerations on the concept of exploitation itself. Although the *caporalato* is rendered particularly critical by the specificities characterizing the agricultural sector with its productive vulnerabilities connected to the demographics and the characteristics of the workforce employed, the exploitation of the agricultural workers does not represent a unique case of coercion and abuse. Rather, the *caporalato* exemplifies a liminal case of the already ongoing process of labor hyper-precarisation earlier introduced by neoliberal post-Fordism and characterized by increasing uncertainty of employment, lack of rights and living conditions. All this needs to be seen in relation with the workers' shrinking contractual strength and with their missed trust and hopes in politics and more generally in the changing capacity of trade unionism (Alò 2010: 164).

8   Conclusion: the *Caporalato* System between Labor Exploitation, Coercion and Neo-slavery

The historicisation of the phenomenon of the illegal intermediation of labor in agriculture together with our ethnographic research suggest that the *caporalato* does not only represent a legacy of the past – an obsolete model of organisation of the agricultural production which has resisted across the centuries as a profitable form of labor coercion. Rather, the existing research reveals the Janus-faced character of this system. On the one side, a historical legacy inherited from the chronic economic underdevelopment of the post-unitarian Italian South, characterized by a scarce, if not virtually absent plan of agricultural reform and a lack of investments in technology, and sustainable development (McBritton 2015). On the other side, nowadays *caporalato* system is representative of the late capitalist modernity: exploitative, easy profit-oriented, flexible, transnational and market adaptive. The result is a system of exploitation and coercion incorporating elements of the past according to new paradigms of profitable performativity and exploitation (Rivera 2010: 205).

In this perspective, our elaboration represents an analytic effort to (re-) frame the illicit intermediation of labor in the Italian agricultural sector within patterns of labor exploitation of migrant labor force, spatial segregation, physical and symbolic violence. We struggle to employ the concept of precarity as representative of this system. Being placed in front of harsh conditions of life and work, our perception is that such term still lacks a clear conceptualisation and fails to grasp, describe and represent the gravity and subordination of what migrant laborers experience in the field of tomatoes in Apulia. We hereby attempted to place the *caporalato* system in between labor exploitation and (neo-)slavery. With respect to the former, we argued that the *caporalato* exemplifies another aspect of the process of labor exploitation typical of the post-Fordism characterized by greater uncertainty of employment and living conditions; the political and cultural void thus created, contributed to the deterioration of the workers' contractual strength. At the same time, it greatly affected the expectations for the future (Alò 2010: 164). Nonetheless, we do not intend to employ the term exploitation in its commonsense perception, i.e. to refer to a restricted range of situations characterized by a particularly unbalanced exchange between work and wage and denoting the pathological traits of such conducts. Rather, we critically reposition the concept of exploitation as intrinsic to the working relationship itself, as a natural, structural element of neoliberal capitalism (Rigo 2015: 7). At the same time, the analysis of the *caporalato* system must not overlook the material and living conditions in which it operates. The experiences and forms of physical and psychological oppression, the violation of the rights and of the workers' bodies pushed us towards advancing an analytical parallelism between conditions of (neo)slavery and the *caporalato*. Slavery is conventionally defined on the basis of the concept of property and ownership. In the case of both ancient and modern slaveries, the slave is commodified as being someone else's property (Viti 2016: 22). Both in the social understanding of slavery and in its juridical sanctioning – as for instance in the Ancient Rome (Casadei 2018: 139), the element of property can be considered as the *trait d'union* between the slave systems of the past and the today's *caporalato* system. The migrant workers' social and juridical status casts them under the subjugation and dependence of the *caporale*. In the past, this relation may have referred exclusively to the working situation insofar as in the total absence of any form of contract or national bargaining, the laborers had no means to exercise their rights. The consolidation of the ethnic *caporalato* has multiplied the forms of precarity and uncertainty of the workers recruited for the seasonal employment. The worker's subalternity is not only due to the lack of legal protection as laborers, but also to their legal and social status of migrants. Either undocumented or with legal residence permits, the *caporale* represents their only viable access to the labor market, forcing migrants into a system of exploitation based on ethnic, racial, and gender oppression (Casadei 2018: 140).

In conclusion, our analysis shows that the *caporalato is not* symptomatic of the cultural and economic Southern backwardness, but a precise mode of production and organisation of labor that is both structural and functional to the neoliberal paradigm that drives the sector.

Acknowledgments

Thanks to the women and men we interviewed and who agreed to share with us their life experiences, knowledge and stories of struggles and hardships. We stand by you. Thanks also to Sergio Goffredo for conducting some of the interviews included in this chapter.

References

Alò, P. (2010). *Il caporalato nella tarda modernità: La trasformazione del lavoro da diritto a merce*. Bari: WIP Edizioni.

Argentiero, V.M., G. Ciccarone, and M. Urgesi (2018). *La terra [che] non tace: storia di braccianti agricole di Ceglie Messapica vittime del caporalato*. (Printed in proper).

Bellizzi, T., and Di Zanni, C. (2018). "Foggia, scontro frontale tra un furgone e un tir: morti dodici migranti. In arrivo il premier." *La Repubblica*, 06-08-2018. https://bari.repubblica.it/cronaca/2018/08/06/news/foggia_scontro_frontale_tra_furgoni_cinque_migranti_morti-20352478.

Botte, A., M. McBritton, F. Olivieri, D. Perrotta, and Rigo, E. (2015). *Leggi, migranti e caporali: prospettive critiche e di ricerca sullo sfruttamento lavorativo in agricoltura*, ed. E. Rigo. Pisa: Pacini Editore.

Brigate di Solidarietà Attiva, G. Nigro, M. Perrotta, D. Sacchetto, and Y. Sagnet (2012). *Sulla pelle viva*. Roma: DeriveApprodi.

Bukowski, W. (2016). *La danza delle mozzarelle Slow Food, Eataly, Coop e la loro narrazione*. Roma: Edizioni Alegre.

Casadei, T. (2018). "Tra storia e teorizzazione giuridica: per un inquadramento dei caratteri della schiavitù contemporanea," in T. Casadei and M. Simonazzi (eds.). *Nuove e antiche forme di schiavitù*. Napoli: Editoriale Scientifica: 135–151.

CGIL-FLAI. (2018). A cura dell'Osservatorio Placido Rizzotto. *Agromafie e Caporalato. Quarto Rapporto*. Roma: Bibliotheka Edizioni.

Ciconte, F., and S. Liberti (2019). *Il grande carrello*. Bari: Gius. Laterza & Figli.

Colloca, C., and A. Corrado (a cura di). (2013). *La globalizzazione delle campagne: Migranti e società rurali nel Sud Italia*. Milano: Franco Angeli.

Colucci, M. (a cura di). (2012). *Giuseppe Di Vittorio. Le strade del lavoro. Scritti sulle migrazioni*. Roma: Donzelli editore.

Colucci, M. (2019). *Storia dell'immigrazione straniera in Italia. Dal 1945 ai nostri giorni*. Roma: Carocci Editore.

Curci, S. (2008). *Nero invisibile normale: Lavoro migrante e caporalato in Capitanata*. Foggia: Edizioni del Rosone "Franco Marasca."

Fana, M. (2017). *Non è lavoro, è sfruttamento*. Bari: Editori Laterza.

Fanizza, F., and M. Omizzolo (2018). *Caporalato. An authentic agromafia*. Foggia: Mimesis International.

INAIL, Istituto Nazionale per gli Infortuni sul Lavoro. (2020). "Infortuni e malattie professionali, online gli open data Inail del 2019." https://www.inail.it/cs/internet/comunicazione/sala-stampa/comunicati-stampa/com-stampa-open-data-2019.html.

istat, Istituto Nazionale di Statistica. (2019). "L'Economia non Osservata nei Conti Nazionali 2014–2017." https://www.istat.it/it/files//2019/10/Economia-non-osservata-nei-conti-nazionali-2017.pdf.

Leogrande, A. (2016). "Il caporalato e le nuove schivitù," *Il Mulino – Rivisteweb*. https://www.rivisteweb.it/doi/10.7377/84339.

Liberti, S. and F. Ciconte (2018). "Il prezzo occulto del cibo a basso costo," *La rivista internazionale*. https://www.internazionale.it/reportage/stefano-liberti/2018/11/19/prezzo-occulto-cibo.

Mancini, M. (2018). "Contrasto penale allo sfruttamento lavorativo: dalla 'Legge 30' alla Legge n.199/2016," in F. Carchedi, R. Iovino, and A. Valentini (eds.). *Agromafie e caporalato*. Roma: Bibliotheka Edizioni: 66–87.

Mangano, A. (2014). *Ghetto Economy. Cibo sporco di sangue*. StreetLib Write.

medu, Medici per i Diritti Umani (2018). "The Wretched of the Earth." https://mediciperidirittiumani.org/en/the-wretched-of-the-earth/.

McBritton, M. (2015). "Lavoro in agricoltura e immigrazione," in E. Rigo (ed.). *Leggi, migranti e caporali: Prospettive e critiche di ricerca sullo sfruttamento del lavoro in agricoltura*. Pisa: Pacini Editore: 101–114.

Meret, S., and S. Goffredo (2017a). "Subverting neoliberal slavery: migrant struggles against labour exploitation in Italy," *Open Democracy*. https://www.opendemocracy.net/en/can-europe-make-it/subverting-neoliberal-slavery-migrant-struggles-agains/.

Meret, S., and S. Goffredo (2017b). "Stuck in Place: Confinement and Survival in Borgo Mezzanone," *Border Criminologies Blog*. https://www.law.ox.ac.uk/research-subject-groups/centre-criminology/centreborder-criminologies/blog/2017/06/stuck-place.

Olivieri, F. (2015). "Giudificare ed esternalizzare lo sfruttamento: Il caso dei lavoratori immigrati nella vitivinicoltura senese," in E. Rigo (ed.). *Leggi, migranti e caporali: Prospettive e critiche di ricerca sullo sfruttamento del lavoro in agricoltura*. Pisa: Pacini Editore: 47–68.

Omizzolo, M. (2019). *Sotto padrone. Uomini, donne e caporali nell'agromafia italiana*. Milano: Feltrinelli.

Perrotta, D., and D. Sacchetto (2012). "Il ghetto e lo sciopero: braccianti stranieri nell'Italia meridionale," *Sociologia del Lavoro* 128: 152–166.

Perrotta, D., and D. Sacchetto (2014). "Migrant farmworkers in Southern Italy: ghettos, caporalato and collective action," *Workers of the World: International Journal on Strikes and Social Conflicts* 1(5): 75–98.

Perrotta, D. (2015). "Il caporalato come sistema: un contributo sociologico," in E. Rigo (ed.). *Leggi, migranti e caporali: Prospettive e critiche di ricerca sullo sfruttamento del lavoro in agricoltura*. Pisa: Pacini Editore: 15–30.

Pisacane, L. (2018). *I lavoratori immigrati nell'agricoltura italiana: fonti e numeri*, in F. Carchedi, R. Iovino, and A. Valentini (eds.). *Agromafie e caporalato*. Roma: Bibliotheka Edizioni: 46–55.

Rigo, E. (a cura di). (2015). *Leggi, migranti e caporali: Prospettive e critiche di ricerca sullo sfruttamento del lavoro in agricoltura*. Pisa: Pacini Editore.

Rivera, A. (2010). "*Io* non mi ribello, quindi *noi* non siamo. Le braccianti e i nuovi patriarchi," in P. Alò (ed.). *Il caporalato nella tarda modernità: La trasformazione del lavoro da diritto a merce*. Bari: WIP Edizioni: 205–208.

Sagnet, Y., and L. Palmisano (2015). *Ghetto Italia. I braccianti stranieri tra caporalato e sfruttamento*. Roma: Fandango Libri.

Salvia, L. (2015). "Labour contractors and migrant labour in Italy's Neoliberal Agriculture," in *XXVI European Society for Rural Sociology Congress, Place of possibility? Rural Societies in a Neoliberal World*. Aberdeen: James Hutton Institute: 146–148.

Sciurba, A. (2013). "Effetto serra. Le donne rumene nelle campagne del ragusano," ADIR. L'Altro diritto. http://www.adir.unifi.it/rivista/2013/ragusa.htm.

Soumahoro, A. (2019). *Umanità in rivolta. La nostra lotta per il lavoro e il diritto alla felicità*. Milano: Feltrinelli.

Stumpf, J. (2006). "The Crimmigration Crisis: Immigrants, Crime, and Sovereign Power," *American University Law Review* 56(2): 367–419.

SVIMEZ – Associazione per lo sviluppo dell'industria nel Mezzogiorno (2011). *150 anni di statistiche italiane: Nord e Sud 1861–2011*. Bologna: il Mulino.

Viti, F. (2016). "Nuove schiavitù," *Parolechiave* 1: 21–36.

CHAPTER 7

Strategies of Overcoming Precarity: The Case of Somali Transnational Community Ties, Spaces and Links in the United Arab Emirates

Abdulkadir Osman Farah

1   Introduction

An increasing number of people around the world live in precarity (Neilson 2015). Those most affected by precarity include people forcefully displaced by conditions of wars and poverty. Though precarity seems not a directly globally organized process, critical studies associate precarious conditions with prevailing global hegemonic neoliberal systems (Harris and Scully 2015). Some regions, countries and people suffer more than others. For instance, in lesser democratic countries in the Middle East and Africa precarity have historically operated under authoritarian organisations from colonial to post-colonial periods.

Over the past two decades, the notion of precarity has become an important concept to explore and articulate the nature of uncertainty faced by millions of people in all aspects of social, political, and economic life (Allen 2009; Casas-Cortes 2014; Standing 2011; Schierup and Jørgensen 2016). Etymologically, according to Casas Cortes (2014: 207), The term precarity is derived "(...) from the Latin root prex or precis, meaning "to pray, to plead," and it commonly implies risky or uncertain situations." The conceptual origin of precarity can be traced back to Pierre Bourdieu's (1963) work on colonial Algeria and later in France in which he described it as a new system of class dominance resulting from the restructuring of the global economy producing new forms of vulnerabilities. In its more recent iteration, the concept gained momentum in Guy Standing's (2011) proposition *The Precariat: The New Dangerous Class*. Standing explains the 'precariat' as a potentially emerging global class that could become a 'dangerous class' following recent intense political populist polarisations often exploiting ethnic cleavages. Apart from the prevailing structural employment insecurity due to markets' demand for flexibility, Standing categorizes migrants representing most of the 'denizens' suffering from special multiple precarities (194) including urban concentration, immobility and for the better-qualified accepting brain-wasting' jobs. Consequently, he suggests, migrants fail to demonstrate agency (24). For Standing precarity – both in its general form as well as its migrant related versions – is the result from neo-liberal market driven transnational subordination of working-class people since 1970s. However, the debate amongst researchers have since shown that the conditions of precarity have a long history preceding Bourdieu's conception (Ettlinger 2007), making precarity the global norm and Standing's work a comment on Western conditions at a particular time in history. Accordingly, precarity has affected diverse population groups (Butler 2006) without sparing those in developing countries in the South (Harris and Scully 2015; Munck 2013; Paret 2016).

Based on these insights, an increasing number of social scientists have explored the nature and dynamics of precarity from a variety of theoretical and empirical standpoints ranging from the immigrant experiences (Goldring and Landolt 2011; Schierup and Ålund 2013; Schierup, Krifors, and Slavnic 2015), social movements (Agustin and Jørgensen 2016; Milkman 2014; Van Dyke and Holly 2010), global labor studies (Burawoy 2015; Arnold and Bongiovi 2013), as well as precarity in the South (Munck 2013). In a recent special issue in *Critical Sociology*, Schierup and Jørgensen examine the extent to which the conceptual precarity proves applicable to a variety of instances. Such instances include experiences of students in China, pensioners and the unemployed in Sweden, labor migrants in Southern Europe, Turkey, Russia, and South Africa, providing an analysis that ventures beyond what is currently referred to as the Global North to includes experiences in and from the Global South (Schierup and Jørgensen 2016).

The above studies, particularly the case studies presented in the recent special issue entitled "Politics of Precarity: Migrant Conditions, Struggles and Experiences," provide an important step for opening a new space for advancing the empirical and theoretical reach of precarity in immigration research. With very few exceptions (Paret and Gleeson 2016; Casas-Cortes 2014), however, most scholarship on immigration, and particularly on precarity, focuses on the ways in which migrants experience precarity instead of the potential ways in which immigrants manage and overcome precarity itself.

Against this backdrop, this chapter seeks to interrogate the circumstances that allows otherwise precarity-impacted communities to flourish, thus seeing precarity as a process in which transnational communities seek to get the best out of challenging contexts and circumstances by, for instance, relating to, with and beyond the dominating coercive systems and their coercive geographies. Employing the case of the United Arab Emirates that prospered from its natural resources and attracted large and diverse migrant groups over the past four decades, it specifically raises the following questions. Firstly, how do the state authorities of UAE produce a system of precarity that imposes social, economic and political restrictions, generating the exploitation of communities as cheap labor? Secondly, how do community members experience and counter such top-down restrictions, often taking an opposing position? Thirdly, how do communities strategize within existing imposed and less imposed circumstances?

With an empirical case study of the strategies of the Somali community in the UAE, this chapter aims to takes the literature on migrant precarity forward in suggesting that migrant communities often experience precarity in a host country where they are excluded in multiple ways. Such exclusions could include social, economic as well as political elements in multi-dimensional coercive geographies. In overcoming such obstacles and spaces, migrants forge diverse social and economic strategies that not only help them in overcoming the challenges but also in benefitting both the host and home countries. For the host country, migrants provide labor force, expand trade to their homelands and attract resources from transnational communities. Consequently, migrant communities transform a situation of precarity in expanding their efforts to incorporating host, home and beyond transnational connections. In short, the aim of the chapter is to show that transnational migrants, such as the Somali community in the UAE, not only respond to the systemic instrumentalisation that considers them as means to an end in the form of dispensable work force but also use transnational communities struggling to exist on their own terms.

Structurally, the chapter consists of seven sections. The two initial sections conceptualize migrant precarity and agency within the volume's conceptual framework of coercive geographies and present the methods used in the research. The third section focuses on the contextual dimension of migrant labor and precarity in the UAE before the following three sections explore how the transnational Somali community in UAE pursue communal ties, create economic spaces and explore transnational links. The final section discusses the implications and concludes the chapter.

2　　Conceptualizing Migrant Precarity and Agency in Coercive Geographies

Overall, the literature focusing on migrant communities' strategies to overcome precarity recognizes the significance of state and society structures in shaping communities. Host states often pursue policy actions aiming to curb community prospects. Among such policies include legal restrictions on who qualifies for residence permit and citizenship status and who does not. Consequently, migrant communities experience legal precarity in what Lemke (2016: 15) describe as heterogeneous group outside the unionized employment sector leading to employment precarity (Goldring and Landolt 2011). Studies confirm the long-term negative impact of legal precarity (Lemke 2016) on job precarity (Wilson and Ebert 2013). Other studies supplement that such exclusion results from the general de-politicisation of the labor force. This happens following the declining collective solidarity that incorporates on what people would term as outsiders, which complicates the processes of overcoming structural and institutional precarity (Paret and Gleeson 2016).

As alternatives to these state-centric approaches, other studies emphasize the civic struggle of migrant communities against existing structural impositions in their conceptualisations and explorations of precarity. While migrants may view temporary precarity as a strategy toward future upward social mobility with the hope of doing better in the long term (Wang, Li and Deng 2017), people (as individuals or groups) also resist both diverse forms of exclusion that undermine political mobilisation and precarity and form "uncertainty reducing" transnational spaces to help communities to transcend systemic coercive spatial restrictions (Pacheco 2019), or what we here call coercive geographies. Such tendencies constitute the core of social change (Eberle and Holliday 2011): the formation of civic and non-civic spaces that operate within the host and homeland societies (Quinsaat 2019), civic organisations and migrant networks' empowerment of communities in everyday life (Chun 2016; Waite 2009; Giralt 2017); the establishment of platforms to assist them in their onward migration, social and economic reproduction as well as gaining political concessions (Rogers Hall and Salamanca 2017); and the employment of diverse strategies such as the formation of traditional ties to help them simultaneously participate and serve multiple purposes (Faist 2000: 11); and the construction of what scholars refer to as "economies of kinship" as well as dynamic contestations and relationships (Baldassar 2007 and Bolognani 2007) that emerge from aggregated social practices reflecting community members' life worlds. According to these studies and their conceptualisations of precarity, the contradicting activities of host states and migrant communities ought thus not be understood as isolated processes within a nation or state, but part of a complex and wider reconfiguration and transformation of societies, which include exclusion on the one hand and subsequent mobilized resistance, community-generated transformations and the formation of new conditions of socialisation and solidarity within the community and beyond on the other (Campbell 2016). However, as Van Hear and Cohen (Van Hear and Cohen 2017) show, associations with kinship loyalty as well as to nation-states overlap and sometimes contradict (Shain 2007). Age, gender, urban dynamics and cultural transformations often also produce a kind of 'weak ethnicity' and thereby challenge relations to history, past traditions and norms (Vathi 2019). Furthermore, the continuing debate on diaspora within diaspora- and the emphasis on ontological security in both the host and home society suggests the need for internal differentiation among transnational communities (Abramson 2019). Additionally, the turn to digitalized social networking transnational sites also require attention to transnational diversity and complexity (Golan and Babis 2019).

Altogether, these ways to conceptualize migrant precarity thus illustrate the need to explore both how feelings and experiences encounter coercive power (Yuval-Davis 2011) and the internal power inequalities and tensions within transnational communities that emerge from both nation-state narrations and diasporic narrations and consolidations (Hundle 2019). Accordingly, this chapter understands migrant precarity as the organisational regimes, coercive or otherwise, generated by the dominant system (state) that seek to position migrant communities in particular coercive geographies designated by the prevailing system, which migrant communities subsequently mobilize as both individuals and as groups to challenge. In other words, migrant communities can thus be seen as approaching the systems in place as social and political opportunity structures and strategize them as such to seek autonomy and get the most out of the prevailing social, political and economic circumstances. Regardless of the strength of the coercive geographies, migrant precarity thus remains, in this perspective, a dynamic process conditioned by continuously transforming and challenging contexts and circumstances of which communities remain an active part. Complex and dynamic, both processes of belonging to and within an organisation also become part of these negotiations. For example, though perhaps sharing common experiences as excluded and in precarious conditions, migrants nonetheless hold diverse capabilities and reflect different trajectories within their communities. Personal experiences, competences, itineraries and dwellings thus also influence on how people get best out of the imposed precarity. Seen in this way, transnational communities work to overcome limitations by creating and joining diverse networks that formally and informally challenge prevailing citizenship top-down exclusions that often rest on ethnicity and nation-state differences. Relying mainly on transnational ties and experiences, migrants seek to assert dignity by actively preventing isolation and marginalisation in the particular coercive geographies they face (Stokes 2004). Over time, informal activities such as informal fiscal contribution, the support of businesses and establishment of connections with the homeland become integrated parts of community activities in which migrants deploy various strategies to manage existing and emerging risks and uncertainties. Therefore, this chapter conceptualizes migrants as precarious individuals and communities who continuously act to complement or subvert imposed and emerging top down restrictions and coercive geographies, and thus seek to transform their own circumstances by strategizing transnational opportunities while simultaneously maintaining certain connections with prevailing nation-state structures.

3   Methodological Reflections on Exploring Precarious
     Migrants' Agency

To better understand and engage Somali individuals and groups with experience of precarity, its implications and challenging these, original data based on interviews were collected in the UAE. The data for the present study was collected through a combination of purposive and snowball or chain-referral sampling (Babbie 1992) from 45 Somali immigrants in 2010–2016 and again from January–February 2018. Diverse informal discussions and focus groups consisting of groups of seven to eight participants in each of six sessions were collected. The purpose was to diversify the formal interview setting and subsequently validate individual interviews.

The data generated through these interviews is unique in the sense that my access reflects that of an insider due to my commonalities with the respondents and therefore the aspiration to access intimate information from their perspective. This reflects the 'insider' effect of how researchers sharing a cultural and probably national identity with the interviewees or someone familiar with transnational lives often is accorded privileged access to 'unfiltered' intrinsic knowledge. While the insider privilege risks compromising the researcher's "(...) proportion of nearness and remoteness (...)" (Simmel 1971: 146), the insider role also confronts situational and relational complexities arising from the researchers and the subjects' presumptions and expectations (Kusow 2003). In general context, the fact that I share both ethnic and national identity with my interviews and participants thus allowed me a degree of accessibility that would have otherwise been difficult, if not impossible, for other researchers to secure and develop.

In extension of the interviews, this chapter also relies on extended (insider) participant observation of immigrants and interactions with community networks in the UAE member states of Dubai, Sharjah, Ajman and Abu-Dhabi. In the UAE, the enumeration of Somali residents is inaccurate. Instead of trying to randomly select probability samples, this study applies snowball techniques reflecting a sociological sampling. In this way, informants participate in the research process, once again pointing to their agency despite being migrants facing precarious conditions. Although the snowball method has its limitations of representative and generalisation (Bryman 2008: 185), the technique, also referred as "theoretical sampling" (Glaser and Strauss 1967), does promote knowledge generated from the members' daily activities, which in this case is central. The descriptions focus on the meaning people attribute to their contexts and to the way in which they sustain their lives. This happens through interviews with individuals, focus groups, observations and participation in community activities. Finally, the chapter also uses reputable web sites as well as online news sites from the media, communities and authorities to understand and explain prevailing opinions within and around the Somali community in the UAE.

4   Migrant Labor and Precarity in the UAE

As many parts of the world, Britain colonized the tribal populations in the Gulf and in 1971 nudged the Emirati sheikhdoms and fiefdoms into formally forming the 7-state union of the UAE: Abu Dhabi, Ajman, Dubai, Fujairah, Ras al-Khaimah, Sharjah and Umm al-Qaiwain. Although these entities formally share and consult on national authority, Abu Dhabi remains the dominant political and economic power, occupying about 87 per cent of the UAE territory and holding over 90 per cent of the UAE proven oil and gas reserves (Heard-Bey 2005).

Centuries prior to the formation of UAE, the Arabian Gulf engaged historical sea trade with the wider Middle East Africa and the Indian subcontinent. In modern times, such connections continued with more people seeking job and business opportunities in the UAE as it became one of the wealthiest countries in the world. Today, approximately 80 per cent of work force consisting of foreigners (Elessawy and Zaidan 2014). However, despite attempts by UAE authorities for policies of 'Emiratization.' there are challenges in achieving these goals (Toledo 2013). Accordingly, extreme migration policies linked to jobs, which make up the labor dimension of the UAE as a coercive geography, force migrants to continuously worry about accessing or renewing residence permit and might face deportation (Jamal 2015). Migrants in the UAE confront precarity from unemployment and low income in several cases which also impacts on whether one obtains a residence permit (Terterov 2006: 218; Smith 2006). The state system classifies the inhabitants into *muwadiniin* (nationals) and *muwafidiin* (foreigners). This classification system qualifies Emirati nationals for public entitlements including employment and other privileges acquired automatically through citizenship rights. In contrast, foreign residents who often undertake the categories of work shunned by the citizens, live with lesser privileges (Peck 1986: 68). Complex mobility altered earlier precarity condition that often depended on peoples' origin, whether European, Arab, Asian or African (Khalaf and Alkobaisi 1999). The legal residence challenges and uncertain employment opportunities impacts not just the Somalis but also many other immigrants (Zachariah, Prakash, and Rajan 2004; Mahmud 2016). Other restrictions include visa uncertainty, impermissibility of family reunion and rarity of intermarriage between nationals and foreigners (Hugo 2004). For most immigrants the conditions of precarity have worsened since the beginning of the oil boom in the Gulf. For instance, within the past decade the UAE implemented governmental nationalisation (tawdiin) strategies combining with extensive neoliberal economic policies (Akinci 2016), effectively making the UAE, particularly the emirate of Dubai, a globalized and multi-sited coercive geography.

Traditionally, Somali people have inhabited an area that stretches beyond Somalia's (1960–1991) borders, living also in Djibouti, northern Kenya and the Somali region in Ethiopia and migrated to countries nearby (East and Central Africa, Asia and the Arabian Peninsula) within the British imperial system's trading networks and circuits (Alpers 2000; Lambert and Lester 2006). During the colonial period, Somali men worked, for example, as employees of the UK's merchant navy. While some returned after sojourns to the UK, others stayed (Kahin 1997: 31). Since the 1960s, significant numbers of Somalis migrated to work in the oil-rich Gulf. The number of Somali migrants has previously been estimated at 400,000 but is currently around 200,000 (Reffer and Salih 2016). For comparison, about 85 per cent of the country's workforce are expatriates from the Indian subcontinent (Singh et al. 2019). The earliest Somali migrants were often people looking for better employment than they could find in Somalia (Marchal 1996). Later, due to diverse state-society transformations in the region – as well as global ideological changes – a second wave of migrants moved to the West, predominantly Europe and the US. In 1977–78, the Ethiopian–Somali War led to economic and political deterioration and eventually the migration of those excluded from economic and political opportunities (Fearon and Laitin 2003). In 1988, the eruption of the civil war generated a major movement during which the better-off refugees went abroad to Western countries such as Canada, the US, UK, Italy, Holland, Sweden, Denmark, Norway, Finland, and Australia. However, most of the refugees, and significantly the poorest, fled to the neighbouring countries, such as Kenya and Ethiopia. More recently, and due to the heavy influx, Somali migration has diversified and become more complex. The recent wave of migration is not only restricted to south-north but also north-south in the pursuing novel transnational formations in relation to both the Gulf and emerging powers such as China, India and South Africa. The recent migration wave confirms the thesis of Somalis becoming a global diaspora (Kusow and Bjork 2007).

As a transnational diaspora in the UAE, Somali communities share similar precarious conditions with other migrants from developing countries though their case is still rather special. This has mainly to do with the lack of a Somali state or government since 1991 that could have provided some sort of intermediary diplomatic role in their relations with the authorities in the UAE – an institutional vacuum that the business elite and traditional leaders had, through informal networking with the natives, tried to fill. Furthermore, the general international migration trend of forced migration (Castles 2003), in which families, women and children are increasingly joining trans-boundary mobility.

Despite the burdens confronting the Somali community, the interviews revealed that not all with Somali background in UAE suffer from such legal and economic precarity. Though few in numbers, some Somali with UAE citizenship enjoy a access to society similar that of the natives. There are also those who over the years obtained western citizenships and live in the country as Westerners. The system often treats them more favourably due to their western status. However, most Somalis in the UAE experience precarity, which may also help explain why Somalis born or raised in the UAE appear not have a particular attachment and sensibility towards the place of their upbringing as is otherwise common. The interviews also suggest that particularly young men experience the burden of precarity as they have to leave the country if they do not secure a job that grants them a residence permit when they reach the legal age of 18 years of age. Accordingly, they, and other AUE-born Somali, confront their situation along the Somali who arrive to with initial high expectations to a prosperous UAE by turning to transnational Somali social networks and communities.

5   Pursuing Communal Ties in a Coercive Geography

When Somalis arrive in the UAE, many of them approach their immediate communities for social networking, accessing job opportunities and even obtaining financial subsidiary in case of unemployment. Others reach out to the wider society. As authorities in the UAE restrict welfare to the citizens and exclude foreigners, engaging the mainstream is not straightforward. Particularly those with higher education and economically better off might reach out, bridging friendship relations and professional networks. So far, communal ties remain essential social formation for the community in managing existing and potential precarities. Communal ties are the first for many to provide basic accommodation and initial living expenses when, for instance, young people arrive in the UAE after hazardous journeys across Yemen and the Saudi desert. Though it is informally organized, the communal support mechanisms build on classic Somali customary law (*xeer*) which involves intensive consultation (*wadahadal*) and inclusion among members (Lewis 1994). As argued by Sheffer (2003), established transnational communities engage modern institutions, while the less established groups might sustain traditionalism building on basic kinship relations. Granovetter (1973) proposes similar conclusions that traditionalism and kinship relations remain part of national and transnational activities. Meanwhile, Itzigsohn and Saucedo (2002) complements that transnational space making consolidates and maintains community belonging. This research shows that kinship remains fundamental for community's social, economic and political meaning making organisational fabric in the UAE. However, the overall objective of such formation is to strengthen the community and provide service for struggling individual members.

As uncovered in the interviews, the core communal activity that sustains communal ties is the contribution to *qaaraan* (fiscal contribution) efforts in which members deduct monthly amount from their income (sources of income) to the least privileged. The term *qaaraan*, in broader sense, refers to activities in which the community shares actual and potential social and economic burdens. In practical terms, each member of a particular kin with a reliable job and income contributes to this communal burse known as *qaaraan* account. In return, the individual qualifies for community support in challenging periods. The communal ties formed in the host country do not fully resemble the traditional, and more hierarchical kinship ties that prevail in the homeland. The current formation is part of a strategic process of overcoming precarity to support the individual contributor while preserving the community's well-being in the host society. The process starts with the identification of the newly arrived and others that claim to belong to particular kin. If immediate identification is not possible, contacts to the homeland ensure proper verification. Apart from confirming lineage ties, additional assessments include people's employability as well as communal solidarity and capabilities. Running such complex community welfare enterprise demands a social organisation. In a traditional Somali context, communities organize through processes of inheritance and charisma. In the UAE, the community appoints temporary leaders, depending on the individual leader's organisational and network capabilities within the host country. While ancestral ties are important, eligibility to access community resources and contribution will depend mainly on employability.

As precarity can impact all members, regardless of status, the community prefers lesser hierarchical and consultative organisation. This does not mean the community is completely egalitarian with no social stratification. Initially, members suffering from unemployment and residential challenges (most of them women, the youth and newly arrived) represent the least privileged. In responding to community needs, community leaders, mostly consisting of traditional leaders and business entrepreneurs, collect resources from privileged members of the community, particularly those with jobs and income, and distribute it to the lesser privileged. Since, almost all members might have benefitted from community welfare schemes or might potentially risk depending on it in the future, people willingly contribute to the collective well-being. Some even consider such traditional insurance system as debt payment procedure that collectively maintains a social security mechanism, in not only preventing social and economic deprivation among the excluded and subordinate individuals, but also eventually generating a sense of belonging and commitment within the community:

> As people get help from their kin, they also contribute. It is a kind of investment. Men lead the traditional system. Their decision is *xeer* [customary law]. After *wadahaldal* [discussion], people accept the verdict and pay their share.
>
> Interview in the UAE, December 2010

Following the collapse of the Somali state in 1991, the community in the UAE became fragmented. Before the collapse, the community interacted with the Somali state, providing a sense of common 'Somaliness.' With the state collapse, kinship relationships and regionalism replaced society and state consciousness, transforming the community from state-linked to stateless transnational community:

> We were better organized in the past. We had a state and a president. When our president visited the UAE, he used to begin his visit by meeting with us and inquiring whether we had any problems. Even the UAE government used to invite us at the official level before the collapse. And our women here in UAE had a women's organisation that was connected to the Somali women's organisation in Somalia.
>
> Interview in the UAE, December 2010

Among the Somali communities in the UAE, this research thus finds that construction of kinship ties functions as a multidimensional process to cope with the empowerment and the inclusion of the part of the community that might need help in overcoming legal or economic precarity.

6   Creating Economic Spaces in a Coercive Geography

The UAE is not a democratic country but has since the 1970s remained relatively stable with some sort of tribal dynamics in otherwise volatile region (Freer 2019). With a vibrant open market, the country attracts professionals, entrepreneurs and investors form around the world. The seven emirates in the union do not, however, share mercantile robustness. While Abu Dhabi dominate the geographical space and the oil sources, Dubai dominates tourism, investment and businesses (Hvidt 2009). This geographical and resource differences among the seven states influences how migrants strategize their presence in the country. While some might work in the oil sectors in Abu Dhabi and run small businesses and trade in Dubai and Sharjah, they prefer to access affordable apartments in Ajman and Ras al-Khaimah. Apart from the restrictive political system and parallel migrant policies, the UAE remains economically flexible and open to the world and its citizens among the wealthiest and socio-economically privileged in the world (Johnsen 2017).

The UAE has an open economy conductive to business entrepreneurship (Herb 2009). Such conditions enable migrants and transnational communities to start small businesses and pursue international trade. The least privileged Somalis start careers with non-skilled, manual jobs. From there they save enough capital to start or join existing small businesses and trade related entrepreneurships. Gradually, they replace the initial monthly remittance to relatives with activities to buy minor shares in import and export businesses or freight goods to relatives back home for further marketing:

> It is easy to get a job in the UAE, if one is not lazy. I came to the UAE through Kenya where I lived a while and learnt the English language that now helps me work for a cargo company. Apart from the residence permit that should be renewed every three years, there are no problems living in the UAE.
>
> Interview in the UAE, January 2010

With community owned small businesses, members access not just employment spaces but also develop and maintain social and economic interconnections. For some, the spaces represent an opportunity for investment, while they expand trade and exchanges with the outside world for others. Similarly, members create investment platforms linking the community with traders and development activities in the homeland. These economic spaces provide services to the increasingly transnational and global Somali community, representing a developmental as well as a contact zone for the homeland and beyond.

Levitt (1998) studied transnational community's adaptability and transmission of social and entrepreneurship platforms and argued that such platforms emerge from the dynamics of host-homeland contexts. In the host country, immigrants confront diverse social, legal and economic challenges. To survive they create a third space where they combine the benefits from host and homeland and at the same time restrict the challenges. Basu (1998) and Levie (2007) also studied how communities generate micro economic activities starting off with informal sources and networks but eventually incorporating formal institutions such as banks and investors, letting the community serve the wider society as well as increasingly globally scattered communities. Consequently, the economic diversification coupled with community entrepreneurial spaces enables the community's adjustment into the mainstream and the surrounding society. Such community expansions both ensure business achievements and confront barriers of national and international exclusion (Naudé et al. 2017).

In the past, Greek communities generated great wealth from their entrepreneurship and trade capabilities (Harlaftis 2007). The tight community connection reduced transaction costs for the Greeks who owned and developed multinational companies. In line with this and also Guarnizo and Smith (Guarnizo and Smith 1998), the fieldwork in the UAE shows that communities engage entrepreneurship not only to accumulate wealth but also to counter the institutionalized precarity of what Guarnizo and Smith refer to 'transnationalism from above' to address often state and corporations' transnational capital flow. Transnational communities often pursue 'transnationalism from below' through the creation of spaces of resistance that informally pursue grass root activism, entrepreneurship and mobilisation. The UAE is not the only space that Somalis, in economic terms, pursue entrepreneurship and investment based on traditional communal solidarity. The experiences in Kenya, South Africa, among other countries, also show that Somali communities come to represent a significant economic factor (Campbell 2006).

Apart from providing employment and entrepreneurship opportunities for the community and other diasporic transnationals residents in the host country, Somali transnational community spaces in the UAE also function as meeting and contact places for the increasingly trans-nationalized Somali community. For instance, the Karaama neighbourhood in Ajman qualifies as a transnational contact zone. This is a vibrant enclave where many Somalis both live and run small businesses. In the enclave, there is a Somali cafeteria-restaurant (Baba cafeteria) owned by a Somali man and his Yemeni wife. Like many other Somali-owned businesses in the country, the core employees include Asians. Outside Baba cafeteria, a father and his son sit together drinking tea. The young man travelled from Texas in the US to meet his father, who had come to the UAE for medical tourism and the chance to meet with his son. They have not seen each other since the outbreak of the civil war:

> I came to the UAE for a health check and for meeting with relatives. I also met my son, who is not willing to come to Somalia for security reasons.
> Interview in the UAE, February 2010

In recent years, the Somali community has also entered service sectors such as the hotel and restaurant industries. This move is in response to the increase of community members with cultural and legal (citizenship) resources and from the West and the richer parts of the world and has provided services to a growing tourism market from the global transnational communities and from the homeland. Such businesses came into being after cooperation between the business elite in the UAE and communities from Europe and North America. One such Somali-owned establishment is the Jubba Hotel, among others. Local Somali businesspersons and Somali-British investors own the hotel that has been open for business for about a decade.

7   Exploring Transnational Links in a Coercive Geography

Business entrepreneurs and traditional leaders remain crucial for community mobilisation. The first provides economic resources for important gatherings and events, while the latter group brings history and continuity. Among other activities, community leaders occasionally organize and sponsor high profile visits from the homeland. Certainly, for their transnational businesses to flourish, both in the host environment and in the homeland, community entrepreneurs often depend on sustained community legitimacy and support. Community leaders also organize humanitarian and political events. During such gatherings, community members show their solidarity to the visiting traditional leaders thereby reaffirming their relationship with the homeland as well as the importance of community cohesion in the host country. Although it is an informal social activity, these events operate with a division of labor. Each sub-group is responsible for the mobilisation and the collection of resources from a specific group:

> If politicians and traditional leaders come here or if somebody needs help, people *waa la abaabulaa* (are mobilized) and organized properly. For instance, the businesspeople are sent to businesspersons, the young people to young persons, the women to the women.
>
> Interview in the UAE, January 2010

Somali transnational community spaces in the UAE include the Sharjah port in downtown Sharjah. The port docks Indian, Iranian and Somali-owned boats exporting goods to and from the Horn of Africa. Somali-owned cranes load cars and electronic materials destined for the Red Sea port cities of Boosaaso and Barbara. During high seasons, business activities around the port employ thousands of Somalis, mainly young men and women who have recently arrived. Some of them entered the country through the same port from which they now earn their income so they can support relatives back home or save for further migration or settlement opportunities in the UAE and beyond. Apart from being an employment centre for the less fortunate community members, the port thus functions as a corridor and lifeline for Somalia. Brokers, known as *dilaal* in Somali, coordinate the shipment activities with mobile phones connecting them to *hawaala* (remittance) businesses, traditional leaders, homeland-host country business elites, ordinary employees, marketing agents in China, India and Japan, and diverse transnational community contacts across the world:

> I have thousands of mobile phones and contacts stored in my cell phone. All of them, one way or the other, link to homeland trade.
>
> Interview in the UAE, January 2010

The *dilaal's* connections and the transnational business deals illustrate the character of athe dynamic space that connect diverse business groups within the UAE and beyond. Somali transnational community spaces in the UAE are less gendered, as the Somali women actively demand equal opportunities. Despite having fewer opportunities when compared to their male compatriots overall, women find ways to participate in the port businesses activities. They take part in the long working hours at the port while also investing in homeland-linked import and export businesses.

The transnational community spaces have regional and kinship characteristics, as the different groups in the transnational communities focus and provide services for diverse regions in the homeland. While the Emirati born Somali youth seek opportunities in the original homeland, due to the fairly short distance to Somalia, homeland's traditional leaders head the opposite direction, often paying visits to UAE Somali transnational communities. The aim of such visits is to strengthen the transnational dimension and the continuity of the kinship ties. During visits, traditional leaders participate in community mobilisations. From their part, communities at times also invite homeland traditional leaders to lobby for their interests at the political level:

> There are cases where the business elite offer accommodation, transport and luxury for members of the different Somali government. This is mostly limited to the times when they have a particular interest and objective. Business tycoons are, in general, not interested in nation and state building.
>
> Interview in the UAE, February 2010

Finally, community members pursue transnational capital transfer in which families invest in the secondary migration of one or more family members to a third country. The aim is to seek better opportunities beyond host-homeland connections mainly in search of citizenship, better education, employment, remittance and family reunion: "We are investing in the children and their education so they can take care of themselves and the family" (interview in the UAE, January 2010).

Parents invest in their children's education, mainly to secure the future of their children but also for their own retirement. However, providing education for young people in a country like the UAE where one who is self-employed has to pay for everything is very difficult. Instead, parents often invest in their children getting an education in universities in India and Malaysia:

> I grew up in the UAE and as a child went to school there. When I reached 18, my father's (family's) residence permit could not help me. I have to get my own through job or education. The option was getting higher education for which my parents could not pay or leaving the country. I was lucky to get the support of relatives to immigrate to the US. In the US, I got both education and citizenship. Now I am again in the UAE with a professional job. This would have been impossible for me to get if I did not migrate.
>
> Interview in the UAE, July 2016

From these platforms people also consider secondary migration and capital transferability. People have to manoeuvre through social agencies and institutions to navigate and link the past with the future. The most privileged get education and citizenship in western countries and then return to the UAE and get well-paid jobs or open businesses for somewhat elevated transnational social belonging and status.

8   Discussion and Conclusion

The continuing conflict in Somalia and the lack of sincere governance in the country sustain large and diverse Somali transnational communities in different parts of the world. Somalis migrated from their homeland due to insecurity and poverty. Later, those who end up in countries where they experience precarity again migrate from their host countries in search of better social and economic conditions. Consequently, a greater number of, for instance, former residents in the UAE, and the wider Gulf, currently reside in Europe and North America. The rationale for this secondary migration reflects the UAE's restriction on citizenship and residence status as well as declining employment opportunities.

This research identified three main transnational community strategies to overcome the social and economic precarity associated with the coercive geography the UAE thereby upholds. The first of such activities relates to the deployment and diversification of a new form of community ties to subvert emerging socio-economic obstacles. Apart from ensuring partial community empowerment for the vulnerable, the emerging community ties also structure the community into a powerful group that often leads (e.g. elders and business elite) and the lesser powerful (e.g. youth, women and new arrivals) that sometimes adhere to what the dominant groups propose. Secondly, the study finds the establishment of community spaces (e.g. business outlets increasingly serving for global community). Such businesses remain diverse in terms of gender, community ties and regional connections. More recently, due to secondary migration and increased return from the West, community entrepreneurship spaces became more mainstreamed. Thirdly, the community is involved in the organisation and diversification of transnational links. With modified form of community ties and spaces, the Somali community engages homeland politics in providing humanitarian as well as developmental support for the vulnerable in the homeland. More recently, the community ventured into capital transferability activities, mainly focusing on secondary migration and the search for transnational education for younger generations.

This research finds that although structures, whether traditional or modern, remain vital for the organisation and the cultural transformation of the community, from the premise of empirical realities and observations, it is obvious that community actions partially remain independent from imposing structures. On one hand, the community preserves and cherishes principles of national and traditional identities, while on the other, community priorities and activities often reflect the processes of finding solutions to contextual social and economic challenges. Apart from the contextual importance, time is also sometimes relevant. The longer community members reside in a host country, the more established they become. However, in recent years, educated youth with dual citizenship mainly returning from west gained status due to their capabilities of transferring cultural capital.

Despite certain limitations of not accessing quantifiable data, this research provides unique insights into how individuals and groups not only adjust to precariat conditions but also strategize to overcome precarity by constructing alternative societal-economic, cultural and political platforms. Somali communities in the UAE and their diverse communal efforts demonstrate creativity in addressing society and state-imposed migration constraints. This research has therefore implications for established assumptions, particularly of immigrants and transnational communities of adjusting/not adjusting into a nation state centric public sphere. The proposition is that state and civil society remain crucial for the acquisition of rights, representation as well as the integration or assimilation processes (Brubaker 2001; Benhabib 2004; Joppke 2007). More broadly, Keohane and Nye argued that private corporations and non-state organized institutions cross boundaries and can operate beyond nation-state jurisdiction (Keohane and Nye 1977). The state-centred conclusions stand in contrast to the literature on transnational formations that rather calls for overcoming the "trap for methodological nationalism" (Beck and Beck-Gernsheim 2008) and in need of stressing the agency of community driven transnationalism from below, equally creating a transnational public sphere (Vertovec and Cohen 2002; Van Tubergen 2015). The findings show that the Somali community, with limited resources, created community ties, spaces and social relations by combining multiple identities and strategies. This calls for the re-examination of static citizenship frames. Societies and states understandably construct legal social, economic and policy frames in administering formal procedures of determining whom to include or exclude. In general, such regulations impact community options. The presented empirical evidence among transnational communities, however, illustrates a community agency with capabilities for transformation and in perpetual search of what Hegel conceptualized as "struggle for recognition" (Hegel 2012).

In order to better understand the dynamics of such communities, we need new methods and frames taking us beyond the dichotomisation of traditionalism vs. moderation as well the rigid categorisation of host vs. home-land environments.

In conclusion, transnational communities strive to overcome precarity – not just in the context of addressing state–society dialectics, but also in the process of creating community spaces that occasionally operate with and around exist-ing local precarities. In expanding the framework of 'various precarities' this chapter proposes 'various strategies of inprecarities' generated and sustained by the community. Such approach helps us to advance the class-oriented cap-ital-centric precarity proposed by Bourdieu (1998) and Standing (2011) and the more specific "political precarity" proposed by Jørgensen and Schierup (2016).

References

Abramson, Y. (2019). "Securing the diasporic 'self' by travelling abroad: Taglit-Birthright and ontological security," *Journal of Ethnic and Migration Studies* 45(4): 656–673.

Agustin, Ó.G., and Jørgensen, M.B. (2016). "For the sake of workers but not immigrant workers? Social dumping and free movement," in Ó. Agustín and M.B. Jørgensen (eds.). *Solidarity Without Borders*. London: Pluto Press: 150–166.

Akinci, I. (2016). "Migrant Dubai: low wage workers and the construction of a global city," *Ethnic and Racial Studies* 40(8): 1–3.

Allen, R. (2009). "Benefit or burden? Social capital, gender, and the economic adapta-tion of refugees," *International Migration Review* 43(2): 332–365.

Alpers, E. (2000). "Recollecting Africa: diasporic memory in the Indian Ocean world," *African Studies Review* 43(1): 83–99.

Arnold, D., and Bongiovi, J.R. (2013). "Precarious, informalizing, and flexible work: Transforming concepts and understandings," *American Behavioral Scientist* 57(3): 289–308.

Babbie, E. (1992). *The Practice of Social Research*. Belmont, CA: Wadsworth (sixth edition).

Baldassar, L. (2007). "Transnational families and aged care: the mobility of care and the migrancy of ageing," *Journal of ethnic and migration studies* 33(2): 275–297.

Basu, A. (1998). "An exploration of entrepreneurial activity among Asian small busi-nesses in Britain," *Small business economics* 10(4): 313–326.

Beck, U., and Beck-Gernsheim, E. (2008). "Global generations and the trap of method-ological nationalism for a cosmopolitan turn in the sociology of youth and genera-tion," *European Sociological Review* 25(1): 25–36.

Benhabib, S. (2004). *The rights of others: Aliens, residents, and citizens*. Vol. 5. Cam-bridge, UK: Cambridge University Press.

Bolognani, M. (2007). "The myth of return: dismissal, survival or revival? A Bradford example of transnationalism as a political instrument," *Journal of Ethnic and Migration Studies* 33(1): 59–76.

Bourdieu. P. (1963). *Travail et travailleurs en Algerie*. Paris: Mouton & Co.

Bourdieu. P. (1998). *Acts of resistance: Against the tyranny of the market*. New York, NY: New Press.

Brubaker, R. (2001). "The return of assimilation? Changing perspectives on immigration and its sequels in France, Germany, and the United States," *Ethnic and racial studies* 24(4): 531–548.

Bryman, A. (2008). *Social Research Methods. 3rd edition*. Oxford: Oxford University Press.

Burawoy, M. (2015). "Facing an Unequal World," *Current Sociology* 63(1): 5–34.

Butler, J. (2006). *Precarious life: The powers of mourning and violence*. London: Verso.

Campbell, E. (2006). "Urban Refugees in Nairobi: Problems of Protection, Mechanisms of Survival, and Possibilities for Integration," *Journal of Refugee Studies* 19(3): 396–413.

Campbell, S. (2016). "Everyday recomposition: Precarity and socialization in Thailand's migrant workforce," *American Ethnologist* 43(2): 258–269.

Casas-Cortés, M. (2014). "A genealogy of precarity: A toolbox for rearticulating fragmented social realities in and out of the workplace," *Rethinking Marxism* 26(2): 206–226.

Castles, S. (2003). "Towards a sociology of forced migration and social transformation," *Sociology* 37(1): 13–34.

Chun, J.J. (2016). "Building political agency and movement leadership: the grassroots organizing model of Asian Immigrant Women Advocates," *Citizenship Studies* 20(3–4): 379–395.

Eberle, M.L., and Holliday, I. (2011). "Precarity and Political Immobilisation: Migrants from Burma in Chiang Mai, Thailand," *Journal of Contemporary Asia* 41(3): 371–392.

Elessawy, F., and Esmat, Z. (2014). "Living in the move: Impact of guest workers on population characteristics of the United Arab Emirates (UAE)," *The Arab World Geographer* 17(1): 2–23.

Ettlinger, N. (2007). "Precarity unbound," *Alternatives: Global, Local, Political* 32(3): 319–340.

Faist, T. (2000). "Transnationalization in international migration: implications for the study of citizenship and culture," *Ethnic and Racial Studies* 23(2): 189–222.

Fearon, J., and David, L. (2003). "Ethnicity, insurgency and civil war," *American political science review* 97(1): 75–90.

Freer, C. (2019). "Clients or challengers?: tribal constituents in Kuwait, Qatar, and the UAE," *British Journal of Middle Eastern Studies*: 1–20.

Glaser, B., and Strauss, A. (1967). *The discovery of grounded theory: Strategies for qualitative*. New Jersey, NJ: Transaction Publishers.

Golan, O., and Babis, D. (2019). "Digital host national identification among Filipino temporary migrant workers," *Asian Journal of Communication* 29(2): 164–180.

Goldring, L., and Landolt, P. (2011). "Caught in the work–citizenship matrix: The lasting effects of precarious legal status on work for Toronto immigrants," *Globalizations* 8(3): 325–341.

Granovetter, M. (1973). "The strength of weak ties," *American Journal of Sociology* 78(6): 1360–1380.

Harlaftis, G. (2007). "From Diaspora Traders to Shipping Tycoons: The Vagliano Bros," *Business History Review* 81(2): 237–268.

Harris, K., and Scully, B. (2015). "A hidden counter-movement? Precarity, politics, and social protection before and beyond the neoliberal era," *Theory and Society* 44(5): 415–444.

Hegel, G.W.F. (2012). *The phenomenology of mind*. North Chelmsford, MA: Courier Corporation.

Herb, M. (2009). "A nation of bureaucrats: Political participation and economic diversification in Kuwait and the United Arab Emirates," *International Journal of Middle East Studies* 41(3): 375–395.

Hugo, G. (2004). "International Migration in the Asia-Pacific Region: Emerging Trends and Issues," in D.S. Massey and J.E. Taylor (eds.). *International Migration Prospects and Policies in a Global* Market. Oxford: Oxford University Press: 77–104.

Hundle, A.K. (2019). "Postcolonial Patriarchal Nativism, Domestic Violence and Transnational Feminist Research in Contemporary Uganda," *Feminist Review* 121(1): 37–52.

Hvidt, M. (2009) "The Dubai model: An outline of key development-process elements in Dubai," *International Journal of Middle East Studies* 41(3): 397–418.

Itzigsohn, J., and Saucedo, S. (2002). "Immigrant incorporation and socio-cultural transnationalism," *International Migration Review* 36(3): 767–798.

Johnsen, S. (2017) "Social enterprise in the United Arab emirates," *Social Enterprise Journal* 13(4): 392–409.

Joppke, C. (2007). "Beyond national models: Civic integration policies for immigrants in Western Europe," *West European Politics* 30(1): 1–22.

Kahin, M. (1997). *Educating Somali children in Britain*. London: Trentham books.

Keohane, R., and Nye, J. (1977). *Power and interdependence: World politics in transition*. 2nd ed. Boston: Little, Brown.

Khalaf, S., and Alkobaisi, S. (1999). "Migrants' strategies of coping and patterns of accommodation in the oil-rich Gulf societies: evidence from the UAE," *British Journal of Middle Eastern Studies* 26(2): 271–298.

Kusow, A. (2003). "Beyond Indigenous Authenticity: Reflections on the Insider/Outsider Debate in Immigration Research," *Symbolic Interaction* 26(4): 591–599.

Kusow, A., and Stephanie, B. (2007). *From Mogadishu to Dixon: The Somali diaspora in a global context.* Trenton, NJ: Red Sea Press.

Lambert, D., and Lester, A. (2006). *Colonial Lives Across the British Empire: Imperial Careering in the Long Nineteen Century.* Cambridge: Cambridge University Press.

Lemke, S. (2016). *Inequality, Poverty and Precarity in Contemporary American Culture.* Cham: Springer.

Levie, J. (2007). "Immigration, in-migration, ethnicity and entrepreneurship in the United Kingdom," *Small Business Economics* 28(2): 143–169.

Levitt, P. (1998). "Social remittances: Migration driven local-level forms of cultural diffusion," *International migration review* 32(4): 926–948.

Lewis, I.M. (1994). *Blood and bone: The call of kinship in Somali society.* The Red Sea Press.

Mahmud, H. (2016). "Impact of the destination state on migrants' remittances: A study of remitting among Bangladeshi migrants in the USA, the UAE and Japan," *Migration and Development* 5(1): 79–98.

Marchal, R. (1996). *Final Report on the Post Civil War Somali Business Class.* European Commission, Somalia Unit, Paris.

Mas Giralt, R. (2017). "Onward Migration as a Coping Strategy? Latin Americans Moving from Spain to the UK Post-2008," *Population, Space and Place* 23(3): 1–12.

Milkman, R. (2014). "Millennial Movements: Occupy Wall Street and the Dreamers," *Dissent* 61(3): 55–59.

Munck, R. (2013). "The Precariat: a view from the South," *Third World Quarterly* 34(5): 747–762.

Naudé, W., Siegel, M., and Marchand, K. (2017). "Migration, entrepreneurship and development: critical questions," *IZA Journal of Migration* 6(1): 5.

Neilson, D. (2015). "Class, precarity, and anxiety under neoliberal global capitalism: From denial to resistance," *Theory & Psychology* 25(2): 184–201.

Pacheco, S. (2019). "The rise of Mexican entrepreneurial migration to the United States: A mixed-embeddedness approach," *Thunderbird International Business Review* 61(2): 197–215.

Paret, M. (2016). "Politics of Solidarity and Agency in an Age of Precarity," *Global Labour Journal* 7(2): n.p.

Paret, M., and Gleeson, S. (2016). "Precarity and agency through a migration lens," *Citizenship Studies* 20(3–4): 277–294.

Peck, M. (1986). *The United Arab Emirates: A Venture in Unity.* London: Westview Press.

Quinsaat, S.M. (2019). "Transnational contention, domestic integration: assimilating into the hostland polity through homeland activism," *Journal of Ethnic and Migration Studies* 45(3): 419–436.

Rogers Hall, K., Salamanca, M., and with contributions from Artists' Bloc collective members. (2017). "Relocating precarity and resiliency within Montreal: the Artists' Bloc of the Immigrant Workers' Centre," *Research in Drama Education: The Journal of Applied Theatre and Performance* 22(1): 116–125.

Schierup, C., and Ålund, A. (2013). "A global migrant precariat: Labour, citizenship and space for civil society." Presented at *Primer Seminario Internacional de Estudios Críticos del Desarollo. Crisis, Desarollo y Trabajo*, University of Zacatecas, 14–15 February 2013.

Schierup, C., and Jørgensen, M.B. (2016). "An Introduction to the Special Issue. Politics of Precarity: Migrant Conditions, Struggles and Experiences," *Critical Sociology* 42(7–8): 947–958.

Schierup, C., Ålund, A., and Branka, L.B. (2015). "Migration, Precarization and the Democratic Deficit in Global Governance," *International Migration* 53(3): 50–63.

Shain, Y. (2007). *Kinship & diasporas in international affairs*. Ann Abor, MI: University of Michigan.

Sheffer, G. (2003). *Diaspora politics: At home abroad*. Cambridge, UK: Cambridge University Press.

Simmel, G. (1971). "The Stranger," in D. Levine (ed.). *On Individuality and Social Forms*. Chicago, IL: University of Chicago Press: 143–149.

Smith, C. (2006). "The double indeterminacy of labour power: labour effort and labour mobility," *Work, Employment and Society* 20(2): 389–402.

Smith, P., and Guarnizo, L. (1998). *Transnationalism from Below*. New Jersey, NJ: Transaction.

Standing, G. (2011). *The Precariat: The New Dangerous Class*. New York: Bloomsbury Publications.

Stokes, G. (2004). "Transnational citizenship: problems of definition, culture and democracy," *Cambridge Review of International Affairs* 17(1): 119–135.

Terterov, M. (2006). *Doing Business with the United Arab Emirates*. Gambela: GMB publishing.

Toledo, H. (2013). "The political economy of emiratization in the UAE," *Journal of Economic Studies* 40(1): 39–53.

Van Dyke, N., and Holly, J. Mc. (2010). "Introduction: Social Movement Coalition Formation," in N. Van Dyke and H.J. McCammon (eds.). *Strategic Alliances: Coalition Building and Social Movements*. Minneapolis: University of Minnesota: xi–xxvii.

Van Hear, N., and Cohen, R. (2017). "Diasporas and conflict: distance, contiguity and spheres of engagement," *Oxford Development Studies* 45(2): 171–184.

Van Tubergen, F. (2015). "Ethnic boundaries in core discussion networks: A multilevel social network study of Turks and Moroccans in the Netherlands," *Journal of Ethnic and Migration Studies* 41(1): 101–116.

Vathi, Z. (2019). "Identifications of Albanian-origin teenagers in Thessaloniki and the role of ethnicity: A multi-scalar perspective," *Global Studies of Childhood* 9(1): 29–41.

Vertovec, S., and Cohen, R. (2002). *Conceiving cosmopolitanism: Theory, context and practice*. Oxford: Oxford University Press.

Waite, L. (2009). "A place and space for a critical geography of precarity?," *Geography Compass* 3(1): 412–433.

Wang, H., Li, W., and Deng, Y. (2017). "Precarity among highly educated migrants: college graduates in Beijing, China," *Urban Geography* 38(10): 1497–1516.

Wilson, S., and Ebert, N. (2013). "Precarious work: Economic, sociological and political perspectives," *The Economic and Labour Relations Review* 24(3): 263–278.

Yuval-Davis, N. (2011). *The politics of belonging: Intersectional contestations*. London: Sage.

Zachariah, K.C., Prakash, B.A., and Irudaya Rajan, S. (2004). "Indian workers in UAE: employment, wages and working conditions," *Economic and Political Weekly*: 2227–2234.

CHAPTER 8

Negotiating Displacement, Precarity and Militarized Confinement in the Mediterranean before Neoliberalism: The Gaza Strip, 1957–1967

Martin Ottovay Jørgensen

1 Introduction

By now, their stories seem common. Having left their homes and families for better lives, four young brown men were apprehended and detained by security forces in a highly militarized borderscape almost at the southern Mediterranean coastline. While seemingly familiar, their stories are not amongst those that have appeared in the last decade of European media headlines, however. Born before the British imperial security forces had been withdrawn from Palestine, the four young men were all Palestinian and had left what remained of their families in Israel in October 1958 to restart their lives initially in the Egyptian-controlled Gaza Strip and, if possible, as migrant labor in the Gulf states (Complaints and Investigations July 1958–April 1959, 28 October 1958). Perhaps surprisingly, they were not apprehended by Israeli military forces at the Israeli border but by a Danish military unit from the United Nations deployed in the Gaza Strip in what was the UN's first peacekeeping operation. Although their stories are old news so to speak, the ambitions and experience of these four young Palestinian men connect to themes in current research on displacement, precarity and confinement in the broader Mediterranean region, namely displaced people's agency, ambitions and experiences in navigating and negotiating the surveillance and security regimes of the coercive geographies across the Mediterranean.

Since the 1980's, it has been possible to follow how the political currents of neoliberalism and populism have securitized migration and refugee movements in the Mediterranean. Against this backdrop, scholars in the research fields of, for example, Migration Studies, Security Studies, Critical Security Studies and European Studies to mention just some have shown how the EU, neighbouring states and international organizations have been both enabled and pushed to enforce regimes of migrant rejection, confinement and expulsion. Additionally, these bodies of scholarship have also shown how these regimes have created entanglements of coercive geographies that criminalize and penalize both 'undesired' displaced and different bodies and the desire for life beyond precarity and conflict in both southern Europe and south-eastern Europe as well as in the Middle East. However, few studies have connected empirically how the various contemporary coercive geographies hark back to earlier regulatory, monitoring and coercive regimes engendered by European imperialism and inter-imperial collaboration in the region such as imperial surveillance technology, migration control and militarized borderscapes (Aas and Gundhus 2015; Barker 2012; Garelli and Tazzioli 2018; Huysmans 2000; Karyotis 2012; Kovras and Robins 2016; Lemberg-Pedersen 2013). Similarly, historians exploring the histories of imperial surveillance technology, migration control and militarized border and security forces in the Mediterranean have also tended to shy away from making direct connections to the contemporary political context of their research (Borutta and Borutta 2012; Huber 2012, 2013; Jackson 2013; Knight 2011; Neep 2012; Thomas 2008).

Despite their powerful analysis of both past and present Mediterranean militarized borderscapes, it can be argued that these bodies of scholarship are still both largely disconnected and mostly concerned with systems rather than how people on the move contest these. Consequently, the contestation of these coercive geographies and their continuous production has yet to fully harness the power of critiques that mobilize history against the current human rights breaches. What is thus also required at this moment, I would argue, is an emphasis on historicizing these militarized borderscapes from below or, as Postcolonial Security Studies scholars Jana Hönke and Markus-Michael Müller put it more eloquently, studies that unpack "(...) the entangled character of transnational fields of postcolonial (in)security governance (...)" (Hönke and Müller 2012: 384) and how these are negotiated in "(...) everyday forms of practice and local agency (...)" (Hönke and Müller 2012: 385).

Against this backdrop, I explore how Palestinian and Bedouin communities in the Gaza Strip negotiated confinement, displacement and precarity within the confines of the multilateral assemblage of Israeli, Egyptian and United Nations regimes of military surveillance and control from 1957 to 1967. Their struggle is one of the many that link the histories of Mediterranean imperial regimes to those of today. By making this connection through an empirical analysis, I hope to invite historical and contemporary scholars to both link their focus on past and present and shift attention beyond surveillance and control technologies to explore how itinerant people negotiate displacement, precarity and militarized confinement.

Conceptually, I frame the volume's overarching notion of coercive geographies within Jana Hönke and Markus-Michael Müller's understanding of the "(...) postcolonial condition of contemporary forms of transnational (in)security governance (...)" (Hönke and Müller 2012: 389). Overall, Hönke and Müller suggest that we are within a global set of "(...) interactions based on unequal power relations in an era that goes beyond the world of colonialism but that has been (and continues to be) decisively shaped by the logic of coloniality" (Hönke and Müller 2012: 385) although these are also continuously opposed by the agency of those governed in each and between postcolony through "(...) tacit forms of resistance and translation (...)" (Hönke and Müller 2012: 394). Embedded in this framing, this take on the notion of coercive geographies allows for empirical studies of how both national and international surveillance and control technologies, militarized confinement and deportation schemes are simultaneously experienced as insecurity and presented as guaranteeing security. Moreover, it also enables analyses that not only link these regimes and how people negotiate them in endless ways, but also does so in a fashion that centers the linkage between past and present regimes of militarized confinement and forms of resistance. Accordingly, the Palestinian and Bedouin communities can here be understood as the 'locals' of the 'postcolony' of the Gaza Strip who tacitly and less tacitly negotiated their displacement, precarity and confinement in various ways by challenging the transnational assemblage of coercive geographies they met in their everyday lives in their towns, villages, fields as well as in the surrounding military bases and camps.

Empirically, I draw upon unpublished records from the UN force that was operation in the Gaza Strip from 1957 to 1967, the United Nations Emergency Force (UNEF); the existing UN military body monitoring the Egyptian Israeli ceasefire, the Egyptian Israeli-Military Armistice Commission (EIMAC); and material from various departments at the UN headquarters in New York. I also draw upon published memoirs by UN soldiers. To contextualize these materials, I turn to research on British, Israeli and Egyptian histories of militarized migration regulation, surveillance and policing and Palestinian nationalism. While all material has gaps and silences (Trouillot 1995), both the records – which have been generated by the UN the process of governing the spaces and population of the Gaza Strip – and the memoirs can this in way effectively be read as a counter-archive.

The exploration of the various Palestinian and Bedouin struggles will unfold in three parts. Firstly, I examine how the Palestinians and the Bedouin negotiated the United Nations' internationalization of the pre-existing occasionally bordering Israeli and Egyptian regimes of military confinement, which had defined the Gaza Strip as a postcolonial coercive geography from 1948 to 1957.

Secondly, I investigate how the Palestinians and the Bedouin negotiated and contested the international regime of militarized confinement the United Nations Emergency Force enforced *along* the Armistice Demarcation Line (ADL), which functioned as the *de facto* border between the Gaza Strip and Israel. Thirdly, and centering the labor aspect, I explore how they negotiated displacement and precarity *within* the Gaza Strip in UNEF's bases and camps as well as their fields, villages and towns.

2   Negotiating the Internationalization of the Coercive Geography of the Gaza Strip, March 1957

When the units of the United Nations Emergency Force entered the Gaza Strip in March 1957, the resolve of the Palestinian and Bedouin communities in towns, villages and refugee camps had been tested for decades. Following the tightening of the Ottoman Empire's grip on Palestine, the subsequent nearly 25 years of British rule had further impoverished, marginalized and concentrated the majority of Palestinians and also constrained Bedouin migratory patterns between the Negev Desert in southern Jordan and the Sinai Desert in Egypt in favour of the growing Jewish settler colonial population. Unsurprisingly, the Palestinians both rioted and revolted leading to an intensifying process of militarization of space and everyday life as well as mobility restrictions up to the Second World War, which brought new hardships. In the subsequent Jewish ethnic cleansing of Palestine in 1948, more than 200,000 people, most of whom were peasants and smallholders, were forced from their homes into the coastal part of the already poor Southern District that became the little and overcrowded postcolony of the Gaza Strip. Thousands of Bedouin were also trapped and occasionally expelled forth and back by Egypt and Israel (El-Eini and Roza 1997; Khalaf 1997; Pappe 2004, 2006). Despite the launch of a UN relief effort, thousands of displaced families faced loss, poverty, disease and under-nourishment in this area only 5–10 kilometres by 40 kilometres (Baster 1955). Thus, many crossed into Israel to get belongings and crops from their former homes while Bedouin returned to their migration pattern. Cairo reacted by both expanding the Egyptian security forces to contain them and forming the Palestine Borders Guard to control the militants (Feldman 2015; Yasigh 1997: 60–64). Similarly, Tel Aviv began jailing Palestinian 'infiltrators' until initiating a 'shoot-to-kill policy from 1951 to 1954, which cost thousands of Palestinian lives and further reduced the number of women crossing the ADL (Korn 2003). Egypt and Israel thus turned the postcolony into a coercive geography that provided neither improved living standards and self-governance nor return while enforcing displacement and immobility. Accordingly, both young male refugees and Egyptian-organized guardsmen increased their number of 'infiltrations.' sabotage actions and attacks, thus provoking Israel in particular. By October 1956, their 'infiltrations' along with the Egyptian purchase of Soviet arms led Israel to both attack Egypt in the Sinai Peninsula and occupy the Gaza Strip (Bartal 2011; Laron 2009; Sayigh 1997: 64–66).

As noted, UNEF arrived in March 1957. However, the Palestinians and Bedouin were not ready to let the UN take control after enduring several months of Israeli occupation, plundering, arbitrary arrests and mass killings that left an estimated 1,000 people dead (Sayigh 1997: 65) in addition to the previous eight years (for which the UN also bore responsibility, having co-legitimized and co-enabled the formation of the Jewish settler colonial state (Ben-Dror 2007, 2013, 2014)). Both UNEF records and memoirs by UNEF soldiers and officers make this very clear. Initially, Palestinians in the towns, rich and poor alike, likely failed to be impressed by UNEF's installation of military governors and use of loudspeaker vans proclaiming in Arabic that the Gaza Strip was under UN control (Burns 1962: 261; Engholm 1996: 231). Similarly, UNEF's use of the former British and Israeli fortified garrison in Gaza City for its headquarters and subsequent suppression of a prison riot initiated by political prisoners probably also did little to improve its standing (Burns 1962: 231; Jensen 2005: 89; Kjeldsen 1958: 54; Sköld 1990: 81). On the second day, however, UNEF's reaction to a protest in Gaza City with thousands of working- and middle-class male and female town dwellers clearly angered the protestors, resulting in the UN unit's retreat into a school behind barricades, sandbags and machine guns mounted on the roof. A day later, another demonstration ended with a UN unit needing backup (that arrived with many soldiers in underwear or kitchen aprons and riot gear). In response, UNEF banned rallies and large public gatherings. Drawing upon their experience of protesting, subverting and resisting the British (Hughes 2019; Swedenburg 2003), the Palestinian working and middle classes and elites alike in turn joined to field an oppositional press and more protests to fight the UN-led joint militarization and reduction of public space. This led the Yugoslavian unit to declare its solidarity and refuse to serve in the Gaza Strip and also forced the Egyptian government to send back the Governor-General and declare UNEF an ally in the Gaza press (Burns 1962: 261–271; Jensen 2005: 91–94). Tellingly, these actions also compelled the UN Secretary-General – who had already noted UNEF to be "(...) on thin ice (...)" (Minutes of Advisory Committee, 7 March 1957) in a meeting with UNEF's Advisory Committee in New York – to go to Cairo (Minutes of Advisory Committee, 16 March 1957). While the Secretary-General and the UNEF Commander managed to reject the Egyptian wish for joint patrols (itself a result of

Palestinian pressure), UNEF had to accept both the Egyptian return and its authority to patrol only on the ADL (Burns 1962: 274–275).

In this way, the Palestinians, native to Gaza or displaced as well as rich and poor, thus reduced the military space UNEF was carving out in the towns of Gaza City, Rafah, Khan Yunis and Deir El Bellah with UNEF's units relocating out of the towns to nearby sites. In extension they also prevented the provisional joint UNEF and UNRWA administration directed from New York as envisioned by the UN Secretariat by bringing the Egyptian forward return by several months (Ottovay Jørgensen 2016: 198–200). However, they were unable to challenge UNEF's composition, which the Egyptian government had been forced to accept due to pressure from the American government. Reflecting its pro-western orientation, UNEF comprized of units from NATO, Commonwealth or other pro-Western states as well as neutral and non-aligned states, some of which had deeper colonial histories (Ottovay Jørgensen 2016: 154–177). Additionally, neither Palestinians, Bedouin nor Egyptians had any say over how UNEF came to resemble the British imperial force in Palestine. As had the British (Hoffman 2013; Hughes 2013; Johnson 2015; Kroizer 2004; Sinclair 2009; Thomas 2008), UNEF deployed light infantry units, reconnaissance units, and light aircraft in addition to the military observers from EIMAC. With nearly 6,000 troops (who all similarly lived separately from the society they monitored and regulated), however, UNEF was a significantly larger force in a smaller area than the permanent British imperial security forces that had covered all of Palestine until the Palestinian revolt in 1936 had necessitated additional forces from other imperial territories (Hughes 2019: 3).

Palestinian resolve also influenced how UNEF set up along the ADL. Prior to UNEF's arrival, internal proposals – produced by American and Dutch EIMAC military observers, who thus drew upon long institutional histories of violent colonialism and imperialism – had proposed a 100 meter wide and 59 kilometer long UNEF zone on both sides of the ADL with permanent and semi-permanent fortified watchtowers with defences and quarters for the units along the ADL, which was to be marked by a full-length bull-dozed ditch with a border fence and several fences in 'trouble areas'(Israel Administration of GAZA, Cable from Acting Chief of Staff UNTSO to UNEF Force Commander 20 February 1957). Whether the UN Secretary-General or UNEF's Commander realized or not, these extreme proposals to control the border zone, and thus Palestinian and Bedouin mobilities, would not only have turned the Gaza Strip into a more extreme coercive geography than already the case. They would also have replicated the British militarization of Palestine with fortified garrisons, frontier forts, border fences and patrol roads (Hughes 2019). Palestinian pressure, however, ensured that UNEF scaled back the most extreme aspects of these proposals and settled for a 59 kilometer and 100-meter wide zone on (the Gaza side of) the ADL with no fence, only some parts of the ADL marked by a shallow ditch, 72 unfortified observation towers with overlapping lines of sight and a field telephone network, a day and night patrol regime as well as some patrol roads and dog units. Nevertheless, the UNEF regime was better geared to enforce confinement in the postcolony of the Gaza Strip than the British had been in imperial Palestine due to the mobile ADL patrols, the real-time communication network and the grid of connected observation towers (Complaints and Investigations April 1957–June 1957, EIMAC Reports 4 April and 15 May 1957), which partly also mirrored the mesh of overlapping Israeli settlements across the ADL (Rotbard 2003).

Altogether, the arrival and set up of the UN force on the ADL added an international component to the existing assemblage of coercive geographies, which both Palestinians and Bedouin would find came to constitute a new and more intense yet familiar borderscape that would impede their mobilities to a higher extent than previously.

3   Negotiating Militarized Confinement along the ADL
       from 1957 to 1967

Although the altered assemblage of coinciding regimes of (in)security would define the lives of many Palestinian and Bedouin from April 1957 onwards, many – men and women as well as children and adults – would also subvert, confront and take advantage of UNEF's presence to challenge their lives of displacement, precarity and confinement. For example, Palestinian boys and male youth from poor families in both refugee camps and ADL villages risked being detained by the UN or killed by the Israelis when stealing apples, melons and grapes from Israeli settlements. The most entrepreneurial would also sell the stolen fruit to UN soldiers, learning quickly which units were open to buying and bartering. Others managed to persuade the UN soldiers to allow them to do their homework away from the overcrowded refugee camps and villages (Complaints and Investigations April 1957–June 1957, EIMAC Report 1 June 1957; Complaints and Investigations July 1957–December 1957, EIMAC Reports 6 and 27 August 1957). While most ADL interactions between adult Palestinians and UNEF soldiers were cursory and undramatic, many also escalated into fist fights, knife fights and occasionally shootings. Some incidents reflected misunderstandings of location, disagreements about UNEF authority or familial responses to young or unmarried Palestinian women being detained by UN soldiers (Complaints and Investigations July 1957–December 1957, EIMAC Reports

1 July and 1 October 1957; Complaints and Investigations January 1958–June 1958, EIMAC Report 3 January 1958; Middle East, Cable from UNEF Commander to Undersecretary of the UN 4 April 1959). Other incidents showed how Palestinian refugees encountered Egyptian, UNEF or Israeli soldiers during the night when returning from harvesting crops on their old lands or stealing from/ attacking Israeli settlements. Upon detection by UNEF's patrols or ambushes, they would engage in firefights to avoid apprehension, which in some cases cost them their lives (Complaints and Investigations April 1957–June 1957, EIMAC Reports 5, 7 and 14 June 1957). Finally, some of the nearly 31,000 Bedouin confined in the Gaza Strip also attacked UNEF's ADL units. Forced into immobility and confinement by British, Egyptian and Israeli security regimes, the Bedouin loathed being immobilized and coerced into refugee camps. Some tried to reclaim their mobility, which in some instances led to violence. Typically, the Bedouin would remove anti-personnel mines and anti-vehicle mines from Israeli and Egyptian mine fields and then place them on UNEF's patrol roads, a tactic they had also used against the British (Complaints and Investigations April 1957–June 1957, EIMAC Reports 15 May and 26 June 1957; Complaints and Investigations July 1957–December 1957, 29 and 30 July 1957).

Overall, however, UNEF's presence – with the Israeli and Egyptian regimes on either side – further reduced Palestinian and Bedouin mobility though enforced confinement. For example, the Danish-Norwegian units conducted 4,180 patrols in six months in their ADL sector alone (DANOR BN IX, 1961). Predictably, the number of Palestinians captured and tried by Israel dropped no less than 16% in the first year after UNEF's arrival on the ADL (Korn 2003). Additionally, the Egyptian police was present in and monitored both everyday life and politics in most towns in the Gaza Strip. On its part, the Israeli air force would also have loud and low flying Israeli jet fighters from nearby air force bases overfly the Gaza Strip, reminding the Palestinians and Bedouin of their simultaneous confinement and displacement. For example, 41% of the 1,157 sightings of Israeli fighter planes between April 1959 and April 1961 in the same Danish-Norwegian sector of the ADL alone were illegal overflights, many of which were as low as 200 meters (Final Reports from DANOR BN VI-IX, 1959–1961). Off the coast, Palestinian fishermen were also often threatened and cut off by Israeli naval vessels (Complaints and Investigations April 1957– June 1957, EIMAC Report 12 April 1957; Reports, Weekly Report for period 16 April to 22 April 1960). Moreover, UNEF units also occasionally missed Israeli settlers attacking Palestinian villages or Israeli military patrols 'infiltrating' the Gaza Strip to test both UNEF and Egyptian responses and response times, adding to Palestinian insecurities (Complaints and Investigations April 1957– June 1957, EIMAC Report 27 June 1957). Inside the Gaza Strip, the Egyptian police also monitored everyone, having set up a 'security society' (Feldman 2011, 2015).

In response to this increasingly militarized and hardening borderscape, especially displaced working- and middle-class Palestinians in the refugee camps grew frustrated with their enforced confinement and the lack of progress on the issue of their right to return. In one expression of this anger, Palestinians fired upon a UNEF camp with around 120–140 soldiers near the ADL (Complaints and Investigations May 1959–December 1959, EIMAC Report 29 November 1959). In turn, the Egyptians began to channel these energies driven by displacement, precarity and confinement away from the ADL – and thus UNEF's military areas – into Palestinian-run organisations and movements. However, some of these organisations – such as, for example, the newly formed Fatah – were both increasingly radical and looking beyond the Arab nationalist project Egypt had hitherto used to absorb Palestinian political ambitions. Hoping to channel Palestinian rage into the Border Guard Corps (which it controlled), Egypt expanded both the number of men from nearly 2,000 to approximately 3,600 and the number of Palestinians. Between 1962 and 1965, Cairo also encouraged Gaza Palestinians to join the Egyptian forces fighting a proxy war with Saudi Arabia in Yemen (Sayigh 1997: 66, 80–94). From 1965 to UNEF's withdrawal in 1967, Cairo likely also avoided a conflict between the newly formed Palestine Liberation Army (PLA) and UNEF about UNEF's areas and facilities. At the heart of the potential conflict was how the Palestine Liberation Organization PLO – which operated in the Arab states hosting displaced Palestinians – had pressured Egypt into accepting that the PLA, which was to operate training bases and field thousands of troops in the states hosting the PLO, would replace the Border Guard Corps. Keen to avoid conflict, however, Cairo deliberately devitalized the PLA, so it was run by Egyptian officers, suffered from a lack of facilities and equipment and was never fully manned, reaching only the same level of troops as the Border Guard Corps of 3,500 rather than the desired 11,500 (Sayigh 1997: 112–142; 1998). Seeking to reduce social pressure in the Gaza Strip, Egypt also initiated a temporary work migration scheme to the Gulf states, which successfully saw thousands of people going to send money home in contrast to previous attempts to resettle thousands of families to Egypt in 1954 and earlier in 1959 that had led to nothing but large demonstrations (Cossali and Robson 1986: 54; Sayigh 1997: 68).

Altogether, it seems fair to say that although every Palestinian and Bedouin in the Gaza Strip were confined within that territory it affected people differently. As can be deduced from the above, the Palestinian elite did not spend much time in the ADL zone or cross into Israel. Rather, especially the displaced Palestinians and the immobilized Bedouin did. Challenging confinement in the unforgiving refugee camps, the coercive geographies of the 'postcolony' and, not least, the broader border landscape, they forced significant concessions and changes throughout the period from 1957 to 1967. At the same time, however, the multilateral assemblage upholding the coercive geographies was neither removed nor replaced (until Israel began occupying the Gaze Strip from June 1967). As will be shown in the following section, a similar dynamic shaped how people in the Gaza Strip contested displacement and precarity in UNEF bases and camps as well as in their towns, villages and fields.

4   Negotiating Displacement and Precarity within the Gaza Strip from 1957 to 1967

Paradoxically perhaps, one of the ways in which Palestinians sought to challenge displacement and/or precarity was through employment with both UNEF and UNRWA, the United Nations Relief and Works Agency. However, the unemployment rate for residents at 30–35% and 80–90% for refugees, which reflected the paralyzed (post-conflict) economics since 1948, meant that any job would have had multiple possible applicants. UNEF also never took on more than 1,200 local employees – the majority of whom were part-time and unskilled – despite being urged by the Egyptians to both hire Palestinians and replace previously hired Egyptians with Palestinians to add more jobs to the area in the same way that UNRWA had added 4,000–7,000 jobs (Estimates 1958, UNEF HQ Analysis of locally recruited civilian staff 23 September 1958, Costs 1957–1967, Cost estimates, 7 May 1965). Furthermore, Egypt did not lift its 1948 ban Palestinians from organizing in unions and striking (despite allowing the formation of a Legislative Council in 1958 and creating a constitution for the Gaza Strip in 1962). Finally, the rising prices – which were driven by the large number of rental contracts and significant purchases of local goods and produce by both UNEF and its international civilian staff with salaries wildly beyond level of the Gaza Strip – would also encourage acceptance of bad working conditions. Food prices, for example, increased about 300% from an already high level from 1963 to 1967 (Costs 1957–1967, Message 'Petition.' 25 July 1966). While challenging, this combination did not hold back the Palestinian UNEF employees, however. If anything, they tried to make the most of their situations whether in the supply and maintenance units in HQ and battalion bases near the larger towns such as Gaza City and Rafah, canteen sections in smaller company camps near small towns and villages closer to the ADL or as guardsmen in officers' villas. Holding various positions in different locations, people applied different strategies. For example, canteen staff in the bigger bases, especially in the largest UNEF base in Rafah, lowered their service levels in response to learning of different salaries for the same jobs or deteriorations in working conditions. In one instance, the Chief Administrative Officer noted that: "(...) it would be playing with dynamite to touch the Rafah kitchens any further than has already been done" (Locals, Personnel Duties and Regulations, Message 'Wage Scales' 5 October 1967). Instrumentalizing the soldiers' need to eat several of their meals in the canteens, the workers used internal pressure: "Furthermore, troop morale can be a very touchy problem and their food is a very important and delicate alement" (Locals, Personnel Duties and Regulations, Message 'Wage Scales.' 5 October 1967). As the problem developed with new contingents, UNEF noted how the workers not only continued but also mobilized without unionizing or striking: "A large number of civilian employees in Camp Rafah have become restive over their lack of progress, lack of pay progression, and inequalities which exist between similar employees from one location to another" (General Administration/Discipline, Message 'Unrest-Civilian Employees.' 29 October 1966). Elsewhere, Palestinian truck drivers would file complaints for unfounded dismissals without the right to organize, which even UNEF's Legal Advisor found problematic: "The fact that our locally recruited labour has been denied trade union rights is an added reason why UNEF should be a 'model employer'" (Local Personnel, Disciplinary Procedures and Action, Privileges and Immunities of UNEF, Message from Legal and Political Advisor to Chief Administrative Officer, 17 December 1962). Another example could be how guards at officers' villas would also use the UN Declaration of Human Rights and the conventions of the International Labor Organization to protest 12-hour work days, 56-hour weeks and dismissals for sleeping following 5% reductions in staff (Staff Relations and Appeals, Message from Chief of Staff to Commander, 16 March 1963). Workers would also break regulations to safeguard their families. Refugees working part-time, in particular, would fail to report their refugee status to UNEF when obtaining work as their salaries would reduce their UNRWA rations without regard for the increasing costs of living (Local Staff Regulations, Message from Chief Administrative Officer to all Unit Commanders and Liaison Officers, 24 January 1958). However, the rising prices affected, UNEF acknowledged, "(...) the middle and lower classes and particularly those in governmental departments and on fixed salaries (...)" (Weekly Reports 1957, 'Summary of General Situation' from Chairman EIMAC to Chief of Staff UNTSO, 22 April 1957).

While most people in the villages of the Gaza Strip had not been displaced in 1948, all lived with the consequences of the ethnic cleansing in 1948 and the violent creation of the Gaza Strip out of a coastal piece of Palestine's southern district. Unable to get support from UNRWA, the poorest of the residents in a

poor district that became even poorer and smaller suffered massively from enforced confinement and immobility, the loss of farmland, the railway, energy
supplies, trade networks and markets, the rising costs of living, and, not least,
the influx of more than 200,000 displaced people, most of whom were also
poor peasants, land tenants and unskilled laborers. Those who had not been
among the nearly 4,000 smallholders and landowners to lose their land in 1948
had no choice but to attend their remaining land, surviving as subsistence
farmers or smallholders and selling what produce they could in town markets
(Filiu 2014: 106). Consequently, many peasants, land tenants and their relatives
working alongside them near the ADL encountered UNEF units regularly. Most
often, they were able to work their land or plots, even if entering the UNEF-
controlled no-go zone near the ADL. As noted previously, however, some would
be either sent away or detained, which occasionally led to fights. Many also
struggled with the loss of land to UNEF's numerous camps, posts, storage areas,
parking lots and roads and the destruction of crops, trees and hedges by UNEF
vehicles. Using communal power, the villagers and some larger landowners accordingly piled pressure on the Egyptians who passed their complaints on to
UNEF. In this way, they forced UNEF to set up a scheme that compensated
hundreds of people financially over several years. UNEF even shifted to direct
payments to prevent the Egyptians from taking credit, which likely appealed to
Cairo given their Palestinian partners' plantation expansions that reduced the
arable land available. Every new UNEF contingent was also ordered to avoid
damage to Palestinian property (Land Claims, Message 'Claims against UNEF'
from UN Legal Counsel to UN General-Secretary, 8 November 1957; Land
Claims, Letter 'Payment of Land Claims' from Legal Adviser to Chief Finance
Officer, 23 May 1960; Land Claims, Message 'Planting of Trees' from Chief Operations Officer, 11 June 1965; Land Claims, "Complaint" from Civilian Claimant
to UNEF, 24 May 1967).

Similarly, middle- and working-class town dwellers also sought to improve
their situations. The small middle class, which consisted of shopkeepers,
tradesmen, teachers, and former Mandate civil servants, was far from wealthy
and many had also been struggling since 1948 as had urban and semi-rural
working-class people such as fishermen, textile workers, unskilled construction workers, irrigation workers, fruit pickers and fruit drivers. Finally, the Palestinians who had been displaced in 1948 but had been able to buy or rent
places in the towns also faced significant challenges (Baster 1955; Sayigh 1997:
44). Especially the aforementioned increasingly expensive rental contracts
and rising costs of living proved challenging following the Israeli occupation.
After six weeks, connected Palestinians took up the problem with their Egyptian contacts. Accordingly, the UN observers in the Egyptian Israeli-Military

Armistice Commission (EIMAC), who also had Egyptian contacts, reported upwards in the system that "The cost of living in Gaza continues to rise as more UNEF funds are spent in the area. Many locals are complaining that there is no rent or price control as formerly." (Weekly Reports 1957, 'Summary of General Situation' from Chairman EIMAC to Chief of Staff UNTSO, 22 April 1957). The situation was not helped by UNEF soldiers partaking in the black-market economy of the Gaza Strip, which was mostly an urban phenomenon. Only four months into UNEF's presence, the Egyptian Governor-General in the Gaza Strip summoned UNEF to discuss this along with the UN soldiers' use of brothels and altercations when off-duty and drunk (Confidential Documents 1956–1960, UNEF Minutes of meeting with Governor General of the Gaza Strip and the Egyptian Liaison Staff, 7 Aug. 1957). UNEF, however, did not address these labor issues. In turn, the Egyptian administration was forced both to hire of middle-class Palestinians and to offer further subsidies for those unable to claim refugee status and thus UNRWA rations (Cossali and Robson 1986: 18–23).

While also confined within the coercive geography of the postcolony, the Palestinian elite – which lived in the towns despite their comparatively large land holdings in the Gaza Strip – benefitted from how the joint Egyptian–UNEF regime upheld displacement and precarity within the coercive geography of the postcolony due to their symbiotic relationship with the Egyptians and the socio-economic inequalities and class differences it both reflected and reinforced. Commenting on Egyptian–Palestinian relations in the Gaza Strip from 1948 to 1967 historian Nathan Shachar notes how "the Egyptians, sometimes in tandem with old rich Gazan families functioned as a superior caste, controlling and taxing every economic initiative, from prostitution – the cheap brothels of Gaza were well known in Cairo and drew many visitors – to the valuable and beneficial projects" (Shachar 2010: 67). Within a few months of the arrival of UNEF, the Palestinian elite was both able to pressure the Egyptian administration into helping them and was placed in society in a way that ensured they would benefit from UNEF's presence. Firstly, the Egyptians were persuaded to exempt the Gaza Strip from taxation. The largest beneficiaries, the Palestinian elite was able to expand its hitherto few and relatively insignificant citrus fruit farms to a rather expansive plantation landscape that came to take up to ten times more land than previously. This expansion not only grabbed valuable arable land. It also offered profits through sales to Egypt, UNEF, UNRWA and the small middle class and allowed the Palestinian elite access to construction materials and industrial equipment, which Egypt would trade for parts of their increased yield in Eastern Europe (Cossali and Robson 1986: 18–23). Secondly, UNEF was also proving beneficial. Case in point, an internal UNEF report observed this dynamic six weeks after arriving, noting that "(...) the business classes are feeling the beneficial effect of the increased spending (...)" (Weekly Reports 1957, 'Summary of General Situation' from Chairman EIMAC to Chief of Staff UNTSO, 22 April 1957). Thirdly, the elite also persuaded Cairo to tolerate Palestinian merchant networks was beginning to ship luxury goods from Lebanon into the Gaza Strip on fishing boats that visiting Egyptians subsequently bought at lower prices than in Egypt due to currency restrictions (Cossali and Robson 1986: 18–23).

Aside the gains enjoyed by the Palestinian elite, the overall picture did not change despite the Palestinian middle- and working-classes' best and multifaceted efforts. Displacement and precarity dominated and created extreme and desperate situations and people. One example of this could be how a group of Palestinians waiting for day jobs outside UN camps stormed the camp out of desperation, leading to one worker being shot to death by the camp guards (Complaints and Investigations April 1957–June 1957, EIMAC Report 18 April 1957). Another could be a 20-year old Palestinian woman, who had been forced to marry a poor and unemployed 50-year old man against her will, and who sought to kill herself by way of Israeli units at the ADL. When interrogated by UN soldiers after being transferred from Israel, she explained: "I crossed the ADL because I am angry with this life and wanted to be killed." (Complaints and Investigations January 1958–June 1958, 'Incident Report' 7 March 1958). Telling of reign of insecurity in the postcolony, thousands of working class and middle class people took part in the Egyptian administration's aforementioned scheme to work in the Gulf states and send home money in the late 1950s onwards.

For Egypt, the scheme also served to reduce the number of labor activists, many of whom would migrate and engage in radical labor politics in the Gulf States (Chalcraft 2011). Despite their profound efforts, the Palestinians (and Bedouin) in the Gaza Strip were thus not able to challenge their overall state of displacement, confinement and precarity. If anything, most were worse off than previously, under the multilateral assemblage of postcolonial (in)security governance in the coercive geography of the Gaza Strip.

5   Conclusion: The Gaza Strip Coercive Geography and Other Postcolonial (In)security Governance Regimes

As demonstrated, the Palestinians and the Bedouin in the Gaza Strip faced hardships due to displacement, precarity and multilateral militarized confinement, within what I have here termed a coercive geography, from 1948 to 1967.

However, the departure of both UNEF and the Egyptian military forces and administration from the Gaza Strip on account of the war in June 1967 did not signal the end of this particular expression of the postcolonial regime of (in-)security governance. If anything, it marked the beginning of a far more brutal new coercive geography under direct Israeli military rule.

Until 2005, the people of the Gaza Strip faced decades of Israeli expansion policies that saw the establishment of more than 20 Jewish settlements and manifestly cruel Israeli military law, which removed any pretence of a justice system and further militarized everyday life. As Sara Roy noted, "(...) the cumulative effect of the nearly 1,000 military orders issued since 1967 inside the Gaza Strip has been to retard almost all economic and social development" (Roy 2006: 45). Facing economic decline, poverty, overcrowding, military rule and intergenerational displacement (to the 5th generation), the residents of the Gaza Strip, once again, turned to riots and revolts in 1987: refugee women in the Gaza Strip threw the first rocks in the first Intifada. Lasting years, this escalatory cycle saw further civic and socio-economic erosion. In 1991, the American invasion of Iraq also cut off the remittances from Palestinian workers in Israel and the Gulf States, which both expanded the supplementary feeding programmes from 8,500 children to 34,000 children and increased the number of people receiving emergency food relief by 70,000 refugee families and 34,000 non-refugee families (Roy 2006). Under international pressure, Israel then engaged in the Oslo Process without being fully committed to any genuine attempt to build peace with the Palestinians. Within a few years, however, the Palestinians launched the second Intifada, prompting Israel to shift its approach to controlling the Gaza Strip and thus how the Palestinians (and Bedouin) were to be kept displaced, confined and without means to retaliate.

In 2005, Israel 'disengaged' from the Gaza Strip, seemingly establishing a permanent border and returning to the former paradigm of 1948 to 1967. However, as argued by Yves Winter, this new stance represented neither disengagement nor an actual border. With both a UN military force and Egypt absent from the Gaza Strip, Israel established what Winter calls a 21st century siege focused on both creating a "(...) new matrix of rule, one that operates through comprehensive closure, punctured by periodic military escalations and the generalized use of extrajudicial assassinations" (Winter 2016: 308) and on generating coercive spaces by "(...) compressing and condensing the circulations and movements that constitute social life and by a general suspension of mobility around the perimeter" (Winter 2016: 310). Each year, this 'disengagement' involved hundreds of systematic killings, the destruction of infrastructure in large-scale military campaigns, the use of militarized surveillance such as drones (on which the Israeli economy is partially reliant), severe restrictions on food imports, and the closure of the border for Palestinian workers who had previously worked in Israel. As intended, the unemployment and poverty rates went up while the GDP went down. Some years later, nearly three quarters of all households received humanitarian aid. In response, the Palestinians built hundreds, if not thousands, of both missiles to counterattack and tunnels to Egypt to procure food, medicine, fuel etc. Alongside the Israeli destruction of these missile launchers and tunnels (which Egypt has also begun to destroy), the Hamas government set up a regulatory regime that Winter sees as representing, "(...) the regularization of precariousness, the legal and administrative normalization of uncertain supply mechanisms, and the institutionalization of officially sanctioned profiteering" (Winter 2016: 316).

Since 2005, several thousand Palestinians in the Gaza Strip have been killed by Israeli forces in military operations, unknown numbers of people have died from the effects of living under siege or have been imprisoned without trial, and an unknown number of properties have been destroyed, all witnessed by the rest of the world. At the time of writing, the coercive geography of the Gaza Strip remains, in the words of Ilan Pappé, "(...) a maximum security prison camp" (Pappé 2017: 219) despite the UN having predicted that the Gaza Strip should be classified as uninhabitable by 2020 (Pappé 2017: 228).

An extreme example of a coercive geography (or a postcolonial regime of (in)security governance in Hönke and Müller's framing), the Gaza Strip points to the imperial histories of the new neoliberal normal across the southern and eastern coastlines of the Mediterranean, in different ways: a large but still growing number of people from numerous Middle Eastern and African postcolonies, challenging and protesting their various circumstances of displacement, precarity and confinement on the one hand, and an increasingly fine-meshed multilateral assemblage of (at times collaborating or overlapping and at others competing) postcolonial regimes of (in)security governance seeking to control and expel itinerant people in a rising number of coercive geographies on the other (while the providers of surveillance and military technologies focus on profit).

Yet, we need a wider perspective. Looking beyond the Mediterranean, the emergence of a global and world-making set of entangled coercive geographies (or postcolonial regimes of (in)security governance) amount to what Michel Agier calls "(...) the management of the undesirable on a planetary scale" (Agier 2016: 18). Accordingly, we need to make our work, as Agier notes, "(...) a political project of contemporary urgency" (Agier 2016: 18). Hönke and Müller are thus correct in suggesting that we need to challenge "(...) the legacies of colonial forms of rule, knowledge production and subjectification that continue to shape our contemporary world, where 'real' colonies have nearly ceased to exist" (Hönke and Müller 2012: 385). Whether historians or social scientists working on historical topics, we have a duty to keep working towards a global emancipatory politics of history that offers the practice of history a horizon beyond itself, and works actively as (part of a broader system of) democratizing practice, no matter the discipline or realm of society.

References

Aas, K.F., and Gundhus, H.O.I. (2015). "Policing Humanitarian Borderlands: Frontex, Human Rights and the Precariousness of Life," *British journal of criminology* 55(1): 1–18.

Agier, M. (2016). *Managing the Undesirables: Refugee Camps and Humanitarian Government*. Cambridge: Polity.

Barker, V. (2012). "Global Mobility and Penal Order: Criminalizing Migration, A View from Europe," *Sociology compass* 6(2): 113–121.

Bartal, S. (2011). *The Fedayeen Emerge: The Palestine-Israel Conflict, 1949–1956*. Bloomington: AuthorHouse.

Baster, J. (1955). "Economic Problems in the Gaza Strip," *The Middle East Journal* 9(3): 323–327.

Ben-Dror, E. (2007). "How the United Nations intended to implement the partition plan: The handbook drawn up by the secretariat for the members of the United Nations Palestine commission," *Middle Eastern Studies* 43(6): 997–1008.

Ben-Dror, E. (2013). "The United Nations Plan to Establish an Armed Jewish Force to Implement the Partition Plan (United Nations Resolution 181)," *Diplomacy and statecraft* 24(4): 559–578.

Ben-Dror, E. (2014). "The success of the Zionist strategy vis-à-vis UNSCOP," *Israel Affairs* 20(1): 19–39.

Borutta, M., and Borutta, S. (2012). "A Colonial Sea: the Mediterranean, 1798–1956," *European Review of History* 19(1): 1–13.

Burns, E.L.M. (1962). *Between Arab and Israeli*. New York: George Harrap and Co.

Chalcraft, J. (2011). "Migration and Popular Protest in the Arabian Peninsula and the Gulf in the 1950s and 1960s," *International Labor and Working-Class History* 79(1): 28–47.

Complaints and Investigations April 1957–June 1957, Gaza Strip, Area Files, Political Affairs, EIMAC, S-0375-0073-0003, United Nations Archive.

Complaints and Investigations July 1957–December 1957, Gaza Strip, Area Files, Political Affairs, EIMAC, S-0375-0073-0003, United Nations Archive.

Complaints and Investigations January 1958–June 1958, Gaza Strip, Area Files, Pol. Affairs, EIMAC, S-0375-0067-0002, United Nations Archive.

Complaints and Investigations July 1958–April 1959, Gaza Strip, Area Files, Pol. Affairs, EIMAC, S-0375-0067-0003, United Nations Archive.

Complaints and Investigations May 1959–December 1959, Gaza Strip, Area Files, Pol. Affairs, EIMAC, S-0375-0067-0004, United Nations Archive.

Confidential Documents 1956–1960, UN Field Operations Service, S-0534-0246, United Nations Archive.

Cossali, P., and Robson, C. (1986). *Stateless in Gaza*. London: Zed Books.

Costs 1957–1967, Staff International and Local, Local Staff Administration, Chief Administrator Officer's Files, S-1773-0000-0192, United Nations Archive.

DANOR BN IX (1961). *DANOR BN IX – October 1960-April 1961*. October 1960–April 1961. DANOR BN, United Nations Emergency Force.

El-Eini, R.I.M. (1997). "Rural indebtedness and agricultural credit supplies in Palestine in the 1930s," *Middle Eastern Studies* 33(2): 313–337.

Engholm, C. (1996). *Fremmedlegionær og dansk oberst: Carl Engholms erindringer i krig og fred 1913-1979*. Lyngby: Dansk historisk håndbogsforlag.

Estimates 1958, Local Staff, Chief Administrator Officer's Files, S-1773-0000-0004, United Nations Archive.

Feldman, I. (2011). "Observing the Everyday: Policing and the Conditions of Possibility in Gaza, 1948–1967," *Interventions* 9(3): 414–433.

Feldman, I. (2015). *Police Encounters: Security and Surveillance in Gaza under Egyptian Rule*.

Filiu, J.-P. (2014). *Gaza: A History*. London: Hurst & Company.

Garelli, G., and Tazzioli, M. (2018). "The biopolitical warfare on migrants: EU Naval Force and NATO operations of migration government in the Mediterranean," *Critical Military Studies* 4(2): 181–200.

General Administration/Discipline 1964–1967, Local Staff Regulations – General Policy, Chief Administrator Officer's Files, S-530-0126-0005, United Nations Archive.

Hoffman, B. (2013). "The Palestine Police Force and the challenges of gathering counterterrorism intelligence, 1939–1947," *Small Wars & Insurgencies* 24(4): 609–647.

Hönke, J., and Müller, M.M. (2012). "Governing (in)security in a postcolonial world: Transnational entanglements and the worldliness of 'local' practice," *Security Dialogue* 43(5): 383–401.

Huber, V. (2012). "Connecting Colonial Seas: The 'International Colonisation' of Port Said and the Suez Canal During and After the First World War," *European review of history* 19(1): 141–161.

Huber. V. (2013). *Channelling Mobilities: Migration and Globalisation in the Suez Canal Region and Beyond, 1869-1914*. Cambridge: Cambridge University Press.

Hughes, M. (2013). "A British 'Foreign Legion'? The British Police in Mandate Palestine," *Middle Eastern Studies* 49(5): 696–711.

Hughes, M. (2019). *Britain's Pacification of Palestine: The British Army, the Colonial State, and the Arab Revolt, 1936–1939*.

Huysmans, J. (2000). "The European Union and the Securitization of Migration," *JCMS: Journal of Common Market Studies* 38(5): 751–777.

Israel Administration of GAZA January to March 1957, Gaza Strip, Area Files, Political Affairs, EIMAC, S-0375-0069-0005, United Nations Archive.

Jackson, S. (2013). "Diaspora Politics and Developmental Empire: The Syro-Lebanese at the League Of Nations," *The Arab Studies Journal* 21(1): 166–190.

Jensen, O. (2005). *Kompagni Larsen: Vordingborg – Ægypten Tur-Retur November 1956 – Maj 1957*. Lyngby: private publication.

Johnson, R. (2015). "Command of the Army, Charles Gwynn and Imperial Policing: The British Doctrinal Approach to Internal Security in Palestine, 1919–29," *Journal of imperial and Commonwealth history* 43(4): 570–589.

Karyotis, G. (2012). "Securitization of Migration in Greece: Process, Motives, and Implications," *International Political Sociology* 6(4): 390–408.

Khalaf, I. (1997). "The Effect of Socioeconomic Change on Arab Societal Collapse in Mandate Palestine," *International Journal of Middle East Studies* 29(1): 93–112.

Kjeldsen, N. (1958). *Fredens soldater*. Copenhagen: Hjemmevaernsfonden.

Knight, J. (2011). "Securing Zion? Policing in British Palestine, 1917–39," *European Review of History* 18(4): 523–543.

Korn, A. (2003). "From Refugees to Infiltrators: Constructing Political Crime in Israel in the 1950s," *International Journal of the Sociology of Law* 31(1): 1–22.

Kovras, I., and Robins, S. (2016). "Death as the border: Managing missing migrants and unidentified bodies at the EU's Mediterranean frontier," *Political geography* 55(C): 40–49. DOI: 10.1016/j.polgeo.2016.05.003.

Kroizer, G. (2004). "From Dowbiggin to Tegart: Revolutionary change in the colonial police in Palestine during the 1930s," *The Journal of Imperial and Commonwealth History* 32(4): 115–133.

Land Claims, Claims outside Contracts, Contracts, Leases, Insurance and Claims, Privileges and Immunities of UNEF, Legal Affairs, Chief Administrator Officer's Files, S-1773-0000-0004, United Nations Archive.

Laron, G. (2009). "'Logic dictates that they may attack when they feel they can win': the 1955 Czech-Egyptian arms deal, the Egyptian army, and Israeli intelligence," *The Middle East journal* 63(1): 69–84.

Lemberg-Pedersen, M. (2013). "Private Security Companies and the European Borderscapes," *The Migration Industry: The commercialization of international migration*. Available at: https://vbn.aau.dk/en/publications/private-security-companies-and-the-european-borderscapes (accessed 22 June 2019).

Local Personnel, Disciplinary Procedures and Action, Privileges and Immunities of UNEF, Legal, Interpretation of Rules and Regulations, Chief Administrator Officer's Files, S-530-0126-0005, United Nations Archive.

Local Staff Regulations – General Policy, Chief Administrator Officer's Files, S-530-0126-0005, United Nations Archive.

Locals, Personnel Duties and Regulations, Personnel Practice and Administration Control, Chief Administrator Officer's Files, S-530-0060-005, United Nations Archives.

Middle East, UNEF/UNEFCA, Code Cables, Incoming, S0370-0032-0002, United Nations Archive.

Minutes of Advisory Committee, Notes on early meetings 1956–1959, UNEF Advisory Committee, Middle East, Urquhart, S-1078-0060-0001, United Nations Archive.

Neep, D. (2012). *Occupying Syria under the French Mandate: Insurgency, Space and State Formation.* Cambridge, UK: Cambridge University Press.

Ottovay Jørgensen, M. (2016). *Revisiting the First United Nations Peacekeeping Intervention in Egypt and the Gaza Strip, 1956–1967: A Case of Imperial Multilateralism?* Aalborg: Aalborg Universitetsforlag.

Overflights, Complaints & Investigations, General Subject Files, Pol. Affairs, S-0375-0060-0007, United Nations Archive.

Pappé, I. (2004). *A History of Modern Palestine: One Land, Two Peoples.* Cambridge, NY: Cambridge University Press.

Pappé, I. (2006). *The Ethnic Cleansing of Palestine.* Oxford: OneWorld Publications Limited.

Pappé, I. (2017). *The Biggest Prison on Earth: A History of the Occupied Territories.* Oxford: OneWorld Publications Limited.

Reports, Pol. Affairs, EIMAC, S-375-0028-0006, United Nations Archive.

Rotbard, S. (2003). "Wall and Tower (Homa Umigdal): The Mold of Israeli Architecture," in Segal, R. and Weisman, E. (eds.). *A Civilian Occupation: The Politics of Israeli Architecture.* Tel Aviv-Jaffa/New York/Babel: Verso: 38–57.

Roy, S. (2006). *Failing Peace: Gaza and the Palestinian-Israeli Conflict.* London, UK: Pluto Press.

Sayigh, Y. (1997). *Armed Struggle and the Search for State: The Palestinian National Movement, 1949–1993.* Oxford/New York: Clarendon Press/Oxford University Press.

Sayigh, Y. (1998). "Escalation or Containment? Egypt and the Palestine Liberation Army, 1964–1967," *International Journal of Middle Eastern Studies* 30(1): 97–116.

Shachar, N. (2010). *The Gaza Strip: Its History and Politics.* Brighton: Sussex Academic Press.

Sinclair, G. (2009). "'Get into a Crack Force and earn £20 a Month and all found...': The Influence of the Palestine Police upon Colonial Policing 1922–1948," *European Review of History* 13(1): 49–65.

Sköld, N. (1990). *I fredens tjänst: Sveriges medverkan i Förenta nationernas fredsbev-arande styrka i Mellanöstern 1956–67.* [Stockholm]: Almqvist & Wiksell International.

Staff Relations and Appeals, Staff Relations and Appeals, Chief Administrator Officer's Files, S-530-0085-0006, United Nations Archive.

Swedenburg, T. (2003). *Memories of Revolt: The 1936–1939 Rebellion and the Palestinian National Past.* Fayetteville: University of Arkansas press.

Thomas, M. (2008). *Empires of Intelligence: Security Services and Colonial Disorder after 1914.* Berkeley: University of California Press.

Trouillot, M.-R. (1995). *Silencing the Past: Power and the Production of History.* Boston, MA: Beacon Press.

Weekly Reports 1957, Reports, Pol. Affairs, EIMAC, S-0375-0028-0003, United Nations Archive.

Winter, Y. (2016). "The Siege of Gaza: Spatial Violence, Humanitarian Strategies, and the Biopolitics of Punishment," *Constellations* 23(2): 308–319.

Yasigh, S. (1997). *Armed Struggle and the Search for State: The Palestinian National Movement, 1949–1993.* Oxford: Clarendon Press.

CHAPTER 9

Science as the Handmaiden of Coerced Labor: The Implementation of Cotton Cultivation Schemes in the Eastern Congo Uele Region, 1920–1960

Sven Van Melkebeke

1   Introduction

In his path-breaking and price-wining manuscript, Sven Beckert recently demonstrated that global cotton production heavily relied on violence and state intervention (Beckert 2015). From slavery in the seventeenth and eighteenth centuries to new forms of forced labor and (colonial) states capable of incorporating rural societies into the capitalist export market in the nineteenth and twentieth centuries.

Coercion and government intervention were connected features of cotton extraction in colonial Sub-Saharan Africa, primarily due to competing better-suited mid-latitude regions around the world. On the one hand, labor exploitation was the 'competitive advantage' *par excellence* to counter lower yields and hence raise production capacities (Porter 1995: 45–47). On the other hand, colonizers also relied on science in an attempt to increase land productivity, to simplify existing land tenure systems, etcetera.[1] This chapter argues that, in the case of the Belgian Congo, agronomical science and coerced labor[2] were entangled dimensions of the cotton story. Moreover, the colonial state increasingly used science to legitimate forced cotton cultivation and land restructuring policies. This increasing reliance on colonial agronomy went hand in hand with a change in the nature of coercion from more direct, physical force towards more indirect, psychological force.

In this book, 'coercive geographies' is defined as the nexus between coerced labor, mobility/migration and state attempts to confine people in clearly

---

1   This is what James Scott defines as colonial high-modernist agriculture: a strong believe in linear progress, science and technology to 'remake' societies in the Global South (Scott 1998).

2   In this chapter coerced labor is defined as: "(...) dominating and controlling workers without actually owning them, featuring physical and psychological violence (or threat of violence), coercion because workers did not have the ability to enter and withdraw from particular labor markets and labor processes, and exploitation of labor through low wages and hard working conditions" (Seibert 2011: 373).

defined spaces. On the one hand, it aims to understand how forms of unfreedom developed, evolved and transformed throughout history and into our contemporary world. On the other hand, it also wants to grasp the resilience of human hope and agency. In the global North, historically evolved social protection and standard employment appear to be crumbling while precarity is normalizing since the spread of neoliberal economic policies in the early 1980s. By contrast, in the global South, welfare and labor security have been an exception for most of the working classes. Moreover, the large majority of workers have been historically excluded not only from wage income but also from its associated entitlements and protections. There already is ample literature that cuts across both colonial and present era and that interrogates forced agricultural labor (including state interventions, agricultural planning and migrations) in the global South and resistance of people to these different 'coercive geographies' (e.g. Keese 2012; Rogaly 2008; Urbano 2017). This chapter aligns with this strand of literature and offers a historical case study of 'coercive geographies' defined as two overlapping but evolving agricultural production systems in which agronomy is (ab)used to coerce people to cultivate a cash crop on a designated plot of land and according to imposed regulation, and how people responded to these coercions.

Cotton cultivation as such has not received sufficient attention in the historiography of colonial Congo, as opposed to, for instance, palm products or rubber. Much of the literature dealing with cotton dates from the colonial period. However, in the 1990s, Osumaka Likaka closely examined obligatory cotton cultivation – introduced in 1917 – in colonial Congo. He mainly highlights harsh coercion and poor working conditions as well as a shift towards more 'developmental' policies – such as films and festivals to promote cotton cultivation – after the Second World War but fails to integrate science (Likaka 1997). As for the scientific part of cotton cultivation, there is a gap in the historiography. In this case too, much of the literature stems from contemporary scientists which results in often very technical accounts that completely neglect African workers. With the exception of Piet Clement, there is also no recent literature on the implementation of scientifically inspired cultivation systems. Clement focuses on the 'indigenous peasantry schemes' – implemented from the late 1930s onwards – and while he hints at a link between obligatory cultivation and these 'indigenous peasantry schemes.' he does not further develop that connection (Clement 2014).

Analytically, this chapter draws on global history theory. The expansion of capitalism was accompanied by the incorporation of 'new' peripheral rural zones into the modern world-system (Moore 2015). With the incorporation of 'new' zones, a process of interaction took place (Hall 2012). Referred to as frontier-processes, these interactions were fuelled by feedback (resistance and agency) of local actors. Thus, frontier-building has to be understood as a process of interaction between formerly unattached social-economic/political/knowledge systems. To improve theorisation of frontier-processes, Jason W. Moore introduced the concept of 'commodity frontier'. By focusing on the production of one specific commodity, he examines the reorganisation of geographical spaces at the margins of the world-system. Commodity frontiers transformed existing land and labor patterns by partially – due to local agency (flight, foot-dragging, reorganizing social relations, etcetera) and interaction – commodifying both. Moreover, commodity frontiers were very effective in the rise of capitalism because "[…] a relatively small volume of capital, backed by territorial power, could appropriate a very large basket of nature's gifts" (Moore 2010).

Examining the development of a new cotton frontier in the Belgian Congo and the impact on, and feedback of, local communities is the aim of this chapter. In doing so, this chapter not only looks at the coercive incorporation of cotton labor and land into the capitalist world-system. It also wants to broaden the theoretical framework of commodity frontiers by integrating science as an important, yet hitherto often neglected, part of capitalist expansion in Sub-Saharan Africa.[3] To achieve that goal, I will draw on published sources as well as on a vast array of largely untapped archival material, held in the African Archives of the Federal Public Service Foreign Affairs, Foreign Trade and Development Cooperation in Brussels: administrative documents, agronomical surveys and sources detailing on land and/or labor issues. The first part of this chapter analyses the Eastern Congo Uele as a new frontier and its importance as a cotton producer. The second and third parts highlight the implementation of two different cotton cultivation schemes, the role of agronomical science, and the entanglement with labor and land issues. The final section examines how Congolese resisted and coped with the introduction of these schemes.

2   Cotton in the Uele Region (1920–1960)

Cotton is not a native Congolese plant. It was introduced in the western Congo by Portuguese traders, likely in the nineteenth century (Brixhe 1958: 13). From the early 1890s, missionaries transported seeds to large parts of the Congo (including Uele) and the Congo Free State unsuccessfully attempted to initiate cultivation. It was not until the take-over of the Free State – due to the rubber scandals (another example of 'coercive geographies') – by Belgium (1908) that

---

3   A notable exception to this tendency is Ross (2017).

TABLE 9.1   Cotton production (Tons) in Belgian Africa and Uele (1917–1959)

Year	Belgian Africa	Uele	Year	Belgian Africa	Uele
1917	532	—	1939	117,633	35,472
1918	524	—	1940	135,689	46,363
1919	650	—	1941	141,566	—
1920	800	—	1942	120,442	—
1921	1,770	200 (A)	1943	132,469	± 34,000
1922	3,105	1,360 (A)	1944	93,664	± 36,000
1923	2,610	1,220 (A)	1945	113,549	33,300
1924	5,130	1,882 (A)	1946	122,734	36,724
1925	9,166	3,505 (A)	1947	121,600	33,657
1926	14,938	6,181 (A)	1948	127,600	± 45,000
1927	17,639	6,236 (A)	1949	149,900	± 48,000
1928	20,207	6,034 (A)	1950	137,300	51,854
1929	21,755	6,962 (A)	1951	137,100	38,582
1930	30,600	8,963 (A)	1952	162,600	44,486
1931	44,822	14,277 (A)	1953	142,200	—
1932	27,700	17,273 (A)	1954	150,000	37,598
1933	46,264	21,600	1955	152,000	42,058
1934	59,160	—	1956	159,000	55,880 (B)
1935	77,781	—	1957	137,000	40,776 (B)
1936	96,105	38,231	1958	150,000	43,320 (B)
1937	110,454	44,387	1959	177,000	—
1938	127,488	47,288			

Notes: (A) 1921–1932: Bas-Uele: before 1932 en after 1955 the Uele region was split up into two separate districts, Bas- and Haut-Uele, with Bas-Uele as main producer. (B) 1956–1958: Oriental Province.

Sources: Belgian Africa: Likaka, Rural Society and Cotton in Colonial Zaire. 42 and Brixhe. 19; Uele: RACCB-442/Uélé (district), Rapports Annuels AIMO, RACCB-719/Uélé (district), Rapports Annuels Agri and Rapport Annuel Sur L'activité De La Colonie Du Congo Belge Pendant L'année..., 1920–58.

cotton production (see Table 9.1 below) took off. Starting in 1913–1914, agronomists tested the suitability of diverse species in Bas-Congo and Maniema (Blommaert 1930: 805). In 1916, the district-administration of Uele failed to start cotton production for the export market (Rapport Annuel Affaires Indigènes et Main-d'œuvre 1917). But a few years later, agronomists succeeded in transporting seeds from Maniema to Uele; this manoeuvre was followed by the first scientific tests (1919) to select the best-suited species (Dejong 1927). The creation of selection station in Bambesa initiated science in the nascent cotton sector of Uele. Tests carried out by this station demonstrated that the *Triumph* variety was best-suited to the region and, as a result, seeds of this variety were eventually distributed – preferably by selection station or by the local authorities – among local Congolese planters (Dejong 1923: 91). It should be mentioned that during the first cotton campaign (1920–1921), planters were forced to cultivate their chiefs' fields, allegedly to 'initiate' and 'educate' them so that from the following campaign they would be prepared to cultivate their own lands (Correspondance coton Uélé, Note 'Le service de la propagande co-tonnière dans les Uélés.' F. Saparano, 7/1932).

Due to the climate, the Congo can be divided into two major cotton produc-ing zones. The Uele region is located in the middle of the northern zone and had to follow an agricultural calendar that differed from the southern belt. In the north (Leplae 1933: 61–62), the cotton season opened with the distribution of seeds to Congolese planters and the preparation of their land from April to June. This was followed by the sowing months July and August in which the first maintenance steps had to be conducted as well. From September to No-vember, maintenance (removal of insects, weeding, thinning out, earthing up) was highly important for the quality and quantity of future harvests. In Decem-ber, planters had to manufacture nets to dry the harvested cotton and fabricate baskets to transport their harvest to the cotton market. From mid-December to the end of March, cotton was harvested, and plant remains were burned in order to prevent insects to survive. Cotton cultivation was a labor-intensive process that was considered the ideal *culture familiale* because it included men and, for 'lighter tasks' women and children (Leplae 1936: 109).

Uele has to be considered a major cotton producing area. The potential of this region attracted contemporary observers and some even compared Uele with successful cotton cultivation in Uganda (Leplae 1933). Indeed, Uele suc-ceeded in attaining higher yields than neighbouring regions which might dem-onstrate locally deviant 'coercive geographies.' In the mid-1950s, for example, the Uele-district reached an average of 450 kilograms per hectare, while in French Equatorial Africa a mere 200 to 250 kilograms was reported (de Dampi-erre 1960: 133).

The Uele region managed to produce around 25 to 30% of the total cotton production in the Belgian Congo and Ruanda-Urundi (see Table 9.1), while Bel-gian Africa was only a minor global cotton producer. In 1921, production only attained 200 Tons (1,770 in the entire colony), but in 1925 production had increased to 3,505 Tons (9,166). Production figures continued to increase, even during the crisis of the 1930s: from 14,277 Tons (44,822) in 1931 to 35,472 Tons (117,633) in 1939. During the Second World War, cotton production decreased, which was a result of imposed rubber cultivation to serve war efforts (Rapport Annuel Affaires Indigènes et Main-d'œuvre 1942–1945). After the war, growth was more gradual and irregular: while still recovering from the war, production attained 33,657 Tons (121,600) in 1947. In 1955, figures indicate an increase up to 42,058 Tons (152,000).

It was estimated that, in 1930, the Uele-district had 91,000 cotton planters (households including women and children), thereby using 30,808 hectares (average of 33 ares per household) (Leplae 1933: 46; Rapport Annuels Agriculture, 1930). Unsurprisingly, figures indicate that accompanied with a decrease in production during the Second World War, cotton acreage also dropped. In 1937, planters in the Uele-district still cultivated 136,698 hectares, while in 1944, only 99,218 hectares were planted with cotton (Rapport Annuel Sur L'activité). It is also not surprising that acreage evolved as uneven as production figures after the war. In 1951, the entire Oriental Province counted 261,714 cotton planters and in that same year, 98,775 hectares were planted in Uele (average of 37 ares per household), while in 1955, this was only 90,924 hectares (Rapport Annuel Sur L'activité).

In 1921, the colonial government decided to divide the cotton zones in *zones d'achats*, or concession areas. From that moment on, Congolese producers were forced to sell their cotton produce exclusively to the company operating in their region (Likaka 1997: 18). In Uele, the first concessionary companies installed were *Belgika*, created in 1920, and the *Société Textile Africaine* (Texaf), created in 1925. The first one continued to buy and process cotton until the end of the colonial period (1960), while Texaf was absorbed by the major cotton company in Uele (and the Belgian Congo more generally), the *Compagnie Cotonnière Congolaise* (Cotonco) in 1931 (Blommaert 1930: 808). Created in 1920 on the joint initiative of the Secretary of the Colony Louis Franck, large financial groups in Brussels and Antwerp, and some textile fabricants in Ghent and Verviers, Cotonco soon developed into a huge concern with various sub-divisions and participations in other firms (Buelens 2007: 439–446).[4]

To ensure processing of the Congolese produced cotton, concessionary companies not only built factories,[5] but also created 'cotton markets' which

---

4 Among the most important stockholders were the Belgian state (10%) and the *Société Générale*.

5 For example, in 1927, already 50 processing factories were operational in the Uele-district (Dejong 1927: 531).

were surveilled and controlled by governmental agents. But because transport infrastructure was limited in Uele – resulting in a high-degree of porterage, at least until the early 1950s – additional *postes volantes* were created, closer to cotton producing villages. The first experiments with these mobile markets were conducted during the Second World War and in 1949, more than 1000 *postes* existed (Rapport Annuel Affaires Indigènes et Main-d'œuvre, 1949).

3   The Regime of Obligatory Cotton Cultivation

The above sketched cultivation cycle was subject to very stringent regulation, prescribed by degrees, and strictly supervized and controlled by European administrators and state agronomists, barely trained African monitors, African chiefs and even company agents. Similar to other colonies, rules were distributed via a chain of command via agronomists over monitors to chiefs, village and family heads and eventually to actual planters.[6]

Cotton was a, if not the most important, *culture obligatoire* introduced and cultivated in the Belgian Congo from 1917 until 1960. The colonial state attempted to ameliorate the material situation of the population and to raise existing agricultural practices' low productivity. The colonial authorities distinguished between obligatory food cropping (mostly rice and bananas) and obligatory cash cropping (mainly palm products and cotton). Colonial experts were unanimous about the value of the first because that would help to reduce scarcities and famines, but they initially disagreed about the second because not everyone was convinced about possible 'enrichment' of the rural masses (Leplae 1936: 95). However, it was believed that obliging Africans to produce a certain export crop would not only improve their living conditions but would also give them an agricultural education.

Once this was settled, obligatory cash cropping was implemented rapidly. In Uele, every *homme adulte valide* (HAV) was obliged to plant cotton on a leap land, chosen by their chief and an agronomist, while the district-commissioner – also advised by an agronomist – decided the size of the plot Congolese households had to cultivate. At the start of the cotton campaigns in the early 1920s, people were forced to plant five to ten ares with cotton; but this acreage

---

6 For (dis)similarities see for example: Thomas J. Bassett, "The Development of Cotton in Northern Ivory Coast, 1910–1965," *Journal of African History* 29, no. 2 (1988); Allen Isaacman, "Chiefs, Rural Differentiation and Peasant Protest: The Mozambican Forced Cotton Regime, 1938–1961," *African Economic History*, no. 14 (1985); Peter F.B. Nayenga, "Commercial Cotton Growing in Busoga District, Uganda, 1905–1923," ibid., no. 10 (1981).

gradually increased to about 25 to 50 ares in the 1930s and to one hectare in some regions of Uele from the Second World War onwards (Likaka 1997: 28; Leplae 1936: 59–60). On these allocated plots, planters were legally enforced to cultivate cotton 60 days a year – and even 120 days during the Second World War. It was only with the degree of 29/12/1955 that this number was reduced to 45 (Mokili 1998: 121). But because cotton cultivation was such a labor-intensive process, 60 days were rarely sufficient. In the early 1930s, it was observed that people sometimes had to work 100 to 150 days a year which in turn endangered food production (D (778) B.II.1).

In addition to taxes, Congolese were forced into cotton cultivation by means of coercion, violence, and sanctions for non-compliance with strict regulations. Local selection stations – or from 1933 onwards, the coordinating *Institut National pour l'Étude Agronomique du Congo belge* (INEAC) – tested cotton in order to increase yields and fight diseases. Agronomists advised the colonial administration on what rules should be implemented and how they should be followed by planters.

As the annual report of 1937 confirms: "We need to bombard the native [with propaganda] in order to make clear when it is time to perform what duty and according to what method." (Rapport Annuel Affaires Indigènes et Main-d'œuvre, 1937). However, sources indicate that not only selection stations engaged in scientific work. In a 1929 letter, Cotonco-delegate Landeghem argues that scientific stations in Uele lacked manpower to perform all assigned tasks and that, therefore, Cotonco would create its own selection stations where more modern agronomical techniques would be developed and imposed on Cogolese planters by its own agronomists (Correspondance générale, Agriculture (510), Lettre Landeghem au Gouverneur-Général, 25/2/1929).

Whether enforced by public or private agronomists, the cultivation scheme was rigid. Once planters had picked up cotton seeds themselves, cultivation could start. Congolese were forced to sow the seeds in straight lines, to dig holes at regular distances and to fill every hole with five to seven seeds. Starting three weeks later, maintenance operations began, following a rigid time schedule. After about four months, planters had to start harvesting, again following severe rules. For instance, they were required to only remove cotton form open capsules. Harvest was followed by drying which had to last for two to three days. In order to fight erosion, agronomists also imposed a rotation schedule for Congolese to follow: a plot of land had to be covered with maize, followed by cotton during the first year. The second year, rice, groundnuts, and other foods crops had to be planted; followed by manioc and bananas during the third year. The fourth year the plot had to be left fallow (Blommaert 1930: 810).

Not following imposed rules and/or time schedules (deliberate or not) was answered with violence and punishments, similar to other colonies.[7] African monitors and chiefs, local European administrators as well as company agents committed abuses against planters. Whipping of men and women was very common, and from 1931 even legalized as a disciplinary measure (Likaka 1997: 54–55). Fines and prison were other means of legal coercion. The annual reports of Uele show an increase in repression towards the end of the 1930s: for instance, in 1938, there were 936 convictions; in 1940 no less than 4089 convictions were reported (Rapport Annuel Affaires Indigènes et Main-d'œuvre, 1939 and 1940). People condemned for non-compliance with rigid agronomical rules were sometimes imprisoned for up to seven days; had to perform unpaid labor for public utilities (construction of roads, deforestation, etcetera); or were fined up to 200 Francs.[8] In addition to legal coercion, women were often raped by monitors, village plundered, etcetera (Likaka 1995: 207).

In Uele, administrators often played a doubtful role. On the one hand, they acted like true company agents, forcing Congolese to sow and harvest, followed by requisitioning the produce in service of Cotonco (Divers coton Uélé, Lettre vice-Gouverneur Moeller au Gouverneur-Général, 6/10/1922). As one observer noted: "The regime is a perfect overprint of the one, referring to rubber, that hitherto provoked such protest" (D (778) B.II.1). Moreover, by limiting competition with other sectors (mostly coffee plantations), Cotonco benefited from governmental support (Rapport Annuel Affaires Indigènes et Main-d'œuvre, 1939). On the other hand, sources indicate that cotton markets were often left unsupervised and that, consequently, planters were at the mercy of companies (Divers coton Uélé, rapport voyage substitue Procureur-Général Leynen, 16/5/1928). Men, women and children had to transport their produce to these markets, often by foot or sometimes by donkeys (Correspondance générale, Agriculture (510), Lettre Gouverneur Province Orientale au Service de l'Agriculture et de la Colonisation, 2/9/1938). Congolese not only had to walk very long distances to reach such markets – according to one observer sometimes more than 20 days (D (778) B.II.1). Fraud and abuses (with balances for example) were also common, as well as people forced to return home with their harvested cotton and without payment: "(...) the native, grumbling under

---

7   There are great similarities between forced cotton cultivation in the Belgian Congo and Mozambique. In fact, Portugal installed a cotton scheme, starting in 1926, that was inspired on the obligatory cultivation scheme Belgium had introduced in 1917 (Isaacman 1985: 18).

8   In the 1930s, only in good harvest years, planters could gain up to 200 Francs (taxes included) a year, so it is clear that fines were extremely severe and could exceed cotton incomes (Leplae 1933: 81). Moreover, increasing repression in the 1930s was clearly an attempt of the colonial administration to maintain cotton production despite falling prices on the world market.

the sun and without hope of returning to his village for the night, has to wait for long hours and even entire days because the buyer, something unbeliev-able, has no money (...)" (Correspondance générale, Agriculture (507), Lettre directeur Régie des Plantations aux Commissaire de district, 20/2/1930). More-over, cultivators often had to return home because company agents deemed the cotton presented insufficient in terms of agronomical quality whether too much dirt, too much moist, not mature enough (Rapport Annuel Affaires In-digènes et Main-d'œuvre, 1938).

4   The Scientifically Framed 'Indigenous Peasantry Scheme'

The above sketched harsh regime had several consequences for the country-side. Obligatory cotton cultivators are considered "(...) the most impoverished segment of the rural society integrated into the colonial economy" (Likaka 1997: 79). However, many Congolese responded to violence and obligation by migrating to industrial centres and cities. For instance, in one territory in the Uele region, more than 7,000 planters had abandoned their fields in 1949 (Rap-port Annuel Affaires Indigènes et Main-d'œuvre, 1949). Although obligatory cultivation continued until the end of the colonial period, it seems that the colonial administration shifted its focus more towards a 'new' agricultural scheme:

> A lot of people are anxiously considering the exodus of rural populations towards large centers (...). This migration will have no serious conse-quences if the men who abandoned their fields are eventually employed in the industry and if we enable those who stayed in their village to pro-duce more and better without extra effort. We consider that our peasant-ries will stabilize rural populations in a slightly improved condition by the use of more rational cultivation methods and more productive seeds (...).
>
> Développement agricole, Note 'Main-d'œuvre et intensification de l'agriculture.'
> G.E. Sladden, 31/12/1949

The intention is clear: supporting industrial development and at the same time stabilizing the countryside and improving agricultural production by relying even more on scientific support. It was believed that rural stabilisation could be achieved by introducing so-called *paysannats indigènes*.

Initiated by the INEAC in 1936, 'indigenous peasantry schemes' were rapidly adopted, appropriated and controlled by the colonial state. While sometimes considered a third and new phase in colonial agricultural development – after precolonial extensive agriculture, improved by the *cultures obligatoires* (Henry 1952: 160–163) – *paysannats* were in reality not merely a novelty, but rather a supplement to, and in many respects a continuation of, obligatory cultivation, albeit more sophisticated in approach. In a recent publication, Clement lucidly summarizes the key objectives: *paysannats* were designed to promote individual land tenure, or at least individualized cultivation (per household on allotted land); Congolese should enter voluntarily as opposed to obligatory cultivation; agriculture required more intensification and methods more modernisation to increase productivity and fight soil erosion – in this the INEAC's role was significant;[9] in addition, it was believed that *paysannats* would increase participants' income while improvement of social services (like health care) were intended to slow down rural emigrations (Clement, 2014: 259). A main characteristic of this scheme was the division of a chosen plot of land into homogenous blocs (lots) destined to follow a rigid rotation schedule with food crops such as maize, annual crops (red areas on Figure 9.1) such as cotton and/or perennial crops (blue areas on Figure 9.1) such as coffee.

The Uele region was among the earliest in the colony where such 'indigenous peasantry schemes' were implemented. Already in 1943, the INEAC installed the first *paysannat* in Babua (Bambesa, northwest of the province) surrounding its cotton selection station (see Figure 9.1). In 1949, no less than 8,879 blocs were allotted in this *paysannat* on an acreage of 80,811 hectares; in 1958, 12,356 lots had been assigned covering 111,204 hectares (Paysannats Indigènes, Agriculture (749) n°o, Rapport INEAC, 1949; Paysannats Indigènes – cartes et statistiques, Résumé de la situation des paysannats de la Province Orientale, 31/12/1958).

In Uele, the assignment of lots followed a regular pattern. Prior to the division of land, European agronomists examined existing land tenure systems and social-political situations at clan-level. Local administrators, in agreement with agronomists and local notables then divided the plot into sub-clan blocs which were further divided into family lots. Subsequently, each household was allocated a certain plot as can be seen on Figure 9.2 (Rapport Annuel Colonial Congo Belge -719/Buta (territoire), Rapport Paysannat Babua, 1951). On these plots, families could reside (or were forced to), or, in other cases, entire villages were relocated towards the *paysannats* (Staner 1955: 536).

---

9   The pioneering role of the INEAC was followed in other colonies. For instance, in 1946, the *Institut de Recherches du Coton et des Textiles exotiques* was founded to conduct research and development on textile plants in French colonies (Bassett 1988: 281).

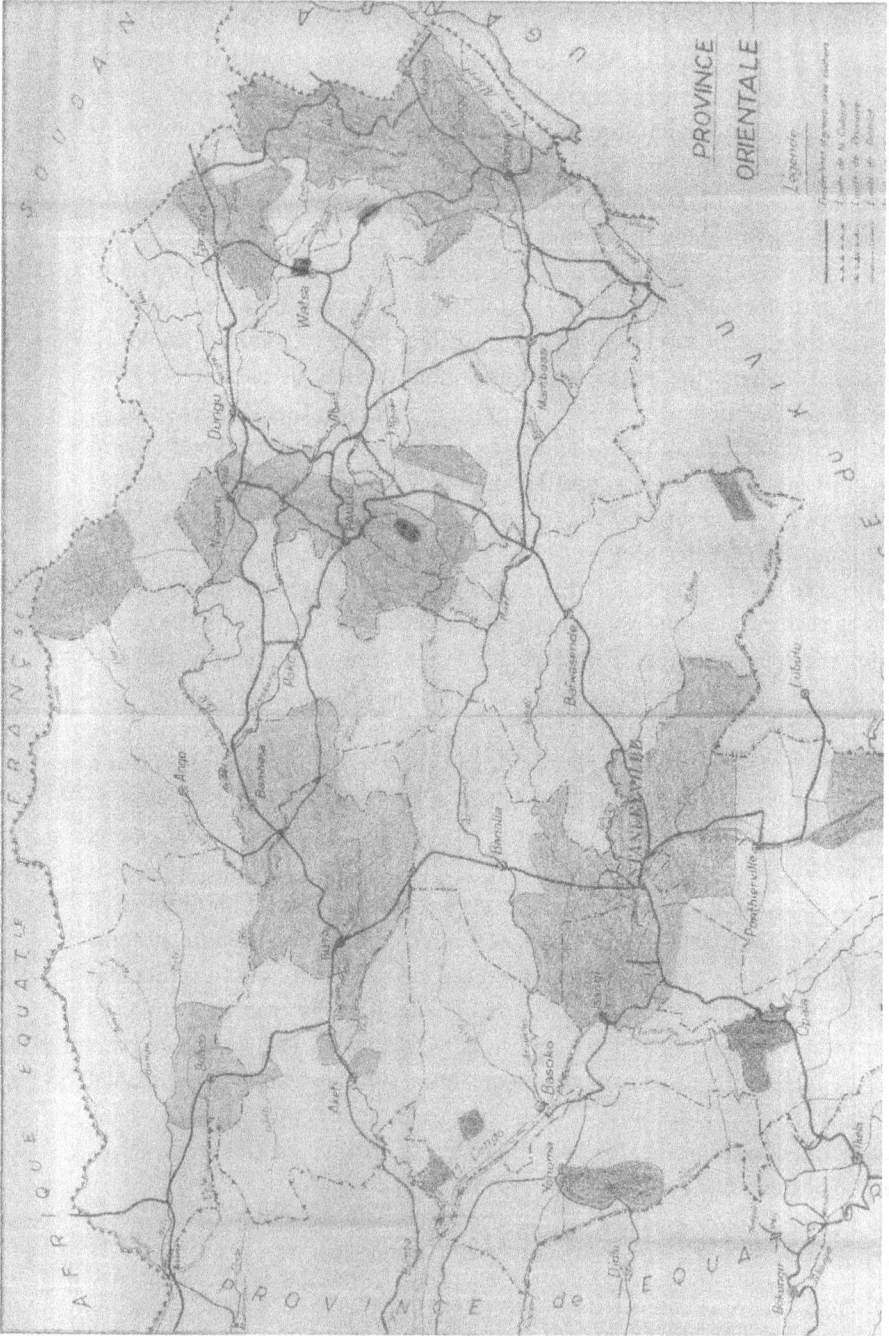

FIGURE 9.1 Paysannats Indigènes in the Oriental Province, 1959
SOURCE: PAYSANNATS INDIGÈNES – CARTES ET STATISTIQUES, CARTE DES PAYSANNATS DE LA PROVINCE ORIENTALE, 29/6/1959. AFRICAN ARCHIVES, THE FEDERAL PUBLIC SERVICE FOREIGN AFFAIRS, FOREIGN TRADE AND DEVELOPMENT

FIGURE 9.2 Distribution of plots, designed on the ground in Babua, 1953
SOURCE: PAYSANNAT INDIGÈNE BABUA, BROCHURE 'LE PAYSANNAT.' 1953.
AFRICAN ARCHIVES, THE FEDERAL PUBLIC SERVICE FOREIGN AFFAIRS,
FOREIGN TRADE AND DEVELOPMENT COOPERATION.

Land allocated to a family was still property of the clan, individual households only had usufruct rights (Paysannats Indigènes Province Orientale, Procès-verbal 'Paysannat.' 21/5/1951). Each family plot had a size between four and a half and nine hectares on which households had to follow a strict rotation schedule. These schedules resembled the ones introduced for obligatory cultivation, although in this case, the rotation cycle was much longer and local conditions (climate, soil) were better taken into account. For instance, in Babua, on leaps of 30 to 50 ares, each family was instructed to plant maize, rice, pumpkins and cotton during the first year, followed by groundnuts and cotton in the second year. The third and fourth year they should plant bananas. After these leaps should be left fallow for several years in order to restore soil-fertility (Staner 1955: 488). But instructions to fight erosion often ended up in obligations.

Congolese were not allowed to plant other cops than those instructed and, moreover "every field where cotton was grown (...) must be covered with food crops obligatorily" (Paysannats Indigènes, Gouvernement Général (6640), 'Quelques commentaires sur le calendrier agricole.' 24/9/1948). Not only the obligation to rotate but also the rigid division of land raised criticism: "assigning land gives the impression of a military camp – does the native feels comfortable with that?" (Paysannats Indigènes, Gouvernement Général (6640), Note 'Paysannats Indignées.' chef provincial du Service Agricole Renard, 12/11/1947).

Not only the obligation to cultivate in a certain scheme indicates the continuation of coercion. Sources indicate that cotton remained primordial, despite the thorough focus on both food and cash crops given in ideal representations of the *paysannat*-scheme: "(...) they [company agents] are almost exclusively occupied with cotton. In the months December to April, although this is the period in which fields have to be prepared with groundnuts and rice, these agents are surveilling the harvest, the destruction of plants, and are buying cotton" (Propagande agricole, Lettre Commissaire de district au Gouverneur de la Province Orientale, 5/2/1952).

This question the objectives of the *paysannats*. Another issue that raises doubt is voluntary participation. Here too it is clear that coercion had not disappeared. According to one observer, the impression of 'freedom' suffices to 'educate' cultivators (Malengreau 1949: 35). Moreover, it seems that people were often recruited instead of freely entering. In a letter sent to the General Governor, the Secretary of the Colony Wigny "(...) interdicted every recruitment in regions [including Uele] with indigenous peasantry schemes and that, in regions where this interdiction is already promulgated, the authorities strictly control its application" (Paysannats Indigènes, Gouvernement Général (6640), Lettre Wigny au Gouverneur-Général, 25/6/1949). Furthermore, in the early 1950s, the colonial administration had turned the *paysannats* into a goal (increasing export) rather than a means to improve agriculture. For instance, in some regions of Uele, the Agricultural Service was instructed to install 100 peasants per month per agronomist (Paysannats Indigènes, Agriculture (749) n°0, Note 'Réflexions sur le paysannat indigène.' directeur INEAC Jurion, [1950s]). Finally, even though cultivation was not obligatory, people unable to prepare their fields, or unable to prepare the instructed superficies, were sanctioned similarly to obligatory cultivation and had to perform labor such as road maintenance (Paysannats Indigènes, Gouvernement Général (6640), Procès-verbal réunion Paysannat Babua, 6/4/1948).

Because the colonial government conceived the 'indigenous peasantry scheme' as a goal, local administrators were anxious about exceeding the 60 days per year limit set for the obligatory cultivation scheme – otherwise *paysannats* would be nothing more than enduring compulsion. In reality, however, this limit was exceeded many times and, in addition, assigned land rather than freely chosen plots, resulted in many Congolese peasants regarding the *paysannats* as *champs de l'état* and cultivating as disguised *cultures obligatoires* (Malengreau 1949: 57–58, 71) What also added to this experience of cotton cultivators, is the continuous strict control of every step, and sanctioning (see also *infra*), in the cotton cultivation scheme, including the rotation schedule. Although participation in these schemes was supposed to be voluntary, (il)legal enforcement of agronomical rules continued. For example, in 1947, in the Buta-territory, 177 Congolese were convicted for not following instructions (Malengreau 1949: 57–58, 71). Moreover, an amalgam of local administrators, agronomists (form the state or the INEAC), African monitors in charge of daily inspections, and even company agents all 'instructed' cultivators and closely surveilled the *paysannats*:

> We have to make sure that we maximally valorize the effort of the peasant: first, in the preparation of his field by means of mechanical aid, by utilization high-productivity seeds, by using fertilizers, adequate insecticides, by providing help for the harvest, by the treatment and good air-conditioning of the product, by an appropriate commercial organization.
> STANER 1955: 538

Strictly controlling Congolese who participated in the *paysannats* and forcing them to cultivate certain crops according to imposed rules and methods did not yet suffice. In the 1950s, the INEAC experimented with a localized cotton variety which promised to increase productivity with 10%, the *Bambesa49*. According to a letter addressed to the Secretary of the Colony, from 1958 onwards, the INEAC would start distributing these seeds to planters in Uele (Agriculture, Lettre directeur INEAC au Ministre de la Colonie, 29/5/1958). Thus, from that moment on, Congolese not only had to plant cotton but were also ordered to cultivate this particular variety.

Finally, the promised raise in revenues is highly doubtful. The introduction of *paysannats* was strongly advocated by cotton companies. Still privileged by their monopsony in purchasing cotton, these companies were the major beneficiary of cotton produced within the *paysannats*. It has been highlighted that in 1959, cotton companies received 46 Francs per kilo exported, while planters – who still had to carry their produce to cotton markets – only gained four to six Francs per kilo (Mokili 1998: 179). Contemporary observers were aware of the continuing low remunerations of cotton planters: Malengreau complains about the fact that prices paid to cultivators were disproportional to the efforts invested; Brixhe admits that despite rationalisation of agricultural methods, the standing of the rural masses did not improve significantly (Malengreau 1949: 53; Brixhe 1958: 78).

5 Congolese Cotton Planters' Feedback

Implementing, enforcing, and controlling, cultivation schemes into rural settings required an extensive colonial staff. However, in Africa, the power of colonial states was arterial rather than capillary which means that state power was weak and often contested (Cooper 1994: 1533). Indeed, many sources indicate that there was a constant lack of agronomical personnel. For instance, a note analysing the cotton situation in Uele shows that at the end of the 1930s, one agronomist was responsible for surveilling the work of nearly 15,000 planters (Correspondance générale, Agriculture (510), 'Note sur la situation cotonnière dans le Bas Uélé et Haut Uélé en 1938–39.' 17/2/1939). Moreover, cotton fields were often dispersed and remote, particularly in the obligatory cultivation scheme. In these circumstances, relying on African notables and monitors who knew local environments, was imperative. However, the latter were merely "(...) agricultural messengers, conveying European instructions to the native. The supervision they exercise often lacks efficiency. They are the allies of those who feed them well" (Rapports Annuels Agriculture, Rapport Annuel Agri, 1932). This suggests that, even within colonial constraints, Congolese cultivators were able to act and react top-down imposed cotton schemes. Some of this feedback has already come to light: people migrating to cities, for instance. But also, the reference made to cotton that was sold too dirty, or to moisty. While this cotton was judged inferior, from a Congolese point of view, these were well-chosen acts of resistance (Correspondance générale, Agriculture (510), Lettre direction Belgika au directeur Cotonco, 2/6/1938).

Planters resisted and coped with colonially coerced labor in many different other ways as well. In this context, most resistance should be understood as 'weapons of the weak' (Scott 1985): small-scale day-to-day forms of not-compliance with forced cultivation. Among these weapons, abandoning and contesting land was common. With the introduction of forced cotton cultivation in the early 1920s, many Congolese fled into nearby forests leaving abandoned villages only with elderly (Leplae 1933: 45). In the 1950s, people still abandoned their plot of land – mostly because assigned plots within *paysannats* were little fertile – and started cultivating food crops elsewhere (Malengreau 1949: 23). On the other hand, in the 1920s, planters prioritized food crops and sowed cotton on less suitable or even completely exhausted soils, "(...) to thwart Europeans" (Divers coton Uélé, Lettre Fisher au vice-Gouverneur-Général, 22/2/1922; Blommaert 1930: 808). Deceiving supervisors was also done by installing 'fake plantations': Congolese made sure that a few beautiful plants were fully visible and surrounded plants on infertile soils (Coton Uélé, 'Rapport annuel sur la culture et le commerce du coton dans les districts des Uélés.' 26/8/1930).

Finally, allocating land often resulted in conflicts within and between rural groups. Relocated villages disrupted clan structures; sometimes land that belonged to a community, was appropriated by the colonizer to install another community; and, due to a colonial lack of knowledge, in some cases clans were installed on a plot of land in the proximity of rivalling clans which inevitable caused disturbances (Malengreau 1949: 49).

At the beginning of the cultivation process, planters managed to resist, on the one hand, by deliberately wasting received seeds: "(...) on several occasions it has been recorded that the native planter has a tendency to exaggerate the number of seeds he requires" (Général, 'Procès-verbal Réunion Cotonnière.' 17/10/1935). On the other hand, Congolese often planted more than the five to seven seeds insisted on by European agronomists which disturbed the growth process (Blommaert 1930: 815). Another 'weapon' planters commonly used was disrespecting dates and imposed regulation. For instance, many sources indicate that Congolese sowed cotton too late – at the end of September rather than in July–August – which resulted in bad harvests and lower yields (Divers coton Uélé, Lettre Fisher au vice-Gouverneur-Général, 22/2/1922; Correspondance coton Uélé, Note 'Le service de la propagande cotonnière dans les Uélés.' F. Saparano, 7/1932). Not following rules during every step of the cultivation process was not appreciated in colonial circles. For example, Congolese cotton planters harvested immature cotton or: "I have seen a case where a planter had uprooted plants, after which he sat down by a tree in order to pull off the fibers of the capsules" (Correspondance générale, Agriculture (510), 'Note sur la situation cotonnière dans le Bas Uélé et Haut Uélé en 1938–39.' 17/2/1939). Additionally, some planters refused to harvest cotton and/or bring their produce to market posts. During a journey through Uele in the mid-1920s, a European cotton expert noticed that many mature plants were left unharvested, or that fibers were laying on the ground, or that people kept harvested cotton in their houses instead of obeying imposed selling dates (Divers coton Uélé, rapport Mr. Fisher 'Voyage Bas-Uélé.' 10/5/1923).

Refusal to harvest or to sell the harvest is not only an act of resistance but is also linked to extreme low prices planters received for their produce. Sources indicate that Congolese supplemented cotton incomes, or even abandoned cotton cultivation completely. People could earn more with selling food crops on local markets than with cotton (Divers coton Uélé, Note 'Coton dans l'Uélé.' rapport voyage substitue Procureur-Général Leynen, 16/5/1928).[10] Moreover, the annual reports of 1939 and 1945 both indicate that cotton planters preferred

---

10   Food crops were often 'illegally' intercropped with cotton. It was not until the 1950s that intercropping experiments were conducted (Likaka 1997: 35).

to cultivate other cash crops (groundnuts, palm products or rice) because these were more remunerative (Rapport Annuel Affaires Indigènes et Main-d'œuvre, 1939 and 1945). Even in the mid1950s, "(...) cotton planters, discouraged by bad harvests, have abandoned cultivation en masse in order to seek revenues elsewhere" (Documentation, 'Fluctuations de la production cotonnière du Nord.' [1955]). Finally, it seems that Congolese planters sometimes sold cotton in Uganda where better prices were paid (D(778) B.II.1). This means that the first either travelled vast distances to sell cotton, or that their cotton was transported, via existing networks, and sold to buyers in British colonial territory.

Congolese also managed to cope with compelled cotton production by reorganizing labor relations. For example, while *cultures obligatoires* were imposed on every HAV, planters in Uele often collaborated: "(...) two or even three people are cultivating a single plot of land and split the revenue (...)" (Coton Uélé, 'Rapport annuel sur la culture et le commerce du coton dans les districts des Uélés.' 26/8/1930). Moreover, intra-household labor relations also changed. It has been pointed out that women and children were heavily involved in the production process which indicates that women were no longer only engaged in food production but had become an important player in cash cropping as well. Furthermore, planters reacted to imposed cultivation schemes by having more wives. Sources indicate that polygamy had increased as a consequence of both obligatory cultivation and *paysannats* (Recrutement familial, Untitled and unnamed document, [late 1930s]; Staner 1955: 536). This indicates that polygamy had become production-oriented and that having more wives implied having a larger labor pool to cope with imposed production criteria. The mere observation that increased polygamy did not only happen in the obligatory cultivation scheme, as argued by Likaka (Likaka 1997: 100), but also with the *paysannats* scheme suggests that both schemes were developed and implemented by Europeans to serve only one goal: raising production in an attempt to compete on the global cotton market.

6   Conclusion

This chapter has examined the implementation of two cotton cultivation schemes in the Eastern Congo Uele region. By using the theoretical framework of 'coercive geographies' it not only highlighted the introduction of these schemes into rural areas, but also the feedback of these rural communities. This chapter has provided a historical case study of labor precarity in the global South. It has highlighted how the interaction between states, companies and local communities (re)shaped both coercion and agency. In doing so, this chapter also filled a gap in the historiography of Belgian Africa, as well as broadened the analytical foundation of 'commodity frontiers' by integrating science into the narrative of capitalist expansion.

It has been demonstrated that the cotton frontier in the Uele region developed from the early 1920s onwards and that this region was a major producer within Belgian Africa, producing one fourth up to one third of the total capacity. Furthermore, cotton producing areas were divided into monopsony zones in which a single company bought and traded cotton produced by Congolese planters. In Uele, Cotonco played a crucial role and was in many respects supported by the colonial state. As a stockholder of Cotonco, it is hardly surprising that the colonial authorities intervened and bluntly used forced (physical and/ or psychological) labor and restrictive land policies to increase cotton production and thus profit margins. However, feedback (both resistance and adaptation) provided by Congolese illustrates that colonial coercion was contested and that top-down impositions were not merely accepted which in turn indicates that colonial policies required adjustments.

Both cotton cultivation schemes have been introduced by the colonial administration with the intention to stabilize rural populations and gain more control. Obligatory cultivation was based on legal enforcements concerning land, time schedules, agronomical rules. Working conditions were harsh and non-compliance was sanctioned severely and often accompanied with violence. The *paysannats*, on the other hand, show resemblances with the first scheme. Here too, land was assigned which people were forced to cultivate. Growing crops had to be done according to strict time slots and in alignment with agronomical instructions which clearly resonated with obligatory cultivation rules. Even though participation in *paysannats* was supposed to be free, people were often recruited, and the colonial administration used sanctions destined for obligatory cultivation. Thus, in Uele, there was a continuation – although overlap is more appropriate – between obligatory cotton cultivation (starting in 1920) and the implementation of 'indigenous peasantry schemes' (from the early 1940s onwards).

The major difference between these two implemented cultivation schemes is the shift from legally coerced labor towards more scientifically framed coercion in which legal enforcement was officially absent. It seems that physical force towards Congolese planters was more used in the obligatory cultivation scheme. Impositions were legalized, violence widespread and used to enforce this regulation based on agronomical science. Whereas for the 'indigenous peasantry schemes.' psychological coercion seems to have been more outspoken. Because the legal framework was no longer officially applicable to this scheme, scientific framing became the major incentive to force people into cotton cultivation. As Congolese always contested and/or adapted to these schemes, the colonial state supplemented obligatory cultivation and the administration – in support of cotton companies – increasingly shifted its attention to science to legitimate coerced labor.

References

Agriculture, Agriculture (133) n°121, African Archives, the Federal Public Service Foreign Affairs, Foreign Trade and Development Cooperation.

Bassett, T.J. (1998). "The Development of Cotton in Northern Ivory Coast, 1910–1965," *Journal of African History* 29(2): 267–287.

Beckert, S. (2015). *Empire of Cotton. A New History of Global Capitalism*. London: Penguin Books.

Blommaert, U. (1930). "Introduction Du Coton Chez L'indigene Au Congo Beige," *Bulletin Agricole du Congo Belge* 21(3): 805–819.

Brixhe, A. (1958). *Le Coton Au Congo Belge*. Bruxelles: Direction de l'agriculture, des forêts et de l'élevage du Ministère du Congo belge et du Ruanda-Urundi.

Buelens, F. (2007). *Congo 1885–1960. Een Financieel-Economische Geschiedenis*. Berchem: EPO.

Clement, P. (2014). "Rural Development in the Belgian Congo. The Late-Colonial "Indigenous Peasantry" Programme and Its Implementation in the Equateur District (1950s)," *Bulletin ARSOM – Mededelingen KAOW* 60(2): 251–286.

Cooper, F. (1994). "Conflict and Connection: Rethinking Colonial African History," *American Historical Review* 99(5): 1516–1545.

Correspondance coton Uélé, Gouvernement Général (12611), African Archives, the Federal Public Service Foreign Affairs, Foreign Trade and Development Cooperation.

Correspondance générale, Agriculture (507), African Archives, the Federal Public Service Foreign Affairs, Foreign Trade and Development Cooperation.

Correspondance générale, Agriculture (510), African Archives, the Federal Public Service Foreign Affairs, Foreign Trade and Development Cooperation.

Coton Uélé, Agriculture (370) n°2, African Archives, the Federal Public Service Foreign Affairs, Foreign Trade and Development Cooperation.

D(778) B.II.1 Papiers Bertrand, Note 'Cultures indigènes.' (1932).

de Dampierre, E. (1960). "Coton Noir, Café Blanc. Deux Cultures Du Haute-Oubangui À La Veille De La Loi-Cadre," *Cahiers d'Etudes Africaines* 1(2): 128–147.

Dejong, E. (1923). "La Ferme De Sélection Cotonnière De Bambesa, Bas-Uélé," *Bulletin Agricole du Congo Belge* 14(1): 90–97.

Dejong, E. (1927). "Le Coton Dans L' Uélé," *Bulletin Agricole du Congo Belge* 18(4): 451–536.

Développement agricole, Plan Décennal (1644) n°71, African Archives, the Federal Public Service Foreign Affairs, Foreign Trade and Development Cooperation.

Divers coton Uélé, Gouvernement Général (12909), African Archives, the Federal Public Service Foreign Affairs, Foreign Trade and Development Cooperation.

Documentation, Agriculture (374) n°13, African Archives, the Federal Public Service Foreign Affairs, Foreign Trade and Development Cooperation.

Général, Affaires Indigènes et Main-d'œuvre (1977) n°88, African Archives, the Federal Public Service Foreign Affairs, Foreign Trade and Development Cooperation.

Hall, T.D. (2012). "Incorporation into and Merger of World-Systems," in Salvatore J. Babones and Christopher K. Chase-Dunn (eds). *Routledge Handbook of World-Systems Analysis: Theory and Research.* London/New York: Routledge: 47–55.

Henry, J. (1952). "Les Bases Théoriques Des Essais De Paysannat Indigène, Entrepris Par L' Ineac Au Congo Belge," in *Contribution À L'étude Du Problème De L' Économie Rurale Indigène Au Congo Belge. Communications Présentées Par La Délégation Belge À La Conférence Africaine De L'economie Rurale Indigène (Jos, Nigérie. – 17–24 Novembre 1949), Numéro Spécial Du Bulletin Agricole Du Congo Belge.* Bruxelles: Services de l'agriculture du ministère des colonies et du gouvernement central du Congo Belge: 159–192.

Isaacman, A. (1985). "Chiefs, Rural Differentiation and Peasant Protest: The Mozambican Forced Cotton Regime, 1938–1961," *African Economic History* 14: 15–56.

Keese, A. (2012). "The Constraints of Late Colonial Reform Policy: Forced Labour Scandals in the Portuguese Congo (Angola) and the Limits of Reform under Authoritarian Colonial Rule, 1955–61," *Portuguese Studies* 28(2): 186–200.

Leplae, E. (1933). *Histoire Et Développement Des Cultures Obligatoires De Coton Et De Riz Au Congo Belge De 1917 À 1933.* Bruxelles: Goemaere.

Leplae, E. (1936). "Transformation De l'agriculture Indigene Du Congo Beige Par Ies Cultures Obligatoires," *La Technique Agricole Internationale* 6(2): 93–116.

Likaka, O. (1995). "Forced Cotton Cultivation and Social Control in the Belgian Congo," in Allen Isaacman and Richard Roberts (eds.). *Cotton, Colonialism, and Social History in Sub-Saharan Africa.* Portsmouth: Heinemann: 200–220.

Likaka, O. (1997). *Rural Society and Cotton in Colonial Zaire.* Madison: University of Wisconsin Press.

Malengreau, G. (1949). *Vers Un Paysannat Indigène: Les Lotissements Agricoles Au Congo Belge: Rapport De Mission.* Bruxelles: Van Campenhout.

Mokili Danga Kassa, J. (1998). *Politiques Agricoles Et Promotion Rurale Au Congo-Zaïre (1885–1997).* Paris: l'Harmattan.

Moore, J.W. (2015). *Capitalism in the Web of Life. Ecology and the Accumulation of Capital.* London/New York: Verso.

Moore, J.W. (2010). "Madeira, Sugar, and the Conquest of Nature in the "First" Sixteenth Century, Part Ii. From Regional Crisis to Commodity Frontier, 1506–1530," *Review (Fernand Braudel Center)* 33(1): 1–24.

Nayenga, P.F.B. (1981). "Commercial Cotton Growing in Busoga District, Uganda, 1905–1923," *African Economic History* 10: 175–195.

Paysannats Indigènes, Agriculture (749) n°0, African Archives, the Federal Public Service Foreign Affairs, Foreign Trade and Development Cooperation.

Paysannat Indigène Babua, Agriculture (80) n°1, African Archives, the Federal Public Service Foreign Affairs, Foreign Trade and Development Cooperation.

Paysannats Indigènes – cartes et statistiques, Résumé de la situation des paysannats de la Province. Orientale, Agriculture (81) n°4, African Archives, the Federal Public Service Foreign Affairs, Foreign Trade and Development Cooperation.

Paysannats Indigènes, Gouvernement Général (6640), African Archives, the Federal Public Service Foreign Affairs, Foreign Trade and Development Cooperation.

Paysannats Indigènes Province Orientale, Agriculture (82) n°5, African Archives, the Federal Public Service Foreign Affairs, Foreign Trade and Development Cooperation.

Porter, P.W. (1995). "Note on Cotton and Climate: A Colonial Conundrum," in Allen Isaacman and Richard Roberts (eds.). *Cotton, Colonialism, and Social History in Sub-Saharan Africa*. Portsmouth: Heinemann: 43–49.

Propagande agricole, Gouvernement Général (17200), African Archives, the Federal Public Service Foreign Affairs, Foreign Trade and Development Cooperation.

Rapport Annuel Affaires Indigènes et Main-d'œuvre, 1917–1945, Rapport Annuel Colonial Congo Belge-442/Uélé (district).

Rapports Annuels Agriculture, Rapport Annuel Colonial Congo Belge -719/Uélé (district), African Archives, the Federal Public Service Foreign Affairs, Foreign Trade and Development Cooperation.

Rapport Annuel Colonial Congo Belge -719/Buta (territoire), African Archives, the Federal Public Service Foreign Affairs, Foreign Trade and Development Cooperation.

Rapport Annuel Sur L'activité De La Colonie Du Congo Belge Pendant L'année, 1920–58. Bruxelles.

Recrutement familial, Affaires Indigènes et Main-d'œuvre (1609)9130 n°4, African Archives, the Federal Public Service Foreign Affairs, Foreign Trade and Development Cooperation.

Rogaly, B. (2008). "Migrant Workers in the Ilo's Global Alliance against Forced Labour Report: A Critical Appraisal," *Third World Quarterly* 29(7): 1431–1447.

Ross, C. (2017). *Ecology and Power in the Age of Empire: Europe and the Transformation of the Tropical World*. Oxford: Oxford University Press.

Scott, J. (1998). *Seeing Like a State. How Certain Schemes to Improve the Human Condition Have Failed*. New Haven/London: Yale University Press.

Scott, J. (1985). *Weapons of the Weak. Everyday Forms of Peasant Resistance.* New Haven/London: Yale University Press.

Seibert, J. (2011). "More Continuity Than Change? New Forms of Unfree Labor in the Belgian Congo, 1908–1930," in Marcel van der Linden (ed.). *Humanitarian Intervention and Changing Labor Relations. The Long-Term Consequences of the Abolition of the Slave Trade.* Leiden: Brill: 369–386.

Staner, P. (1955). "Les Paysannats Indigènes Du Congo Belge Et Du Ruanda-Urundi," *Bulletin Agricole du Congo Belge et du Ruanda-Urundi* 46(3): 467–551.

Urbano, A. (2017). "A "Grandiose Future for Italian Somalia": Colonial Developmentalist Discourse, Agricultural Planning and Forced Labor (1900–1940)," *International Labor and Working-Class History* 92: 69–88.

CHAPTER 10

Life on the Run: Coercive Geographies in Denmark–Norway, 1600–1850

Johan Heinsen

1 A History of Escape

In the night of 12 March 1723, two convicts by the names of Fridrich Schmit and Christian Møller worked silently to create a small opening in the roof of Copenhagen's naval dockyard prison. This penal institution was located within a large naval complex in what is today the heart of city. Because of the two convicts' involvement in previous escape plots, they had been placed in a small room apart from the rest of their fellow inmates who slept in two large dormitories. Furthermore, they had been placed in heavy bolts and fetters to hinder them in making new attempts at escape. Yet, during the morning routine the following day, when all inmates were mustered in the prison courtyard and the usual search of the facility commenced, the prison warden found only the broken irons and the makeshift exit, 15 by 9 inches wide. Schmit and Møller were gone (Standretsprotokoller 1722–1724, note from Matthias Schlieman 13 March 1723).

Rigorous interrogations revealed nothing. As the room from which the two men had escaped was connected to one of the dormitories by an open doorway, the examiners knew that some of the other inmates must have had knowledge about the escape. Yet, all were "so hardened that they refused to tell the proper truth." This infuriated the naval authorities who ran the prison, but, despite being collectively flogged, the convicts continued to deny having any knowledge of the escape whatsoever (Standretsprotokoller 1722–1724, court minutes 13–15 March 1723).

Meanwhile, Møller and Schmit were on the move. They found themselves nested within a series of concentric thresholds searching for ways to cross (Heinsen 2017). Managing to also exit the guarded city gates of Copenhagen, Schmit and Møller moved north. Their hopes were to go to Sweden – a destination favored by both prison breakers and military deserters in the period. However, in order to hinder escapes from the Danish monarch's territories, laws dictated that owners of vessels were not allowed to leave boats in a seaworthy state along the coast.

When in the late evening of 17 March Møller and Schmit reached the fishing village of Snekkersten just south of Elsinore, they thought themselves in luck. Lurking about in the dark on the beach they came across a small fishing vessel. As they attempted to drag it into the sea, someone heard them. The village fishermen chased the two convicts. Schmit lagged behind his friend and was caught. Møller reached the woods and was gone. He was never found again. Schmit, on the other hand, was forced to surrender. The fishermen watched him all night, and handed him over to the authorities in the morning, likely receiving a cash reward for their efforts. Scars on his forehead from having been branded gave away his identity as a convict (Standretsprotokoller 1722–1724, note from Kronborg 18 March 1723).

In his pockets, Schmit carried two letters. Both were passports. One was from the mayor of the Swedish city of Helsingborg on the other side of the Sound, permitting Schmit to be ferried across the border. It was dated 1 March 1723. The other passport was in the hand of Oluf Judichær, the admiral overseeing the dockyard. It was a release passport for a convict named Niels Christensen Bastrup, proclaiming that as this man had been pardoned by the King, he was allowed to move about as a free man. This passport was dated 10 March 1723 (Standretsprotokoller 1722–1724, evidence presented on 1 April 1723).

The convict by the name of Niels Christensen Bastrup had never been pardoned. Like the passport from the mayor of Helsingborg, the release passport was a fake. As Schmit was escorted back to Copenhagen and placed in the prison's dungeon – the so-called "Black Hole" – he proved much less hardened than his fellow inmates. On 1 April, he was forced to give up his story to the interrogator. Besides Møller, two other convicts had been part of the plot, but had not managed to get away. In lieux of crowbars, they had used the very bolts in which they had been placed to hinder further escape as their tools. A piece of stolen ship's rope had served them as they lowered themselves from the roof into the prison courtyard, before climbing the palisades. The noise of a patrol had kept their two comrades back. Schmit and Møller had been chased on the docks by a guard but had managed to shake him off in the dark. Silently, they had crept past another guard at the gate by Nyhavn in order to exit the sequestered dockyard premises. The sources do not tell us if they used their forged documents when they left the capital through a city gate at Vesterport, but we know that as they moved North, they avoided the main roads. They managed to pay for a meal at a farmer's house under the guise of being pigs' dealers. They offered up the same story several times over the next days as their circuitous itinerary led them from one small village after another. Not until reaching Snekkersten had they found a vessel to steal. Slyly, Schmit argued that the entire plot had been conjured up by Møller. Portraying absentees as the instigators of escape plots was a common strategy in situations like these (Standretsproto-koller 1722–1724, interrogations 1 April 1723).

However, Schmit's attempt to argue that the escape had not been planned in advance was undermined by the passports. He was forced to describe how the convict Bastrup had made a fake wooden seal of the Admiralty office. The Swedish seal had been harder to fake as it had a coat of arms on it. They copied it from an original by covering it in grease, then creating a mould from lacquer. This mould had then been used to make the proper imprint in the sealing wax. Bastrup confessed to the whole thing but argued that it was Schmit who had convinced him to do it on the premise that he would then make sure to bring him along when they escaped. The group had even discussed the prospect of counterfeiting money once they would arrive in Sweden. Bastrup had a skilled hand and Møller was a convicted coiner. On account of Bastrup's testimony, Schmit was sentenced to have been the originator of the plan. Already carrying a life sentence, his punishment was three years in fetters far heavier than the regular irons carried by all convicts in the prison. The rest were flogged and Bastrup was sentenced to have his hand severed for his forgeries. However, in the end Bastrup's hand was spared by royal mercy, probably so as not to render him unable to perform the manual labor at the docks (Standretsprotokoller 1722–1724, sentence 14 April 1723 and resolution 1 May 1723).

The classical tenets of liberalism might have taught us to read this story as an expression of something universal: that the travails of Møller and Schmitt reveal an innate quest for personal freedom that is essentially human but is thwarted by an oppressive state. And surely, history teaches us that states were build from coercion. As recently argued by James C. Scott, even the earliest agrarian states relied on human bondage (Scott 2017: 150–182). Yet, to view the story as an expression of the ahistorical nature of states and their subjects is to overlook how the key elements of the story – the prison, the need for personal documentation, mobilities defined as illicit, a border enforced – were the his-torical products of what was by then a relatively recent turn involving the state, the labor market and the population. The period from the middle of the six-teenth century to the nineteenth century was defined by experiments that cre-ated coercive geographies, not only in Scandinavia, but all over Europe and its empires.

Global labor historians have imprinted on us that this period in history was defined by the forced migrations and mobilizations of enslaved, indentured or convicted labor. That process of mass coercion formed a prerequisite in the creation of global capitalism (Rediker and Linebaugh 2000; Beckert 2014; Donoghue and Jennings 2015; Anderson 2018). This scholarship emphatically shows that the basic premise of both classical and marxist economics which stipulates that capitalism is incompatible with unfree labor is empirically untenable and that many of the concepts with which we conceptualise class and class struggle are particular to a short period of industrial capitalism in the west, but fail to encompass the complexities, coercions and grey areas within labor relations throughout history and across the globe (van der Linden 2008; De Vito, Schiel and van Rossum 2020). Following this new line of reasoning, scholars have recently begun highlighting how desertion was a common but reflexive form of resistance on the part of the coerced and the displaced and can be interpreted as a genuine struggle for agency (van Rossum and Kamp 2016; Rediker, Chakraborty and van Rossum 2019). This reinterpretation of escape runs counter to an older more traditional marxist view that saw desertion as a "weak" sometimes even cowardly form of class struggle. Thus, forced labor and displacement was countered by the attempts of millions to wrestle themselves out of the grips of colonial masters and to forge new lives through illicit mobility. Hence, escape offers a prism to understanding social relations of the early modern world, just as it does in our present.

Such histories have focused largely on colonial settings. Arguably, illicit mobility was key in struggles against slavery and helped create enduring cultures of resistance as evident from the multitude of cases of mass escape and marronage unearthed by scholars. Yet, while these new conceptualizations have created histories that help us understand the long lineages of contemporary struggles against confinement, coercion and precarity in a wide range of geographies, relatively little systematic attention has been paid to how the geographies of Europe itself were structurally remade in the period as well.

Elements of that remaking echo in how European states today deal with issues of mobility and transgression. For instance, while we tend to think of recent developments in migration policies as a fundamental change in how Western liberal democracies deal with migrant populations and labor, the instruments put to use by those states as they enforce their borders – among them confinement, policing, documentation of personal identity, deportation – often took on their earliest recognizable shapes in the period from the sixteenth to the nineteenth century. They are inheritances of a Europe that had a market economy for goods and labor, but was neither liberal, nor democratic and in which workers were, by definition, not free. In this way, many practices of control exercized by contemporary states were initially institutionalized in a world that ran on very different rationalities than those we perceive to be the basis of modern European societies. The states that created them were war machines, often global empires and some – such as Denmark–Norway – were constitutionally absolutist. The legal traditions reflected in these geographies did not revolve around civil rights but around the interests of both state and private employers. Thus, while they were designed with very different aims than those they currently serve, these fundamental building blocks of control reflect a specific constellation at the nexus between the state, its territories and the individual that carries inheritances from these much older types of state. In this way, exploring this earlier history helps us historicize the present and to see current politics less as a discontinuity and perhaps more as a return within a deep history of ebbs and flows.

This chapter sketches the story of how this coercive geography was made and tested from a highly specific vantage point: the history of escape from the early prisons of Copenhagen – at that point the capital of the composite state of Denmark–Norway. While the penal system of the period was certainly symptomatic of the deep structures that imprinted on a host of different types of labor and power relations, the story could have been told with a focus on any of these other types of labor coercion including agricultural, urban or military service. Similar stories could also have been told – with only minor variation in form and pace – focusing on other European states. The age of coercion and confinement explored in the following pages was far from confined to this small Northern European theater. However, focusing on escaped convicts holds the advantage that convicts came from all of the above-mentioned sectors and upon escape often sought to re-join them. Therefore, the escape stories found in eighteenth century court records form a useful heuristic for coming to grips with how the different systems of control created to police specific groups of workers and their mobility came together to form a single coercive geography. The focus on Copenhagen is also specifically useful as the capital was Denmark's main garrison city whose bulwarks formed an important element in the control of the urban population. From the peace treaty at Roskilde in 1658 onwards, it was also positioned at a border, since the territories on the other side of the Sound became Swedish. Subsequently, the slender body of water separating the two competing kingdoms also separated two competing states and their labor markets, providing the opportunity of a fresh start for runaways from all sectors of society. Thus, that competition helped create both barriers and pathways across this early modern borderscape.

2   Creating Confinement

In the early modern period, carceral institutions emerged as an important tool in how states enforced restraints on mobility. Revisionist historians of the second half of the twentieth century conceptualized the prison as an invention of the late eighteenth century. In doing so they crafted a strong, but flawed narrative that has imprinted heavily on how the history of the prison has been interpreted across the social sciences. While Michel Foucault explained the emergence of the prison by relating it to new notions of discipline and the self, Michael Ignatieff also related it to the industrial revolution (Foucault 1977; Ignatieff 1978). Hugely influential, both interpretations have come under close scrutiny by historians, yet still form a common enough historical framework that a recent state-of-the-art prison ethnography proclaims that "incarceration as the central modality of retributive justice has existed for little more than two centuries" pointing to the revisionist narrative and exclaiming that until that point punishments were almost without exception "corporal and public" (Fassin 2017: 14). However, the genealogies of Foucault and Ignatieff must be understood from the particular perspective of France and England respectively. The rather sudden turn of those two states towards carceral measures in the eighteenth century came late compared to other European states. In fact, it only created forms of bondage that had strong parallels in already existing forms of punishment in Scandinavia, the Netherlands, Germany, Austria and Spain and which had in many of these places been practiced for more than a century (Gibson and Poerio 2018). In several of those places, imprisonment combined with hard labor had already either largely supplanted or co-existed with the spectacular corporal punishments often assumed to be the antithesis of carceral institutions.

Generally, what we might then call "the early modern prison" came in two forms that can be distinguished by the labor performed. The best studied are the institutions in which convicts performed intramural labor. The Dutch pioneered a form of this institution in the 1590s often called "spinhouses" because of the wool production taking place within them. They are commonly referred to as "prison workhouses" in anglophone literature. Throughout the first decades of the seventeenth century, this type of institution was adopted and adapted throughout the Low Countries as well as by German and Scandinavian authorities, with the first such institution on Danish soil opening in 1605. They generally mixed productive and rehabilitative aims and were commonly conceptualized as households. (Spierenburg 1991; Larner 2018) Thus, the chastisement endured was akin to that which the child in a god-fearing family should expect from her parents. Initially, some of these institutions directly targeted children and adolescents who could be raised as good christians and taught the profession of spinners. In this way, the prison workhouse was both a school and a factory. The inmate populations not only tended to mix children and adults, but also the criminal and the poor. Thus, only a few of these institutions can technically be considered penal institutions, if one adopts a purist definition. In his pathbreaking study, Dutch historian Pieter Spierenburg put such a definition to use, and argued that the first criminal prison – meaning a purpose-built prison designed for convicted offenders – was the rasphouse of Amsterdam which opened in 1654. They were forced to rasp dyewoods imported from America. Only male offenders with an actual sentence entered this prison workhouse. Countering the revisionist view that the prison was born in the second half of the eighteenth century, Spierenburg thus gave a firm birth certificate to the prison as we understand it (Spierenburg 1991: 143).

However, Spierenburg effectively neglected the fact that outside of the Netherlands the prison workhouses had to compete with a different kind of institution: one designed around extramural labor activities. Only men were subjected to this form of punishment. What they experienced is sometimes conceptualized as "public works" punishment and argued to harken back to Roman traditions of "opus publicum" (Sellin 1976; Krause 2003). The earliest appearances of this type of punitive labor are from Copenhagen (1558), Ulm (1560) and Almadén (1566). In the anglophone literature the latter case – in which convicts were used side by side with enslaved workers in the mercury mines of Spain – is the most well known, and it has been argued that other European practices sprang from it (Spierenburg 2015: 113). It was clearly related to already existing practices of using convicts as galley rowers, which was at the time spreading across the Mediterranean. However, the chronology does not support the hypothesis that Europe's convict labor institution sprang from this origin. In fact, nothing seems to suggest that the three emergences in the mid-sixteenth century were directly related. Instead, it appears that they shared the same structural preconditions: that of a utilitarian response to labor shortages.

All three strands developed and mutated. Spain would eventually develop a penal practice known as "presidio" punishment which saw convicts used as manual laborers at fortresses across Spain's colonial possessions (Pike 1983). By the early seventeenth-century, experiments with mobilizing chained offenders in Ulm developed into a tradition known as *Schellenwerke*. From its Southern German origins, it spread south and became widespread in Switzerland (Fumasoli 1981). Eventually, Habsburg Austria even transposed the model into Transylvania and combined it with forced displacement along the Danube (Steiner 2015). Generally, the inmates lived in facilities that also doubled as prison workhouses for other groups of inmates and much like the workhouses the populations tended to mix the criminal and the poor. In some cases, the most egregious offenses were instead punished with galley service under foreign rulers (Schuck 2000). For those not exported from these landlocked territories, the work took place in chains outside, often consisting of cleaning streets etc. The name derives from the bells that were commonly attached to the chains.

On the surface, the parallel strand that developed in Scandinavia and spread into Northern Germany appear similar enough that historians have sometimes conflated the two (Krause 1999). Yet, nothing suggests that authorities in Ulm had drawn inspiration from Denmark. What happened to the North was, in a sense, more clean cut: convicts and criminalized groups were coerced into performing labor directly for the state, almost always to the advantage of the military sector. It was often understood in terms inherited from medieval notions of enslavement (Stuckenberg 1893; Heinsen 2018). At first these measures were directed at the criminalized wandering poor then by the start of the seventeenth century they were put to use for other groups such as thieves and deserters. In the middle ages, the poor had generally been accepted and charity considered a virtue. However, in the sixteenth century, Europe saw a general turn towards the criminalization of poverty and wandering especially that expressed itself in repression of begging and vagrancy. A Danish law code from 1558 called for local masters and officials to force the capable to work and even allowed for the enslavement of repeat idlers (Secher 1887–1888: 42–43). Private parties do not seem to have adopted this measure, but instead the state itself took the reins as construction work in the armament of Copenhagen, prompted the King to call for the forced conscription of "wandering beggars" later that year (Bricka et al. 1885–: 1556–1560:204). From 1566 onwards, much of such labor was performed at the naval dockyard in Copenhagen. Here the coerced helped build and maintain the Danish King's navy (Bricka et al. 1885–: 1566–1570:70).

What was happening was two-fold: Effectively, it became illegal for those deemed undeserving to refuse to serve a would-be employer, and punitive labor became a way of enforcing such labor coercion and immobilization. Thus, from this combination of criminalization and impressment a regular prison system emerged. Penal labor was institutionalized at the dockyard of Copenhagen and in the seventeenth century adapted to include prisons at military fortresses throughout the realm. By the late seventeenth century, it became common to refer to such prisons as "slaveries" and the inmates as "slaves" (slaver) even in official correspondence (F. Slavesager 1698–1794). Similar forms of punishment had by then been adopted in Northern Germany and in Sweden were the "slave" moniker followed. There was a heavy concentration of these institution around the Sound, were the labor of convicts were used by both Denmark–Norway and Sweden in efforts to strengthen against the other. Despite not being total institutions in the modern sense due to the extramural character of the labor, they were very much clear-cut penal institutions.

Thus, prisons as we know them formed across Europe against a backdrop of myriad practices marrying labor coercion, mobility control and confinement. While such practices have since mutated over and over again, and the heavy focus on labor extraction has slowly dissipated, the seeds to the prison system that is today being turned into a powerful tool in the repression of migrants all over Europe can be traced back to the second half of the sixteenth century. Then, as now, it was used to coerce poor people on the move.

3   Escaping an Early Modern Prison

The distinction between prison workhouses and these extramural convict labor institutions is key when studying escape practices. While escapes were common from institutions where labor took place inside the prison itself, they often grew massive in scale in extramural institutions. Working outside allowed frequent chances to escape. Even if labor was performed under supervision and in chains, its nature provided inmates with possibilities of exit. Thus, Schmit's escape was uncommon in being an escape from the prison building itself. Usually, convicts would run from the outdoor worksites during the day.

Escaped convicts were everpresent in debates about crime and punishment (e.g. Lütken 1813; Hvidberg 1814; Tøttrup 1815). This did not express a moral panic, but a very real concern. Studying the inmate registers of *Trunken* from 1690 to 1740, I have found that almost one in five convicts managed to escape at least once from this prison (see Heinsen 2017: Chapter 5). Unsurprisingly, all of Schmit's co-conspirator later managed to get away in other plots. Schmit himself also ran again on several occasions, though he was caught every time. Eventually, he was sent to a smaller slavery at Kronborg as authorities crafted an internal deportation scheme in which the most troublesome convicts circulated between prisons in order to break up inmate organization (Bøger over Bremerholms fanger 1722–1739).

There was a direct correlation between an inmate's sentence and his propensity to run. Thus, those who served only short sentences were much less likely to try escaping than those with life sentences. Further, if the convict had been branded or otherwise defaced, the likelihood of flight became even greater. This latter phenomenon can be explained by the simple fact that defaced convicts – who always served life sentences – were seen as socially dead and unfit for pardons. Thus, they knew that their only way out of prison was to run (Heinsen 2017: Chapter 5). As early as the beginning of the eighteenth century we see clear traces of a prisoner subculture in the prison, in which inmates cooperated in large scale on escape plots, keeping internal discipline, beating up snitches, etc. (Engberg 1973; Heinsen 2018). The escape plot in 1723, in which a large group of fellow prisoners collectively refused to reveal the makeup of the plot, is one of the earliest known cases.

Thus, as in many other settings, escape was not as difficult as we might imagine (van der Linden 2016). On the run, however, convicts faced a number of difficulties, sometimes put in place to police them specifically, at other times to police the mobile poor in general. The painstaking preparations of Schmit and his conspirators need to be understood in light of these measures. Document forgeries are a recurrent theme in cases against runaways. Sometimes passports were written by the same people who ran. At other times runaways bought documents from other inmates (F. Justitsprotokoller 1779–1783: 276). In some cases we see that prison breakers managed to buy passports after having already escaped, but the prices cited in such cases were often higher than the relatively modest sum that a passport cost on the inside.[1] The reason for this price disparity is simple: convicts did not receive pay for their work in the early eighteenth century. This changed by the middle of the century, but then the pay was still only barely enough for the convicts to subsist on. Therefore, prices were generally low within the black market of the prison. At the same time, forging passports could earn a convict a reputation and some seem to have done so as a way to gain status within the convict hierarchy (Standretsproto-koller 1722–1724, minutes 8–9 July 1723).

The need to forge documents again point towards workings of the coercive geography that all mobile poor moved within in early modern Denmark. Thus, it was created by the same forces that had created the prison itself. By the mid-sixteenth century Danish rulers had begun reigning in the mobility of the poor in other ways than by incarceration. This happened not only in Denmark, but all over Europe (Beier 1985; Krogh 1987). Anti-vagrancy laws in Denmark–Norway imposed demands for documentation on the poor. Those who were seen as deserving poor were given proofs that they were allowed to beg within a given town or parish. Nobody else were allowed to receive private alms. Effectively, this created a system that persisted into the nineteenth century, in which those defined as being deserving were allowed to receive aid and in which mobility was by definition suspect as assistance hinged on belonging to the native community. By the early eighteenth century, begging in all forms were in theory outlawed as the poor were now to receive alms only through the

---

1   For instance, convict Rasmus Schmidt paid 24 shillings for a passport while on the run in 1775 (F. Justitsprotokoller 1773–1779: 391–393). In no case from within prisons is the price of a passport cited as having been more than 8 shillings.

poor commissions. Private almsgiving was criminalized although this measure proved impossible to enforce effectively (Hansen 2008).

Other types of documentation came into use as well. Most notable was the need for passports for people on the move. For instance, a royal proclamation from 1582 demanded that no ships at the island of Bornholm in the Baltic Sea were allowed to take on passengers unless they could show passports from authorities specifying that they were allowed to move about. Further, the King demanded a watchful eye on vessels and oars. This all happened because of "roving people" and "escaped criminals" were said to use the island as a refuge. Fines were put in place for people who violated such prescriptions (Bricka et al. 1885–: 1580–1583:537). This is one of the earliest examples of compulsory documentation in Scandinavia. Over the next decades it became common practice. For instance, after one of the earliest known collective prison breaks in Denmark in late 1621, the King sent out missives to his magistrates to ensure control at the common ferry crossings on the island of Zealand. The way of identifying the runners was to be their lack of passports (Bricka et al. 1885–: 1621–1623:194).

By the middle of the seventeenth century, such measures of control were also applied to the workforce of Denmark's growing army. The majority of soldiers were at this point migrants. Mercenary soldiers signed away their freedom for eight years at a time. In this time span they had no rights of resignation. About two thirds were recruited in Germany which made German soldiers the period's largest migrant labor force in Denmark. They were stationed in garrison cities all over the realm, with Copenhagen itself being the centre of this military geography. They were severely underpaid, and in order to make a living many were given passes that allowed them to seek short-term employment in Copenhagen or around the countryside. This also helped to keep the cost of labor low, so besides being a policy meant to keep a large army in reserve, it can be seen as an attempt to suppress wages at large. Policy dictated that only 40% of these foreign soldiers were allowed to marry – possibly in order to keep them from staying, when their contracts ran out. The testimonies left by these migrants articulate experiences of coercion – sometimes likened by themselves to slavery (Petersen 2002; Nübling 2005; Krogh 2017). Control of this large group of male workers was a key concern of lawmakers. They were disproportionally overrepresented among inmates in the prisons.[2] They generally served long sentences as the crimes that brought them before court were

---

2   All statistics presented are based on Bøger over fangerne på Bremerholm # 1–16 in the archive
    of Holmen's chef, Rigsarkivet and Slaverulle # 32–40 in the archive of Københavns Stokhus,
    Rigsarkivet.

typically either theft – explained by their poverty – or desertion – explained by their lack of autonomy. This also means that they were further overrepresented among those convicts who became prison breakers (Heinsen 2018). Ex-deserters turned prison breakers knew what they faced as they ran.

Laws on desertion called for punishments of all who assisted deserters, not only knowingly, but also unknowingly (Forordning om deserteurer 1703). When the testimonies of prison breakers speak again and again about difficulties of finding vessels it was because of desertion laws which commanded everyone to chain or lock up their vessels and to take away oars. Those same laws consolidated the practice of offering cash rewards to people who apprehended or presented information that could lead to the apprehension of deserters. In a few cases, we know that prison breakers were actually apprehended by civilians on suspicion that they were soldiers on the run. Rewards were also paid in cases of prison breakers (F. Justitsprotokoller 1783–1791: 405).

For prison breakers and deserters alike, neighboring Sweden (and to a lesser extent Germany to the south) presented an alluring opportunity. The reasons for this are tied to questions of control, but also labor. First and foremost, Swedish authorities were not on the lookout for the runaway, so there was a much smaller chance of being caught. Secondly, the Swedish military offered a chance to start over. Many convicts managed to establish new lives in Sweden. We know this because quite a few grew so confident in their regained freedom that they returned years later to Denmark only to be apprehended (F. Justitsprotokoller 1783–1789: 233). Thus, border crossing was a way to reset the score and create a new identity. This dynamic is wellknown in many border regions of early modern Europe. Thus, it was common practice for deserters (and through the same flows also prison breakers) to be recruited upon arrival in new places. (Kamp 2016) The standing armies of early modern Northern Europe had an insatiable appetite for recruits and would rarely question the personal history of a foreigner.

If a runaway on Zealand was unable or unwilling to cross the Sound, the regiments stationed around Denmark and the fact that their recruitment was organized by each regiment itself created a structure that could be used by people on the run. Thus, upon recruitment the mercenary soldier received a considerable sum in ready money. Many ex-military convicts sought out this opportunity after escaping, but signing on came with its own risk, as recruitment officers were, at least in theory, to ask the would-be recruit for papers, and at times lists of the names and – increasingly – physical descriptions of deserters and prison breakers circulated (Standretsprotokoller 1722–1724, interrogations 8 January 1724). Thus, this was another threshold at which there was a need to be able to present a false identity. Cases are known in which the recruit showed forged papers, but then gave a different name from the one in the documents. This could reflect the fact the relatively low levels of literacy among the poor in the period. Thus, one might have documents to present, but be unable to read them (F. Justitsprotokoller 1779–1783, 8 December 1780).

If successfully recruited, the daring could then repeat the process by running again in order to go for the bounty of signing up somewhere else. Such bounty-jumping is a well-known phenomenon across early modern Europe's military labor market. Other recruited prison breakers deserted their new regiments for other reasons. In several cases, caught prison breakers explained that they had run because they encountered people who knew their prior identity (Standretsprotokoller 1727–1732, interrogations 29 June 1728).

Similar problems were faced by people, who opted for returning home. In the period, Copenhagen's prisons saw inmates arrive from all across the realm, so some had a long way to move and many thresholds to cross. For those who came from Zealand or other nearby places, it was easier and even more tempting to return home. However, people in the local community in some cases challenged the claims of the prison breaker of having been pardoned and many were returned (Olafsson 1905). Others opted for creating new identities in new places in rural Denmark. However, just as recruitment agents were demanded to question the identity of recruits, so were private employers, usually by being proscribed to consult the so-called conduct books that any would be employee could be forced to present and in which an employer would – at the end of contract – give his evaluation of the employee. Sometimes such documentation was also conceptualized as a way of hindering criminals and escapees from being able to hide (Forordning om Passer og Skudsmaale 1701).

The private labor market was very different from what we know today. Only certain groups were allowed to perform casual wage labor. These were tenant cottagers and mercenary soldiers who had either been given the right to seek temporary employment or had served out their capitulation and been given a discharge pass. If the convict had a way to present themselves as either of these things, they could roam and take whatever jobs they could get. However, the general rule all over Scandinavia was that employment took the form of servitude (Ågren 2017). Servitude was highly regulated and contracts were, by law, set to be at least six months. During this time, the servant was part of their master's household (Østhus 2013). Anti-vagrancy laws defined the vagrant as those among the poor who were not in the service of an employer if such a position was to be had. Therefore, the majority of the propertyless faced the options of binding themselves to a master for a set amount of time, or to run the risk of performing day to day casual labor, yet formally be considered a vagrant and be subject to persecution. Not only did such laws – at least in theory – tie everybody to a fixed place in the social order. It also undermined the possibility of bargaining on the part of the potential servant. Effectively, the mobile poor ran afoul of the law, if they did not accept the terms of conditions set by employers.

The coercion experienced by servants in Denmark became even worse by the creation of the conscript army. From 1701, it became the sole privilege of landlords to choose who were conscripted from local communities. Only those, who had already leased farms and married were legally excluded. Thus, servitude now came with the risk of being singled out to serve in the conscript army. We know of convicts who effectively entered local communities, but then ran because of fears of being drafted (F. Justitsprotokoller 1773–1779, 1 February 1775). By 1733 this construction evolved. Now all men under 40 were tied to the estates on which they had been born. If they decided to move without the landlord's permission, they would join the ranks of the runaways (Løgstrup 1987).

Effectively, a runaway needed two things to have any reasonable chance of success: a plausible identity that could be documented and the ability to fill a need for labor in whatever community they arrived in so as not to prompt suspicion. Many convicts did succeed in entering new labor relations upon escape. We can deduce the strategies of the successful from those who failed and in subsequent interrogation described where they had been. Despite the criminalization of casual labor, many employers would need seasonal employees, especially during harvests. Other convicts managed to become servants proper. Presenting a new identity would often need to work only once. If a farmer was willing to take a runaway on, they might then become an accepted part of local communities and sometimes acquired non-forged paperwork in their fake names. This possibility speaks to the fact that the interests of private and employers and state were not always completely in sync, even if the measures of coercion exercized by the state as a rule served employer interests. We know of at least one person who managed to convince the local priest that he had not been confirmed, before receiving this religious ritual in his fake name (F. Justitsprotokoller 1773–1779: 502). In other cases, we even know of an apprehended prison breaker who upon a subsequent escape ran back to the same employer (F. Justitsprotokoller 1773–1779: 66).

The sum of all of these legal measures was that by the eighteenth century no subject of a master (i.e. everyone but a very small elite) was, in principle, to move from one local community to another without being granted permission in writing. Whether part of the military, urban or rural labor markets legal mobility hinged on interlocking systems of documentation that had developed ad hoc over two centuries and which worked to tie workers to the written word of their employers – whether state or private. In effect, this entailed a definition of personal identity and belonging that revolved around the question of place of origin and employment. This worked against the mobility of prison breakers and other runaways, and the prison itself enforced this structure, as forgeries of any kind could lead to sentences of hard labor. As this construction of identity defined at the nexus of spatial and hierarchical belonging solidified it proved to have tremendous staying power.

4   Tightening the Grip

During the eighteenth century, it became even harder to be on the run. While many of the restrictions in place upon mobility originated in the sixteenth century and had been foundational to the creation the prison itself, the grip was now beginning to tighten. More than ⅔ of all escapees in the early decades of the eighteenth century stayed free. However, by the end of the century that rate had dropped to around ⅓. In the nineteenth century, it fell even more. Such numbers serve as a powerful index of the process of making a coercive geography. While we cannot calculate success for other types of runaways in the period because of insufficient source materials, we have no reason to suspect that their success rates did not also drop.

There are many reasons for this development. The Danish state repeatedly tried to close the Swedish route. Beginning in the early eighteenth century they signed repeated cartels with Sweden for the exchange of both deserters and escaped criminals. However, these were only intermittently enforced, and men crossed the border into freedom throughout the century. Thus, the border continued to be a problem for Danish authorities. Other measures were taken. The first substantial Danish border control was therefore a ship that was stationed to continually patrol the Sound for vessels with deserters and runaways. When at times the ship was unable to patrol because of ice, foot patrols were posted on beaches or on the ice itself in order to prevent crossings (F. Justitsprotokoller 1783–1791: 258). In this way, the border became harder, as authorities attempted to keep their runaway workers in. As such, permanent border control in Denmark – as in many other places – was born as an instrument of labor control.

Attempts at enforcing document control at the borders have also left considerable traces. Thus, among the men who made up the convict populations of the prisons we encounter quite a few fishermen and other vessel owners sentenced for ferrying deserters and convicts. From several of their cases, we get the sense that the absence of vessels to be stolen meant that ferrying run-aways in need of transportation actually became a business for some along Zealand's eastern coast.[3] Judging by the frequency of such cases, there seems to have been an increased focus on such practices as the eighteenth century went on. Similarly, there were repeated attempts to enforce laws about de-manding documents of people roaming highways or entering the major cities.

New forms of knowledge aided the attempts at confinement. As newspa-pers grew increasingly common from the 1760s onwards, it became standard practice to advertise runaways of all kinds. Such practices have been well re-searched in colonial settings but were a stable feature in European societies as well (Maxwell-Stewart and Quinlan 2019). The Copenhagen newspaper *Kongelig Alene Priviligerede Adressekontor* carried thousands such advertise-ments during the last decades of the eighteenth century. Here prison breakers shared the pages with runaway servants, deserted tenant farmers, missing sail-ors, absentee apprentices, absconding soldiers etc. No type of source testifies more dramatically to just how bonded the early modern workforce was. Adver-tisements carried ever more detailed physical descriptions of escapees. For instance, we know that prison breaker Niels Hansen who ran in 1774 was "short of stature with a smooth face, black curly hair and brown eyes." His most uniquely identifiable feature was his limp, as several of his toes had "frozen off" (Kiøbenhavns Kongelig alene priviligerede Adresse-Contoirs Efterretninger, 11 March 1774). Hansen was then advertised again in 1790, having deserted once again. He was by then described as "small in height, has blackish hair, has slen-der limbs and face" (Kiøbenhavns Kongelig alene priviligerede Adresse-Contoirs Efterretninger, 28 June 1790). If branded, the state of a convict's scars could also be noted, while other runaways were identified on account of spe-cific ways of talking or recognizable mannerisms. Most importantly perhaps, the bounty was also advertised as the control mobilized in this way still needed incentives. When in the early nineteenth century, description protocols be-came common practice in the prisons, authorities would have a firm language of identity available to them. Such protocols would register similar character-istics as well as features such as scars and tattoos (Signalementsprotokol 1807–1832). They formed a powerful language of unique identity long before photog-raphies, fingerprints and dna. In this way, a visual dimension was added to the structure of identification outlined above.

Deportation as a practice also gained new relevance. Banishment had been in use as a punishment for as long as there are written sources, but usually

---

3   We find traces of quite a few such cases in the various entry books of the prisons in
    question.

banishment meant being expelled from the local community to which one belonged. The prison itself often supplanted this practice as those banished from a local community had effectively presented a problem in the eyes of the state, as the practice simply created more roving poor. Now banishment changed form, as it became common for authorities to give conditional commutations to foreign offenders serving prison time, on the premise that they were sent by ship to either German or Swedish ports and never returned again. We know a few cases in which such people actually did return – prompting authorities to hand out new prison sentences (Mandtal over Forbedringshusets lemmer 1773–1790, #899). Then, by the nineteenth century, this practice morphed and through the century several thousands native Danish subjects were released from prisons on the condition of letting themselves be transported overseas and never return (Bertelsen and Kirkebæk 2014). The most common destination was USA. This was not a transportation scheme in the traditional sense, given that the destination was not a territory of the Danish sovereign.

One final development contributed to the increasing difficulty of staying on the run: the slow advent of the police as a crime fighting institution. All over Europe policing was being professionalized. While police had existed in Copenhagen since 1683, it was only in the eighteenth century that police officers became involved in actual crime fighting and investigation. And whereas the police had initially been limited to Copenhagen, every city worth its name had a small police force by the early nineteenth century. In this way, the state became somewhat less dependent on suspicious employers, ferrymen and recruitment agents (Pedersen 2014). Yet, from studying court proceedings against runaways, it still appears relatively rare that police themselves identified a person on the loose. They did however provide those who suspected that a person might be a runaway with an easy way of having the person apprehended (F. Justitsprotokoller 1783–1791: 460). Further, the police did actively enforce rules against vagrancy and working with pauper authorities they mass incarcerated beggars which severely limited the strategies of runaways wanting to stay away from prying eyes.[4]

5   Conclusion

This essay has been an attempt to sketch out an early history of control over labor and mobility in Scandinavia by tracing the difficulties and options of

---

4   This is evident from the musters at Copenhagen's prison workhouse. See Mandtalsbog for Børne- og Rasphuset samt for Tugt- og Rasphuset 1772–1778 and 1778–1811.

convict runaways from Copenhagen's prisons. In doing so, it traces a history in which both state and employers found new ways to discipline and control itinerant labor – these include institutions of confinement, new modes of identification, border patrols and deportation practices. Incidentally, this culminated at the same time that nominally free wage labor started to become increasingly common. In this light, the period around 1800 is defined by still more fine-combed measures of labor coercion and its control on mobility. This runs counter to the common narrative presented in Danish whig historiography, in which the late eighteenth century heralds Danish modernity as the remnants of serfdom eroded and the market for land was liberalized.

In turn, studying the themes of this volume in a deep historical perspective raises questions about the current situation of labor (im)mobility, coercion and state policies of confinement; it asks where current instruments of coercion and restraints on mobility have come from, what exactly has changed since and why historical forms of control seem to be so inherent to state practices. It should not be understood as an argument that modernity originated in early modern Scandinavia, but rather as a plea for deeper archeologies questioning modernity as such. Historicized in this way, what appears to be a rather sudden and somewhat erratic turn towards a regime of confinement – on the surface at odds with the core tenants of liberal democracies – becomes something much more central to the workings of Western states in their many iterations across historical periods. Without neglecting the paradoxes of the present, we need to understand that modern states have inherited many of their tools from the ruthless utilitarianism of military-fiscal states and their mercantilist economic politics. Thus, the paradoxes sometimes are echoes of the past. Deep spectral resonances reverberate in the politics of our contemporary world.

References

Anderson, C. (ed.) (2018). *A Global History of Convicts and Penal Colonies*. London: Bloomsbury.

Beckert, S. (2014). *Empire of Cotton: a global history*. New York: Knopf.

Beier, A.L. (1985). *Masterless men: The vagrancy problem in England 1560–1640*. London: Methuen.

Bertelsen, J., and Kirkebæk, B. (2014). *Uønsket i Danmark – bortsendt til Amerika*. Copenhagen: SFAH, 2014.

Bricka, C.F. et al. (eds.) (1885–). *Kancelliets brevbøger*. Multiple vols. Copenhagen: Reitzel.

Bøger over Bremerholms fanger 1722–1739, Holmens chef (Søetaten), Rigsarkivet.

De Vito, C., Schiel, J., and van Rossum M. (2020). "From Bondage to Precariousness? New Perspectives on Labor and Social History," *Journal of Social History*, 1–19.

Donoghue, J., and Jennings, E. (eds.) (2015). *Building the Atlantic Empires: Unfree Labor and Imperial States in the Political Economy of Capitalism, ca. 1500–1914*. Leiden: Brill.

Engberg, J. (1973). *Dansk Guldalder, eller Oprøret i Tugt-, Rasp-, og Forbedringshuset*. Copenhagen: Forlaget Rhodos.

F. Justitsprotokoller 1773–1779, Forsvarets Auditørkorps, Auditøren for Københavns Garnisonskommandantskab, Rigsarkivet.

F. Justitsprotokoller 1779–1783, Forsvarets Auditørkorps, Auditøren for Københavns Garnisonskommandantskab, Rigsarkivet.

F. Justitsprotokoller 1783–1791, Forsvarets Auditørkorps, Auditøren for Københavns Garnisonskommandantskab, Rigsarkivet.

F. Slavesager 1698–1794, Auditøren for Kronborg Fæstning, Generalauditøren, Rigsarkivet.

Fassin, D. (2017). *Prison Worlds: An ethnography of the carceral condition*. Cambridge: Polity Press.

Forordning om deserteurer. 13 October 1703. Copenhagen.

Forordning om Passer og Skudsmaale. 19 February 1701. Copenhagen.

Foucault, M. (1977. Org. 1975). *Discipline and Punish: The birth of the prison*. London: Penguin.

Fumasoli, G. (1981). *Ursprünge und Anfänge der Schellenwerke: Ein Beitrag zur Frühgeschichte des Zuchthauswesens*. Zürich: Schultess.

Gibson, M., and Ilaria Poerio, I. (2018). "Modern Europe, 1750–1950," in Anderson, C. (ed.). *A Global History of Convicts and Penal Colonies*. London: Bloomsbury: 337–370.

Heinsen, J. (2017). *Mutiny in the Danish Atlantic World*. London: Bloomsbury.

Heinsen, J. (2018). *Det Første Fængsel*. Aarhus: Aarhus Universitetsforlag.

Hansen, P.W. (2008). "Den strafværdige gavmildhed: Synet på almissegivning, betleri og fattiglove i 1700-tallets Danmark," *Fortid og Nutid*, 173–197.

Hvidberg, O. (1814). *Noget om Tyverierne især i Kiøbenhavn*. Copenhagen.

Ignatieff, M. (1978). *A Just Measure of Pain: The penitentiary in the industrial revolution 1750–1850*. New York: Columbia University Press.

Kamp, J. (2016). "Between Agency and Force: The Dynamics of Desertion in a Military Labour Market, Frankfurt am Main 1650–1800," in van Rossum, M. and Kamp, J. (eds.). *Desertion in the Early Modern World*. London: Bloomsbury: 49–72.

Kiøbenhavns Kongelig alene priviligerede Adresse-Contoirs Efterretninger, 11 March 1774.

Kiøbenhavns Kongelig alene priviligerede Adresse-Contoirs Efterretninger, 28 June 1790.

Krause, T. (2003). "Opera Publica," in Gerhard Ammerer, G., Bretschneider, F., and Weiß, A.S. (eds). *Gefängnis und Gesellschaft: Zur (Vor-)Geschichte der strafenden Einsperrung.* Leipzig: Leipziger Uni-Vlg: 117–130.

Krause, T. (1999). *Geschichte des Strafvollzugs: Von den Kerkern des Altertums bis zur Gegenwart.* Darmstadt: Wissenschaftliche Buchgesellschaft.

Krogh, T. (1987). *Staten og de besiddelsesløse på landet 1500–1800.* Odense: Odense Universitetsforlag.

Krogh, T. (2017). "Larcenous Soldiers: Crime and Criminal Cultures in Copenhagen in the First Half of the Eighteenth Century," in Krogh. T., Kallestrup, L., and Christensen, C.B. (eds.). *Cultural Histories of Crime in Denmark, 1500–2000.* London: Routledge.

Larner, A. (2018). *The Good Household Gone Bad.* Ph.D.-dissertation. Aarhus University.

Lütken, F. (1813). *Om Tyverierne i Kjøbenhavn.* Copenhagen.

Løgstrup, B. (1987). *Bundet til jorden: Stavnsbåndet i praksis 1733–1788.* Odense: Landbohistorisk Selskab.

Mandtal over Forbedringshusets lemmer 1773–1790, Tugt-, Rasp-, og Forbedringshuset på Christianshavn, Rigsarkivet.

Mandtalsbog for Børne- og Rasphuset samt for Tugt- og Rasphuset 1772–1778, Tugt-, Rasp-, og Forbedringshuset på Christianshavn, Rigsarkivet.

Mandtalsbog for Børne- og Rasphuset samt for Tugt- og Rasphuset 1778–1811, Tugt-, Rasp-, og Forbedringshuset på Christianshavn, Rigsarkivet.

Maxwell-Stewart, H., and Quinlan, M. (2019). "Voting with Their Feet: Absonding and Labor Exploitation in Convict Australia," in Rediker, M., Chakraborty, T., and van Rossum, M. (eds.). *A Global History of Runaways: Workers, Mobility, and Capitalism, 1600–1850.* Oakland: University of California Press: 156–177.

Olafsson, J. (1905). *Islænderen Jon Olafssons oplevelser som bøsseskytte under Christian IV.* Copenhagen: Gyldendalske Boghandel.

Pedersen, K.P. (2014). *Kontrol over København: Studier i den sene enevældes sikkerhedspoliti 1800–48.* Odense: Syddansk Universitetsforlag.

Pike, R. (1983). *Penal Servitude in Early Modern Spain.* Madison: The University of Wisconsin Press.

Rediker, M., and Linebaugh, P. (2000). *The Many-Headed Hydra: The Hidden History of the Revolutionary Atlantic.* London: Verso.

Rediker, M., Chakraborty, T., and van Rossum, M. (eds.) (2019). *A Global History of Runaways: Workers, Mobility, and Capitalism, 1600–1850.* Oakland: University of California Press.

Schuck, G. (2000). "Arbeit als Policeystrafe: Policey und Strafjustiz," in Härter, K. (ed.). *Policey und frühneuzeitliche Gesellschaft.* Frankfurt am Main: Klostermann: 611–626.

Scott, J.C. (2017). *Against the Grain: A Deep History of the Earliest States.* New Haven and London: Yale University Press: 150–182.

Secher, V.A. (1887–1888). *Corpus constitutionum daniæ: Forordninger, recesser og andre Kongelige breve, Danmarks lovgivning vedkommende, 1558–1600.* Copenhagen: Selskabet for udgivelse af kilder til dansk historie.

Sellin, J.T. (1976). *Slavery and the Penal System.* New York: Elsevier.

Signalementsprotokol, 44, 1807–1832, Københavns Stokhus, Rigsarkivet.

Slaverulle, boxes 32–40, Københavns Stokhus, Rigsarkivet.

Spierenburg, P. (1991). *The Prison Experience: Disciplinary institutions and their inmates in Early Modern Europe.* Amsterdam: Amsterdam University Press.

Spierenburg, P. (2015). "Prison and Convict Labour in Early Modern Europe," in De Vito, C., and Lichtenstein, A. (eds.). *Global Convict Labour.* Leiden: Brill: 108–125.

Standretsprotokoller 1722–1724, Overadmiralitetsretten, Admiralitetet, Rigsarkivet.

Standretsprotokoller 1727–1732, Overadmiralitetsretten, Admiralitetet, Rigsarkivet.

Steiner, S. (2015). "'An Austrian Cayene': Convict Labour and Deportation in the Habsburg Empire of the Early Modern Period," in De Vito, C., and Lichtenstein, A. (eds.). *Global Convict Labour.* Leiden: Brill: 126–143.

Stuckenberg, F. (1893). *Fængselsvæsenet i Danmark 1550–1741.* Copenhagen: Gad.

Tøttrup, F. (1815). *Afhandling om det i de offentlige Blade i Maji 1814 fremsatte Spørgsmål: Hvilke ere de meest hensigtsmæssige Midler til, i en stor Stad og navnlig i Kiøbenhavn at forebygge og afværge Tyverier?* Copenhagen.

van der Linden, M. (2008). *Workers of the World: Essays toward a Global Labour History.* Leiden: Brill.

van der Linden, M. (2016). "Mass Exits: Who, Why, How?," in van Rossum, M., and Kamp, J. (eds.). *Desertion in the Early Modern World.* London: Bloomsbury: 31–48.

van Rossum, M., and Kamp, J. (eds.) (2016). *Desertion in the Early Modern World: A Comparative History.* London: Bloomsbury.

Østhus, H. (2013). *Contested Authority: Master and servant in Copenhagen and Christiania, 1750–1850.* Ph.D.-dissertation. European University Institute.

Ågren, M. (eds.) (2017). *Making a Living, Making a Difference: Gender and Work in Early Modern European Society.* Oxford: Oxford University Press.

CHAPTER 11

Assembling Coercive Geographies in Comparative Context

Johan Heinsen, Martin Bak Jørgensen and Martin Ottovay Jørgensen

Dear miners, they will slave you
Until you can't work no more
And what will you get for your labor but a dollar in the company store
A tumbledown shack to live in
Snow and rain pouring through the top and you have to pay the company
rent and your payments will never stop

> Traditional, US, no year

∴

1 Introduction

In this book, we have sought to historicize the relation between mobility, labor and confinement. We do so through a conceptualization of *coercive geographies*. As written in the introduction coercive geographies is our attempt to bring together space, precarity, labor coercion and mobility in an analytical lens that examines *spatialities that work to create moments of coercion through practices that limit or otherwise define the mobility of a subject*. The focus on practices that the concept entails serves as a way to open up the way such spatialities constitute and produce a host of different experiences of coercion through concrete actions and instances. We contend, that coercive geographies are best understood, not by resorting to abstract categories or statuses, but by analyzing what is actually done, by multiple actors, in such (spatial) relations at multiple, sometimes serial, at other times parallel moments. Throughout the nine chapters providing the empirical bulk of the book we have tested this concept and applied it on both historical and contemporary cases. As editors, we have not enforced strict homogeneity in the way the concept has been put to use, but rather give the author(s) of each chapter space to adapt the concept to reflect the circumstances of the chapter. Our goal here is not to make a sharp distinction between then and now but rather to historicize the present relations of mobility, labor and confinement and to show its links

to coercive geographies from varied pasts. In other words, we have tried to argue that both past and present remain unfinished business, as practices have
and will continue to mutate. We have not argued that the present-day coercive
geographies are direct continuations of former ones but rather, that we can
identify echoes, convergences and resemblances. Thus, history can help us
come to terms with what is happening today, just as the rapidly changing contemporary world, can help us understand pasts that were themselves changing
and in flux. Coercive geographies were and are always processual – continuously made and remade, contested and asserted through social practices and
lived experiences that blur the dichotomy of past and present. In this way, our
ways of gauging the past and the present inform each other through uneven
exchanges.

2   Lessons Learned

Three of the chapters included in this volume relate to migrant workers' position in the agricultural supply chain. Apostolos Kapsalis, Konstantinos Floros
and Martin Bak Jørgensen's chapter focuses on Bangladeshi strawberry pickers
in Manolada, Greece, Karin Krifors' chapter looks at Thai berry pickers in the
Swedish forests, and Susi Meret and Irina Aguiari offer an analysis of the conditions of (especially) West African agricultural workers in Italy. The three cases
can be placed within a continuum of exploitation and mobility. The most regularized conditions exist for the Thai berry pickers. The Bangladeshis in Greece
are trapped in a semi-legal condition where their labor is regularized through
a temporary permit but their residence is not. A socio-legal status for migrants
that has been termed 'para-legality' by Apostolos Kapsalis, as the regulation
"constitutes a parallel state of tolerance (of labour) into illegality (of residence)
[...] as it appears that the residence status remains irregular throughout the
duration of the work permit" (Kapsalis 2018: 78). In Italy the hidden economy
amounts to €211 billion in 2017 (Meret and Aguiari, this volume) of which the
share of irregular work amounts to €79 billion. The business of the *caporalato*
system accounts for €5 billion of this. The *caporalato* system is the focus for
Meret and Aguiari's chapter, which describes how migrant workers are forced
to endure conditions that Meret and Aguiari liken to a form of modern-day
slavery. Their description of the *caporalato* system is an example of a coercive
geography. Their description of this system as a 'convergence of spatial coercion, ethnic segregation, and the geographical organization and dispersion of
a dispossessed workforce (through the intersection of class, gender, and racial
oppressions) are made indispensable to maintain and reproduce the profits

within the contemporary agri-business sector' (Meret and Aguiari, this volume) also describes the conditions Bangladeshi workers face in Manolada. The coercive geography in all three cases entails segregation. Just as in so many past systems of forced labor and enslavement, outsider status constituted through physical displacement is key to these practices of exploitation. And just as in so many historical examples, the Transatlantic plantation complex key among them, that outsider status has to be produced and maintained, through practices that confine the workforce even after their initial displacement. Understanding the complexity of that reproduction is crucial. These are geographies comprising spatial, economic, cultural and political segregation. In all three cases, the migrant workers live in remote settlements and makeshift camps away from the general population. Workers have few if any labor rights. They are physically separated from the rest of society with a wide array of legal, economic and cultural mechanisms of exclusion in force to enforce that separation. As a product, they are not conceived as people with legal rights. Most of all they represent an indispensable source of cheap labor to the local agricultural labor markets. Referring again to Harald Bauder, the political economy of neoliberal globalization creates a condition where the excluded are unsafe and vulnerable, but not superfluous – they are indeed valuable due to their vulnerable position and thus particularly exploitable (2006).

All three papers, and to some extent the volume as a whole, demonstrates how coercive geographies – while often produced by much larger processes of removal and difference – are intimately tied to highly specific power relations and coercive practices within very local geographies. In that way, these practices must also be understood against the backdrop of particular and situated histories in order to understand how these conditions of exploitability have come to be. In all three cases – to various degrees – migrant labor is regulated not by labor regulations but by actors whose action define the workings of these coercive geographies. In the *caporalato* system, the *carporale* (a middleman or 'gangmaster') is the link between the worker and a larger system of labor exploitation and coercion, deeply embedded in neoliberal economy. In Greece, these intermediary actors are termed *masturas*. A migrant intermediary also referred to as a group-commander. *Masturas* are paid to secure employment, a place in the camp, to secure papers. *Masturas* keep protesting workers away from work for eight or nine days. However, protests are scarce as such will lead to deprivation of work in a setting where work is the only way for the workers to ensure legal residence. In Greece, irregularized workers who can document a seven-year presence can apply for a 'residence permit for exceptional reasons.' *Masturas* are the ones who can help document presence, which makes workers accept exploitation from *masturas* and bosses in return for proof of legal existence. In the berry industry in Sweden it is the 'madam's monopoly on knowledge and transnational networks that facilitates berry picking in Sweden for the Thai berry pickers. A 'madam' refers to a Thai woman living with a foreign (Swedish) husband. Although not all berry pickers had an exploitative relationship with a 'madam.' The system with a middleman is also recognized in Sweden. The coercive geography characterizing berry picking in Sweden is different from the ones in Italy and Greece. In Sweden, Krifors describes it as a migration corridor where Thai workers become berry pickers as a result of complex infrastructures of diaspora and social networks, commercialization and professionalization, as well as a state lenience where no claims on social rights are made. The three cases illustrate how relations of mobility, labor and confinement are shaped and institutionalized within the agricultural supply chains in both north and south of Europe. Some of these relations are shaped in the recent years whereas the *caporalato* system has resisted across the centuries as a profitable form of labor coercion.

Individually, all three papers tell stories of our present moment. Collectively, they evoke deep links to myriad pasts of exploitation in agricultural production. The middleman or gang master as a character producing and enforcing vulnerability to exploitation through displacement has had more historical faces than can be grasped by a single study. Thus, history shows itself here both in the very concrete trajectories of specific places and in distorted reverberations of centuries of globalized violence. While slavery is often used politically as an abstraction to which such present conditions of labor coercion can be likened or against which its brutality can be measured, these specific stories also echo the nineteenth century and events in the wake of the collapse of Transatlantic slavery. Across the globe, Imperial authorities and plantation managers solved the labor shortages that followed abolitions by putting in place new forms of exploitation that bound, nominally free, Asian and African workers to soils through systems of debt and indenture that depended deeply on physical displacement and societal alienation, underlined by actual or potential physical compulsion, in the places where labor was to be performed. The forms of labor coercion that came to litter the colonized globe were themselves echoes of older forms. As argued by historian Alessandro Stanziani, the systems of indenture revolved around adaptations and mutations of old forms of servitude creating "forms of bondage inspired by status inequalities entrenched in Europe" (Stanziani 2014: 196). Thus, these forms carry deep links to the many forms of servitude that, rather than free wage labor, were the norm across Europe before the nineteenth century and which across Europe bound the lower classes to masters and places. In their globalization, however, these new "old" forms of dependency almost always depended on middlemen with localized knowledge and networks. Key were what historian Enrique Martino, in his studies of labor recruitment in the Gulf of Guinea, has labelled "economics of deception" in which recruiters and agents "armed themselves with varying degrees of deception, creativity, theatrics, and the most intimate of illicit relations, double-dealing and betrayal" (Martino 2015: 94). The resulting forms of migrant labor instituted extreme forms of precarity that could effectively make for a substitute for enslavement. Like the present cases discussed here, these systems too hinged on creating workforces that were valuable because of their vulnerability. In this way, this volume echoes previous histories of the globalization of labor and the role of coercion in that process. Linked to this evolving research agenda, the contributions demonstrate that capitalism, in its many forms, does not equate a workforce enjoying anything resembling a historical passage from bondage to "freedom" as stipulated by economics of old, but rather many workforces subject to heterogeneous precarities as they live and work confined within and across coercive geographies.

That confinement is the leading theme of the second group of chapters chapters focuses on border work, mobility and citizenship. The chapters by Vasileios Spyridon Vlassis, Leandros Fischer and Abdulkadir Osman Farah taken together show how coercive geographies are configured also by border regimes. As we saw in the first bulk of chapters a precarization of labor and states accepting (and even being dependent on) illicit labor relations shapes particular local geographies. The three chapters here offer a different reading. Vlassis argues that borders are not static, fixed or permanent. As Étienne Balibar argues, they are 'polysemic in nature' (2002). Borders therefore, including the external borders of the European Unions are better understood through the 'bordering practices' constituting the borders at a given time. Such a focus accommodates the plurality of actors and processes at play in shaping the border, be they state or non-state actors, migrants or other forms of actors, as well as their distribution in geographical terms (Vlassis, this volume). Nicholas de Genova calls for a focus on bordering, as a verb, an activity that "involves productive activity, a kind of labor" (De Genova 2016: 47). Borders, mobility and stuckedness are central for Fischer's analysis of the multiple links between migrant autonomy and austerity on Cyprus. The island is an ideal case to study such links due to the geographical position as an insular borderland along major migratory routes, its politically ambiguous status, as well as its character as a crisis-hit peripheral European society (Fischer, this volume). In this chapter, Fischer shows how many migrants today face both a class journey of downward social mobility, as well as a sense of existential stuckedness. Nevertheless, migrants may decide that the best survival strategy might be to 'wait out the crisis.' Waiting out can include an acquiescence to worsened living condition, effectively leading to an internalization of coercive structures and the blurring of distinctions between what constitutes free and unfree labor. Although 'free' migrants find themselves confined into certain labor niches through a complex set of legal mechanisms institutionalizing precarity. Fischer shows how downward mobility may result from processes along the intersection of race and class. At the same time, it is the product of state practices that seek to regulate the flow of migration, not only through the reception and the deportation center and through legal measures like working restrictions. He argues that the coercive geographies behind the current confinement of populations in reception and deportation centers are not solely intended to deter further migratory flows but to classify migrants and regulate their entry into local economies. Irregularized migrants face racialization, geographical confinement and labor restrictions, while those able to procure citizenship through a golden visa scheme can experience the island as 'expats' (Fischer, this volume). Categorizing people and making them countable, moveable and (ultimately) deportable is also a central aim for the screeners and FRONTEX officers in the Hotspots at the Greek islands investigated by Vlassis. The screening process is part of the border practices constituting the border through filtering and sorting mechanisms rendering the migrant subject known and governable for the EU's apparatus of migration governance. It is a coercive practice shaping both mobility and immobility.

Likewise, stuckedness is central for Farah's chapter. In his analysis of the Somali transnational community in the United Arab Emirates (UAE), he interrogates how precarity is experienced on an everyday basis and how it can be challenged. The UAE has attracted large and diverse migrant groups over at least the past four decades. At the same time migrants have next to, none rights except for working permits. The UAE has produced a system of precarity that imposes social, economic and political restrictions, generating the exploitation of communities as cheap labor. The intersection of restrictive migration and labor policies shapes the coercive geographies of the UAE. As noted in the introduction of this volume immigration controls function both as "a tap regulating the flow of labour" and as "a mould shaping certain forms of labour" (Anderson 2010: 301). However, Farah also shows how coercive geographies are contested through migrants' agency. Migrant precarity, he argues, remains a dynamic process conditioned by continuously transforming and challenging contexts and circumstances of which communities remain an active part (Farah, this volume). Taken together the three chapters show how mobility and immobility are constituted in tandem. The classification of migrants within a particular coercive geography situate them within relations of mobility, precarity and stuckedness, which migrants can navigate within with a limited set of options.

The third and final part of this volume, starts from historical cases as it interrogates the questions explored through contemporary practices in the first two. Van Melkebeke takes us back to the question of labor in the fields, but this time those worked to serve the global cotton industry of the first half of the twentieth century as capitalism expanded in Belgian Congo after the Belgian state had taken over the colony from the Belgian king. As labor intensive cotton production was introduced as an obligatory cash crop to the Uele region it came to be supervised and controlled by colonial administrators informed by science, but dependent on an entire chain of relations before reaching the actual planter, including African middlemen such as monitors and local chiefs. The obligation to cultivate cotton came as a form of taxation, but it was undergirded by violence. It changed the geography both literally, as cultivation was standardized and land re-distributed, and figuratively as it introduced a host of disciplinary measures that included the whip, penal labor and rape. It also reshaped gender relations, as production-oriented polygamy flourished. Coercion kept being a stable feature of cultivation in the region even when cultivation was conceptualized as non-obligatory in what became known as the 'indigenous peasantry schemes.' In this way, Melkebeke shows continuity in terms of practices of precarization. However, he also stresses how colonial state control was fragile. The dependence on middlemen whose supervision left colonial authorities frustrated left the system open to continuous shows of everyday resistance. Thus, the very geography itself was also shaped by agency, as the planters regularly abandoned and contested the land, or sowed cotton on the least fertile lands, prioritizing food crops.

Like the chapter by Melkebeke, the contribution of Ottovay Jørgensen revolves around coercive geographies that are both literal and figurative, though his exploration speaks more to the second part of the book as his contribution turns to the question bordering, but through analysis of the historical case of The Gaza Strip from 1957 to 1967. Like Melkebeke, Jørgensen stresses the question of agency in the face of the making of coercive geographies, as he explores how Palestinian and Bedouin communities negotiated and challenged practices of confinement carried out as part of military surveillance and control schemes shaped by deep legacies and continuities of colonialism in a region shaped first by Ottoman imperial dispositions and later by British rule. These schemes were brutally disruptive to life in the area, creating what has rightfully been conceptualized as a prison camp. The story he unfolds is one of borders, camps and patrols in which mobility became increasingly limited, but also one that was challenged every step of the way, both through everyday forms of resistance and violent retaliation. This coercive geography was at the same time one of rapidly changing labor relations. As outside forces employed thousands of workers in a climate in which inflation and unemployment lead to a marked worsening of labor conditions in the area, workers still mobilized in a variety of ways despite the illegality of unionizing or striking. Highlighting how militarized security links present and past through practices of both confinement and displacement, Jørgensen brings the perspective to the present highlighting how the practices of confinement created or perpetuated after World War II, have lived on.

While Jørgensen takes us forward in time, Heinsen takes us back. Not only in time, going all the way back to what in European history is referred to as the early modern period, but also to the Europe whose present coercive geographies were discussed in the first parts of the book. Heinsen traces a history in which many of the elements that define this volume were crucial to the way early modern states – the conglomerate state of Denmark–Norway being his particular point of interrogation – operated. These are elements that the previous eight chapters have shown in various assemblages across the modern world of the twentieth and twenty-first centuries: borders, personal documentation, carcerality and policing. Heinsen shows that all of these were already at play before the world became anything that we would normally consider "modern." The absolutist states of early modern Europe crafted coercive geographies that, in subtly varied ways, tied everyone to someone else, and most people to the land. Heinsen argues that the prison camp, partly evolving from forms of convict labor emerging in the sixteenth century, served both states and masters in disciplining their subjects. Of course, as the essay takes prison breakers as its departure, the ensuing geography was challenge. The border emerged as a key instrument to Danish lawmakers as they sought to combat that challenge – just as it was in the attempt to limit the criminalized mobility of other coerced forms labor in both agricultural and military contexts, such as the practices of desertion of migrant mercenary soldiers. In this way, where the bulk of the present volume has been focused on relatively recent trajectories and assemblages of coercive geographies, Heinsen shows that such processes have been taking place for at least five centuries. What he offers is, however, not an origin story, but rather a view of history as continuous assemblage in which heterogeneous elements are brought into play to serve a variety of purposes for those with the power to put coercive geographies to use. Thus, while states and economies have mutated multiple times, the attempt to keep people in check through practices limiting their mobility and controlling their productivity emerges over and over again as an evolving theme through history.

3   Leaving No One Behind (Apart from Migrants and Refugees) –
      Coercive Geographies during the Pandemic

Not only our conceptualization of coercive geographies but also the analysis of such in the spring 2020 became embedded in the context of the Covid-19 pandemic. Both the pandemic itself as well as the political responses of national authorities to contain the virus and protect the citizens in the respective countries have direct consequences on several of the cases we deal with in this book. In many ways Covid-19, as both a virus and as a particular kind of governance, has accentuated the coercive geographies we investigate in this volume. At the same time, it has created new forms of immobility and confinement. One very visible consequence is the lockdown measures taken by most countries around the world, which has led to forms of confinement for people who might not ever have experiences this kind of confinement before. Of course, there is a difference between this kind of time limited confinement and the ones the people our chapters deal with experience and live by every day. Nevertheless, there are also overlaps and consequences, which have led to deepened forms of precarization for the most precarious and vulnerable workers. In no country has neoliberal market economy been able to restore order and sustain the economy. The private sector has been dependent on financial aid packages and in a very short time, we have seen the implementation of policy measures which previously would have been characterized as 'socialist.'

In 2015 the UN's 2013 Agenda launched the 'Sustainable Development Goals' with 193 countries committing themselves to pursue the goals under the beautiful but lofty statement 'leave no one behind.' The SDGs are for all of us. Reality, as so often, has turned out to be different from the ideals. One consequence of the pandemic has been the opposite. The policy initiatives implemented during these first months of the pandemic do not offer the same protection for 'all of us.' The lack of a universal health coverage in the US has developed into a health crisis. Before the pandemic, 87 million people were uninsured or underinsured in the US. Now the situation is even direr. Over just a month, more than 26 million Americans have lost their jobs and now face a crisis unique among advanced countries: for most of them, their healthcare was tied to their jobs. In America, unlike any other major country, when you lose your job, you lose your healthcare (Sanders and Jayapal 2020). The consequence is that, up to 35 million Americans are estimated to see their health coverage disappear due to economic recession caused by Covid-19. Migrant workers as so often before are among the most precarious groups. Caught between needing an income, not having a health insurance and often not having the documentation for staying in the country. The US is not the only country where we can witness such a development. In the global South, we can find daily examples on the devastating and lethal effects of the pandemic. Not from the virus itself but from the effects of economy, lack of access to health or even just sanitary conditions – clean water and soap is not a given – and collapse of various parts of the labor market. Even the informal ones.

There is a huge gap between the ideals of leaving no one behind and the actual attempts to secure this happening. The failure to do so leads to a strengthening and expansion of the coercive geographies globally.

4   'Human Waste' or 'Essential Workers'

In *Wasted Lives*, Zygmunt Bauman (2004) suggests that the border politics of globalization categorizes many people as 'human waste' – people dumped into the refuse heaps of asylum systems, refugee camps or urban ghettoes. Although, as Gillian Wylie rightly contends (2014), this characterization risk being determinist and debilitating, squeezing out human agency by exclusionary globalization, it is difficult not seeing this categorization reshaping during the pandemic. While workers are hailed as 'essential' for society they at the time find themselves in low-paid jobs, not having access to sufficient protection kits. Despite the claim 'leave no workers behind.' few efforts are actually made. The UK based Focus on Labour Exploitation (FLEX) did an assessment of the economic impact of the Covid-19 pandemic on the most vulnerable groups of workers: Workers in low-paid and insecure work, Migrant workers, and Women workers (FLEX 2020) and shows the brutal results and a 'continuum of exploitation.' Amongst the findings the assessment shows that:

> The vital financial support measures introduced by government since the outbreak fail to cover significant groups of workers, leaving them at risk of destitution and more vulnerable to exploitation. [...] Unable to afford food and other basic necessities, [...] low-paid workers become extremely vulnerable to labour exploitation, as they find themselves with no viable alternatives and are unable to say 'no' to unsafe and/or abusive working conditions. Low-paid workers in sectors classified as 'key' or 'essential' are being pressured to accept unsafe conditions. Demand for workers in sectors that are already high risk for labour exploitation could lead to a rise in exploitation rates in the UK, including modern slavery offences.
>
> FLEX 2020

Europe's largest agricultural economies, including the United Kingdom, France, and Germany, rely on foreign agricultural workers. About 70,000–80,000 workers, mainly from Romania and Bulgaria, travel to the United Kingdom each year to work. 98% of all agricultural workers in the UK, estimated, are from these two countries (Doward 2020). Likewise, around 300,000 seasonal workers travel to Germany each year, mainly from Eastern Europe. France requires about 800,000 farm workers to harvest, of which two-thirds come from Central and Eastern Europe, Tunisia and Morocco.

Death is a feature of coercive geographies. Confinement, precarity, coercive labor conditions and lack of rights all add to lethal consequences. However, the Covid-19 pandemic has added a necropolitical dimension to our discussion. The notion 'necropolitics' was coined by Achille Mbembe's (2003) and emphasizes 'death.' Necropolitics is not an historical exception. Studies applying necropolitics have shown how necropolitics is not just about killing but rather about who is left to die through decisions taken by the state. John Round and Irina Kuznetsova show how precarity renders migrants both visible and invisible in Moscow. They are invisible through being *sans papiers* but visible when the state puts blame on 'the migrant' as the carrier of disease, as criminal, and as a racialized object of disgust. We see these kinds of narratives accentuating during the pandemic. In Italy, Matteo Salvini, the former Minister of the Interior of the far-right League party, called on the Italian Prime Minister to resign, accusing him of promoting the spread of the epidemic by accepting the landing of humanitarian ships in its ports (Dayant 2020). Leaders of far-right parties in France, Germany and Spain have also asked for border closures to limit the expansion of Covid-19. 'Necropolitics' is thus a framework through which the state views migrants as diseased, criminal and deviating. Writing from the perspective of US–Mexican border-scape before the pandemic, Ariadna Estévez argues that poverty, violence and other precarious living conditions for migrants and marginalized populations along the US–Mexico border make up what she terms a:

> necropolitical dispositif of production and administration of forced migration—in other words, a set of policies and laws enacted to produce situations, times and places that force people to leave their homes or that lead them to situations and places of death.
>
> ESTÉVEZ 2018: 2

She argues that the consequence of this is the emergence of 'disposability pockets.' which refers to "people who live around open-air garbage dumps waiting for some informal work to come their way, or around sewers and improvised migrant shelters" (ibid.: 13). She argues further that disposability pockets are areas of spatial injustice in which vulnerable populations, especially migrant ones, are forced to live in inhumane conditions and work in illegal labor markets with the tacit approval of the government (cf. 'institutionalized migrant precarity.' Floros and Jørgensen 2020).

Necropolitics and disposability pockets can be related to coercive geographies during the pandemic. We see immigrants being blamed for carrying the disease across borders, despite being referred to as essential due to their place in the food-supply chain. In the US migrant fieldworkers have been told to keep working despite stay-at-home directives, and given letters attesting to their 'critical' role in feeding the country (Jordan 2020). The 'essential work' letters that many now carry are not a free pass from immigration authorities. The general regulations still allows ICE to deport undocumented field workers at any time but local law enforcement authorities state the letters can give immigrant workers a sense of security that they will not be arrested for violating stay-at-home orders (ibid.). In sum, caring less about the workers' personal safety, than their work.

This discussion also is directly relatable to the cases that are discussed in this volume. In Sweden between four and six thousand berry pickers from Thailand would normally arrive within the next months. This year none will arrive. In one way, this removes a precarious supply chain. The industry expects prices to go up and thus make it more interesting for Swedish 'free pickers.' It could also open up a space for EU workers accepting lower wages however, if the internal borders of the EU open again during the summer. Moreover, the Thai berry-pickers counting on this income will now be in economic distress at home. The effects of all this are yet to be seen.

In Greece, the strawberry season began in March, as did the Covid-19 pandemic and there are now at least 7,000 to 10,000 agricultural workers living and working in the Manolada area. Work has not stopped at this time due to pandemic but has been minimized. Production has dropped approximately by 70%, with large quantities of strawberries being thrown away. The reduction at strawberry production has a direct impact not only on producers but also on the agricultural workers, whose economic survival depends on this job (Generation 2.0 2020). Some employers distribute gloves and masks, according to information from the local authorities. Some workers have them, some do not. Social distancing is implemented through no longer transporting the strawberry pickers by truck but letting them walk to the fields. Sometimes entailing very long distances. There are now restriction of movement and the compulsory use of movement certificates where agricultural workers must carry employer certificates. Employer certificates requires a passport, which is something many of the workers do not have leaving them both within funds for living and new immobility. The vast majority of the Manolada workers, working in the fields for at least a decade are 'invisible' to the Greek state (Malichudis 2020). At the peak of the season 2019 it was estimated that at least 8,500 migrant workers were found in the wider area, while the number of foreigners legally employed in prefecture of Ilia (often referred to as Manolada), was just about 500 (ibid.). People live in makeshift camps and huts with very poor sanitary conditions. Each hut continues to accommodate approximately 10 to 20 people, depending on its size (Generation 2.0 2020).

In Italy the Italian Minister for Agriculture Teresa Bellanova recently stated that in times of Coronavirus "we truly realize that it is we who need the immigrants," rather than them who need us (in Meret and Goffredo 2020). As in other countries, the Minister is referring to the increasing demand for migrant workers in agriculture to help Italy maintain a fully operative food and agricultural production and supply chain. It is estimated that Italy needs more than 370,000 workers to harvest agri-food products this year (ibid.). More than one million agricultural workers are in Italy today. About 28% are immigrants. However, the real number is higher than the official one. The number of immigrants employed in agriculture is well above the workforce of 400,000, with an estimated 16.5% employed through informal contracts and 39% working at much lower wages than the regulated contract (ibid.). Like the conditions in Greece, the immigrant workers live in makeshift camps without electricity or running water. Also, here it is impossible to respect the basic health conditions of social distancing sought by the authorities or keep sanitary requirements. The positioning as 'essential' comes with new immobility. Where they normally would follow the harvest seasons, picking tomatoes in the South and peaches and apples in the North they are now stuck, as the recent regulations require them to stay at home. As stated by Susi Meret and Sergio Goffredo, "these essential workers that today are advised by authorities to continue working and whose toil is necessary to keep the food and agriculture sector running, live in extreme deprivation and often without valid documents" (2020). These are just some of the myriad of examples that show mobility, rights and labor relations are changing as a consequence of Covid-19.

Coming to an end, the (interdisciplinary) conceptualization of coercive geographies as a way of defining and analyzing mobility, labor and confinement can be used to show that perhaps we should not read the current developments as a dichotomy between 'human waste' and 'essential workers.' The politics taking place during the pandemic is even bleaker and shows that workers easily can be both at the same time, especially so immigrant workers. Caught between a rock and a hard place, these workers in many countries are cut off from the protectionary schemes, have lost their financial means of survival, experience new immobility and yet are portrayed as needed and essential and regularized with the right to work but no other rights or long-term protection. Once again showing the need to politicize the past and historicize the present, the pandemic in this way has deepened and expanded the coercive geographies.

References

Anderson, B. (2010). "Migration, immigration controls and the fashioning of precarious workers," *Work, employment and society* 24(2): 300–317.

Balibar, E. (2002). *Politics and the Other Scene*. Reprint edition. London: Verso.

Bauder, H. (2006). *Labor movement: How migration regulates labor markets*. Oxford: Oxford University Press.

Bauman, Z. (2004). *Wasted Lives: Modernity and its Outcasts*. Cambridge, UK: Polity.

Dayant, A. (2020). "Covid-19 and migration: Europe must resist a populist pill," *The Interpreter*, March 23, 2020: https://www.lowyinstitute.org/the-interpreter/covid-19-and-migration-europe-must-resist-populist-pill.

De Genova, N. (2016). "The 'Crisis' of the European Border Regime: Towards a Marxist Theory of Borders," *International Socialism* 150: 31–54.

Doward, J. (2020). "Fruit and veg 'will run out' unless Britain charters planes to fly in farm workers from eastern Europe," *Guardian*, March 28, 2020: https://www.theguardian.com/environment/2020/mar/28/fruit-and-veg-will-run-out-unless-britain-charters-planes-to-fly-in-farm-workers-from-eastern-europe?fbclid=IwAR3ZHVmj6zMbynTnjLy8NXpfAhsUUrf3uDJvI83VcZCA7n2nH4yt3TkcfaA.

Estévez, A. (2018). "The necropolitical dispositif of production and administration of forced migration at the United States-Mexico Border," *Estudios Fronterizos* 19: 1–18.

FLEX (2020). *New Briefing: No Worker Left Behind – how might the COVID-19 pandemic impact worker exploitation?*: https://www.labourexploitation.org/news/new-briefing-no-worker-left-behind-how-might-covid-19-pandemic-impact-worker-exploitation.

Floros, K., and Jørgensen, M.B. (2020). "Tracing the future of migrants' labour relations. Experiences of institutionalized migrant precarity in Denmark and Greece," *Political Geography Journal*, pre-print. https://doi.org/10.1016/j.polgeo.2019.102120.

Generation 2.0 (2020). *Report on the situation at Manolada | March 2020*: https://g2red.org/report-on-the-situation-at-manolada-march-2020/.

Jordan, M. (2020). "Farmworkers, Mostly Undocumented, Become 'Essential' During Pandemic," *The New York Times*, April 2, 2020: https://www.nytimes.com/2020/04/02/us/coronavirus-undocumented-immigrant-farmworkers-agriculture.html.

Kapsalis, A. (2018). "The development of Greek migration policy and the invention of "para-legality," in labour relations of immigrants," *Κοινωνική Πολιτική* 9: 67–87.

Malichudis, S. (2020). "Thousands of agricultural workers in Manolada are "staying home" – in shacks," *Solomon Mag*, April 3, 2020: https://solomonmag.com/publications-en/a-story-we-shared-en/reportage/thousands-of-agricultural-workers-in-manolada-are-staying-home-in-shacks/.

Martino, E. (2015). *Touts and Despots: Recruiting Assemblages of Contract Labour in Fernando Pó and the Gulf of Guinea, 1858–1979*. Dr.phil. dissertation, Humboldt Universität zu Berlin.

Mbembe, A. (2003) "Necropolitics," *Public Culture* 15(1): 11–40.

Meret, S., and Goffredo, S. (2020). "Replenished grocery stores tomorrow rely on migrants' work today," *Open Democracy*, April 27, 2020: https://www.opendemocracy.net/en/can-europe-make-it/replenished-grocery-stores-tomorrow-rely-on-migrants-work-today/.

Round, J., and Kuznetsova, I. (2016). "Necropolitics and the Migrant as a Political Subject of Disgust: The Precarious Everyday of Russia's Labour Migrants," in Schierup, C.U., and Jørgensen, M.B. (eds.). *Politics of Precarity: migrant conditions, struggles and experiences*. Leiden: Brill: 198–223.

Sanders, B., and Jayapal, P. (2020). "The pandemic has made the US healthcare crisis far more dire. We must fix the system," *The Guardian*, May 2, 2020: https://www.theguardian.com/commentisfree/2020/may/02/us-healthcare-system-coronavirus-pandemic-bernie-sanders-pramila-jayapal.

Stanziani, A. (2014). *Bondage. Labor and Rights in Eurasia from the Sixteenth to the Early Twentieth Centuries*. New York and Oxford: Berghahn.

Wylie, G. (2014). "Human Waste? Reading Bauman's Wasted Lives in the Context of Ireland's Globalization," in Brennan, L. (ed.). *Enacting Globalization*. London: Palgrave Macmillan: 57–66.

Index

CPSIA information can be obtained
at www.ICGtesting.com
Printed in the USA
JSHW042048291021
20020JS00003B/3